THE
Good Health
Microwave
Cookbook

THE
Good Health
Microwave
Cookbook

Carl Jerome

Introduction by C. Wayne Callaway, M.D.

BANTAM BOOKS
New York • Toronto • London • Sydney • Auckland

THE GOOD HEALTH MICROWAVE COOKBOOK

A Bantam Book / December 1990

Library of Congress Cataloging-in-Publication Data

Jerome, Carl.
 The good health microwave cookbook / Carl Jerome and C. Wayne Callaway.
  p. cm.
 ISBN: 0-553-07069-X
 1. Microwave cookery. I. Callaway, C. Wayne. II. Title.
TX832.J44 1990
641.5′882—dc20   90-34713
                                                       CIP

Published simultaneously in the United States and Canada

PRINTED IN THE UNITED STATES OF AMERICA

RRH   0 9 8 7 6 5 4 3 2 1

For Barbara Kafka,
who holds the lamp that lights our way

Contents

Soups

VEGETABLE SOUPS

Fish

Poultry

Meat

Breakfast

Desserts

PUDDINGS

ICE CREAMS, SORBETS, AND MOUSSES

POACHED AND FRESH FRUITS

CAKES AND COBBLERS

Jams, Jellies, and Other Condiments

Acknowledgments and Thanks

Special thanks to my agent and friend Sam Mitnick, who guided every word in this book during the three years it took from conception to publication.

Special thanks to my editor Fran McCullough, who guided every word in this book, quite literally, from proposal to publication.

And special thanks to my friend Bryan Harrison, who guided every word in this book from keyboard to monitor, and from monitor to printer, and who enthusiastically ate almost every recipe in this book.

Thanks also to Kristine Mehring for her assistance in providing the nutritional data for this book, and to Biagio Abbatiello, Saud Al-Sowayel, Chris Benton, Brother International Corporation, Robert Burnett, Marguerite Callaway, Andrew Coile, Frank Cook, Lisette and Jimmy Corro, Brandon Cross, Natalie Cunningham, Terry Dale, Judy Dugan, Lynn Fischer, David Fye, Robert Galano, Ellen Haas and the staff of *Public Voice*, Korynne Halverson, Karen Harrison, Howard Helmer, Charles Hollingsworth, John Kalesh, Jill Lai, Karen MacNeil, Brian Mahoney, Louis Mahoney, Julian Morris, Michelle Mundth, Rachel Newman, Coleen O'Shea, Phyllis Richman, Tom Seitsema, Bill Stern, Margaret Stern, Michael Such, Carol Sugarman, Kathleen Silvassy, Karen Timmons, Michael Turgatt, Jerry Wager, Arlene Wanderman, and Catherine Whitney.

Preface

My first venture into microwaving took place fifteen years ago. I tried to melt some frozen butter in a friend's microwave and ended up with creamy lumps swimming in a puddle of burned, glistening fat. Unimpressed, I waited well over a decade to buy myself a microwave. That was three years ago. Within a few short months, quite to my astonishment, the microwave became the single most important appliance in my kitchen because no other appliance is as well suited to cooking great contemporary food as the microwave oven. And how do I define great contemporary food? First, it must *taste* great. And second, considering our present knowledge of nutrition, it must be food that is good for us. The lipid-laden, sodium-saturated dishes of the past, no matter how good they may seem to taste, can no longer be considered great food. The microwave allows us to preserve flavor, texture, and color, to cook without added fat, and to reduce our need for salt—and it does it in minutes. But I'm getting ahead of myself.

While I was teaching myself to cook in a microwave by painstaking trial and error, my friend and colleague Barbara Kafka asked me to help her with some of the testing for her first microwave cookbook, *Microwave Gourmet*. And it was she who opened my eyes, and the nation's, to the enormous potential of the microwave. With her extraordinary insightfulness, Kafka explored the potentials of microwave cooking and set down the foundations that would allow future microwave writers, like me, to understand this new form of cooking. Kafka broke more new ground in *Microwave Gourmet* than any other food writer in this century.

When I returned home, after spending a month working in Kafka's New York kitchen, I did an exhaustive review of the literature, perusing hundreds of microwave cookbooks in the collection of the Library of Congress and finally writing a story assessing the value of these books for the *Washington Post.* Unfortunately, unlike Kafka, authors of those early microwave cookbooks all tried to force the microwave to mimic traditional cooking techniques; no one seemed to understand the unique cooking abilities of this new appliance.

For example, early microwave recipes for making chicken stock would place the chicken and vegetables in a bowl with water, microwave it on HIGH until it came to a boil, then reduce the power to MEDIUM and microwave until the stock was done. This mimicked the traditional stove-top method for making stock— bringing the water to a boil over high heat and then lowering the flame so the stock simmered. But microwaves can penetrate directly *into* the meat, bones, and vegetables to extract their flavors, as I had learned from Kafka, so why not cook the stock entirely on HIGH? The microwave astounded me. In only about 40 minutes I could make a richly flavored stock by just placing the ingredients in a bowl and microwaving them on HIGH. In fact, the microwave extracted flavor so well that the meat itself was now tasteless, to be discarded along with the bones.

The more I microwaved, the more strongly I felt that wholly new recipes were needed, recipes designed to take advantage of the special cooking abilities of the oven.

This book is the result of the decision to write a book of recipes designed uniquely for the microwave. There are over 400 recipes and variations, all created to take advantage of the singular cooking abilities of the microwave oven. No mimicking, no adapting. Just recipes that use the potential of the microwave oven to its fullest. And because I believe that home cooking should basically be simple and easy, virtually all of the recipes in this book are simple to prepare.

But this book is more than just a collection of easy-to-follow microwave recipes. It is more than just another microwave cookbook. It is more than a diet or health book. It is a cookbook with a culinary point of view, a new approach to fine home cooking that I hope will be the style of cooking in the year 2000. In the past, efforts to create healthy recipes have been considered diet books, for a special audience. But great cooking in the 1990s and on into the next millennium is not only about great-tasting food, most of which can be prepared quickly and easily, but also about food that is good for us, food that follows the public health recommendations of the *Dietary Guidelines.* Dr. C. Wayne Callaway, one of the authors of those guidelines and one of the most respected physician nutritionists in America today, explains those seven simple guidelines in his introduction to this book.

One of the most important discoveries I made while I experimented with the microwave was that by its very nature the microwave encourages its user to prepare healthful food. It cooks without the need for added fat, and the excessive amount of fat in our food today is our major dietary consideration. The microwave enhances flavors, in large part because it cooks foods without the need for added water—which drains foods of their flavor—thus minimizing the need for salt. An excess of sodium, which is a part of salt, is another major dietary concern. The microwave cooks fresh vegetables magnificently. It cooks cereals, grains, dried beans, and peas perfectly in one simple step while preserving their natural textures and flavors. As we reduce the fat in our diets, we need to replace those lost calories with more calories from vegetables, grains, beans, and peas. The microwave cooks fish fabulously; it cooks poultry and game well. And we know that we need to be eating fish and poultry more frequently. The microwave cooks fruit better than any other appliance. Fruits microwave quickly and easily, and they retain their natural textures and fragrances, which are often lost in traditional cooking techniques like poaching. The microwave cooks some lean red meats adequately. The microwave is a terrible baker. High-fat, high-sugar foods, such as cakes and pastries, taste rubbery and awful when microwaved, which is fine, because we need to be restricting our consumption of them. So the more we cook in the microwave, the more we use the microwave for what it cooks best, the better our diets will be.

Even if you have never cooked in a microwave—indeed, even if you have never cooked before—you'll find it easy to prepare the recipes in this book. If you can chop, stir, and set the timer on the microwave oven, you can prepare the recipes in this book. Microwave cooking is, after all, the easiest way to cook. It requires less technical skill than sautéing or frying, for example, which require the cook to frequently adjust the temperature, watch for browning, and to know when to raise or lower the heat to produce a crisp, properly browned surface in the same time that it takes to cook the food to the proper degree of doneness. Microwaving is easier because it is less participatory. Once food is placed in the microwave, all you have to do is test it for doneness.

I learned to cook in the early 1970s from the dean of American cookery, James Beard, a man who loved butter more than life itself. But in 1977, after reading the Senate subcommittee report on the relationship of health to nutrition, I began to change the way I cooked and ate, for I realized that the only way to live a high-quality, healthy life was to eat properly.

My diet became lighter. I reduced the Beardian lakes of butter sauces to small puddles. Gradually over the next decade I began to understand that good eating and good health are one and the same. Gradually I changed the emphasis of my eating from high-fat, low-fiber to high-fiber, low-fat. And in the last few years, thanks to the microwave, I have been able to cook great-tasting, healthy foods more easily than ever.

But while I was shifting the focus of my cooking, I was absolutely unwilling to compromise any of the principles of good taste that I had learned from Mr. Beard. And as you will see when you prepare the recipes in this book, microwaved food sparkles with natural, fresh flavors, aromas, and textures.

During the seven years I worked with Mr. Beard, as his assistant and colleague in his cooking school and public demonstrations, we used butter and olive oil with great abandon. We bathed everything in fat. I have now grown to understand that we were actually smothering the natural flavors and textures of the food we cooked. Mashed potatoes, for example, with their delicate sweet flavor and natural starchy texture, were prepared with so much butter and cream that they lost their freshness, in both taste and texture. Now when I make mashed potatoes, I add skim milk, and sometimes a little stock, rather than cream and butter, and I can taste the potatoes.

I also came to realize that healthy people don't analyze the nutrient content of their food. Instead they just follow a few simple rules that allow them to cook well. For me, those rules are: Eat a variety of foods. Try never to repeat a food for at least three days. Serve more vegetables and starches and less meat, fish, and poultry. Avoid high-fat dairy products. And use fat only as a condiment.

That's right, I now use fat—butter and olive oil—as a condiment. I think of fat in much the same way I think of capers and anchovies. Every now and then, when I think it would add an important taste or texture to a recipe, I use it. But for most of my cooking there is no need for added fat. This practice was difficult before I began to use my microwave as the primary cooking appliance in my kitchen, for so many traditional cooking methods require fat—sautéing, frying, roasting, grilling, and, to a lesser degree, stewing and fricasseeing.

General information about microwave ovens and microwave cooking can be found in the appendix. Information about microwaving specific foods is explained in the chapter and recipe introductions. Once you understand the basic principles of second-generation microwaving, you can use them to create your own recipes. One thing I promise you: if both taste and health are major concerns for you, and your kitchen time is at a premium, you'll cook this way the rest of your life, with great pleasure.

Carl Jerome

Introduction

For over 20 years now, in my capacity as endocrinologist and nutrition specialist, I have addressed the diet and nutrition concerns of thousands of patients. One of the most frequent complaints I've heard is that it's hard to find pleasure in eating healthful foods. The language my patients use to describe food often reflects this sense of conflict. They will confess, with guilty smiles, that they have been "bad," naming a favorite food they ate as a treat. Clearly they believe that "good" food is drab and pleasureless, a point of view I have never shared. I am not an expert on cooking, however, so it has been difficult for me to show people how they can eat great-tasting food that is also good for them. For this reason I am especially enthusiastic about the way Carl Jerome has used the microwave to transform the experience of healthy eating.

I learned firsthand of Carl's microwave magic several years ago, soon after I arrived in Washington, D.C., from the Mayo Clinic, to begin work as director of the Center for Clinical Nutrition at George Washington University Medical Center. While still at Mayo, I had been "loaned" to the National Institutes of Health and had served as nutritional coordinator for the U.S. Department of Health and Human Services during the development of the first edition of the *Dietary Guidelines for Americans* (1980). More recently I served on the committee that reviewed the guidelines and advised the secretaries of agriculture and health and human services on revisions for the third edition, published in 1990.

Carl knew of my work, and one day he called and introduced himself. He asked if we could have lunch to discuss a concept he was working on. But, he added, instead of meeting at a restaurant, would I mind coming over to his house so he could cook lunch for me?

I was intrigued by this unusual invitation. It was the first time I had ever been invited to a business lunch that my host offered to prepare. I agreed, and it turned out to be a wonderful meal and a productive meeting.

I had expected Carl to prepare a healthy gourmet meal, since that was his specialty. What I didn't expect was that he would cook every bit of it in a microwave oven while I was in the kitchen watching. There was moist breast of chicken with salsa, lemon-scented balsamic rice, and crisp, perfectly cooked broccoli. For dessert he served individual cheesecakes with fresh raspberry sauce. It was one of the best meals I had ever eaten.

Like many people, I considered the microwave to be a necessary evil in the busy American household, not a valuable asset for preparing healthy food. I had believed, until that lunch, that microwave food was as tasteless as fast food. I was amazed to see how easily and quickly Carl had fixed a meal that was nutritionally sound and tasted great. It seemed to me that this kind of microwave cooking is the wave of the future, and I said so to Carl.

Our lunch that day was cooked without oil or butter, something Carl showed me you can do in the microwave. The vegetables were cooked quickly and without added water so they retained their flavor, texture, and vitamins. Carl explained that his goal was to show people how to use the microwave to prepare great-tasting, healthy food and to kill the myth that healthy food is the equivalent of gummy brown rice and tasteless tofu.

I realized Carl had found the answer to many of the concerns expressed by my patients. I was pleased that he was so nutrition-conscious; when he asked me to write this introduction, his primary concern was that readers be able to maximize the nutritional benefits of his recipes.

DIET AND HEALTH: GUIDELINES FOR AMERICANS

During the last 10 years we have come a long way toward establishing definitive guidelines that the average American can follow to achieve a healthy diet. Today there is consensus in the scientific community regarding the major diet and health issues. This is reflected in two authoritative reports released in 1989: *The Surgeon General's Report on Nutrition and Health*, published by the U.S. Department of Health and Human Services, and the *Diet and Health Report*, prepared by the Food and Nutrition Board of the National Research Council. I had the privilege of serving as a member of the editorial advisory board for *The Surgeon General's Report* and as senior science consultant for the *Diet and Health Report*.

The two reports are in agreement on all fundamental issues. Together they provide a scientific basis for the latest revision of the *Dietary Guidelines for Americans*, which I mentioned earlier.

The guidelines are surprisingly simple and, more important, delightfully unobtrusive. For most people, following them will not involve radical changes. Certain of the guidelines have become so common in our dietary practices that the latest revisions come as no surprise.

When my colleagues and I wrote and, later, revised the *Dietary Guidelines*, we did not intend them to be rigid rules for eating. Their purpose is to help people avoid proven nutritional pitfalls and achieve a healthy balance in their diets. The guidelines are as follows:

- Eat a variety of foods.
- Maintain healthy weight.
- Choose a diet low in fat, saturated fat, and cholesterol.
- Eat vegetables, fruits, and grain products daily.
- Avoid excess sweeteners.
- Avoid excess salt and sodium.
- Alcoholic beverages do not improve the diet.

Eat a Variety of Foods. You need more than 40 different nutrients in your diet, and the best way to get them is to eat a variety of vegetables, fruits, grains, lowfat milk and milk products, meats, poultry, and fish.

During the past 20 years there have been many fad diets promoting the so-called miracle qualities of certain isolated foods. Unfortunately, many people have substituted fad foods for a balanced diet. But failure to achieve variety in your diet almost always leads to nutrient deficiency and related health problems.

Maintain Healthy Weight. Many of my patients are concerned primarily about achieving a healthy weight. Unfortunately, they are often convinced that healthy weight means "the thinner the better," a popular cultural standard that has led to a multitude of health problems—which I discuss in my book, *The Callaway Diet: Successful Permanent Weight Control for Starvers, Stuffers and Skippers.*

What does it mean to have healthy body weight? Medically, we define it as that weight at which you are minimally at risk for weight-related health problems. Traditionally you have calculated this figure by using the standard weight-for-height tables. However, in recent years we have found that, although the weight tables may have some validity for groups of people, they are inadequate for judging the healthy weight of individuals.

Nutrition professionals now consider a number of factors, including your age, health history, and any current medical conditions in defining healthy body weight. There is also recent evidence that the distribution of body fat may be more important to health than the amount of body fat. Research indicates that fat located in the belly is associated with diabetes, high blood pressure, heart attacks, and strokes, while fat in the hips and thighs has not been linked to any of these medical conditions. This is not to say that how much you weigh is irrelevant. But today an evaluation of healthy weight is not limited to the number on your scale.

Choose a Diet Low in Fat, Saturated Fat, and Cholesterol. Dietary fat is viewed as the culprit in a number of health conditions, including heart disease, obesity, and certain types of cancer. Saturated fat is the major contributor to high blood cholesterol. Dietary cholesterol also raises blood cholesterol, although it does not appear to raise it as much as saturated fat.

While the recommendations call for moderate consumption of all kinds of fat, polyunsaturated and monounsaturated fats do not raise and may even lower cholesterol. However, there are other reasons to keep intakes of these fats to moderate levels. High-fat diets may contribute to obesity, and there is new evidence that reducing overall fat may lower the risk of some types of cancer.

The *Diet and Health Report* of the Food and Nutrition Board supplies specific recommendations: 30 percent or less total daily calories from all fat, less than 10 percent total daily calories from saturated fat, and no more than 300 milligrams per day of dietary cholesterol. The recipes in this book are very low in fat and cholesterol. In fact, one of the greatest health benefits of the microwave is that it allows you to cook without adding fat.

Eat Vegetables, Fruits, and Grain Products Daily. A decline in fat intake goes hand in hand with an increase in carbohydrates and fiber-rich foods, such as whole grains, starchy vegetables, and legumes. And, as I discovered firsthand, microwave cooking is wonderfully suited to the preparation of these foods.

The *Dietary Guidelines* recommend that adults eat daily at least three servings of vegetables (including dry beans and peas), two servings of fruits, and six servings of grain products, such as bread, cereal, pasta, and rice. These foods provide energy, primarily from carbohydrates, and a rich mix of vitamins, minerals, and dietary fibers.

Consuming a good balance of high-fiber foods is essential to a healthy diet—and these foods also contain essential vitamins and minerals. Certain fibers are beneficial to bowel functions; others may help to reduce blood cholesterol levels. There is also evidence, although it remains inconclusive, that some dietary fibers may have potential for preventing colon cancer.

Avoid Excess Sweeteners. There is nothing inherently bad about sugar, which has been blamed wrongly for a whole host of ills. In fact sugar's only absolute negative seems to be that it helps cause dental cavities—especially when it is consumed in the form of sticky, tooth-clinging foods.

However, a high sugar consumption will upset your nutrient balance. The so-called empty calories that sugar provides take the place of foods that include the vitamins and minerals your body needs. Also, many foods that are high in sugar, such as candy, cookies, and cake, are also high in fat and low in fiber content.

The value of artificial sweeteners is highly questionable. Contrary to popular belief, they have not been proven effective as calorie and body weight reduction aids. Indeed some studies show that people who use artificial sweeteners are more likely to gain weight in any given year than people who don't.

Avoid Excess Sodium. It is estimated that about one third of American adults have or will develop high blood pressure. As many as half of this group with high blood pressure are what we call "sodium sensitive." When they reduce their salt intake, their blood pressure declines.

Cutting down on sodium involves more than taking the saltshaker off the table, since many processed foods are high in sodium. Microwaving, which helps to bring out the full flavors in fresh foods, thus reducing the need for salt as a flavor-enhancer, can help America cure its salt habit. The *Diet and Health Report* specifies the consumption of no more than 6 grams of salt, about 1 teaspoon, or 2,400 milligrams of sodium daily.

Alcoholic Beverages Do Not Improve the Diet. Like sugar, the calories in alcohol are empty calories, and for this reason alone too much alcohol will rob you of the nutrients your body needs. Furthermore, alcohol consumption (even at a level of two drinks a day) may be a factor in strokes, heart attacks, cirrhosis of the liver, and some types of cancer. Both the *Diet and Health Report* and *The Surgeon General's Report* recommend that pregnant women not drink at all, since alcohol may cause neurological damage and mental retardation in infants.

While we cannot say with certainty that a low to moderate intake of alcohol is harmful, neither the dietary guidelines nor any other recommendations suggest that it is good for you.

ABOUT THE NUTRITIONAL INFORMATION IN THIS BOOK

As I mentioned earlier, when my patients try to put the *Dietary Guidelines* into practice, they often speak of sweeping their kitchens clear of "bad" foods and stocking up on "good" foods. But the new thinking reflected in Carl's approach abandons the great nutritional food fight where ingredients are separated into "good" and "bad." No food is good or bad in and of itself. It is the overall diet that matters. The best way to achieve your diet and health objectives is to learn how to balance a variety of foods over the course of time so that your overall eating pattern is the best it can be.

For example, a pat of butter is virtually 100 percent fat, but that in itself does not make the pat of butter a "bad" food. More relevant is how much of your daily calories the pat of butter represents—or how many pats of butter you eat.

We have used this principle in presenting the nutrient content information for the recipes in this book. For each recipe the most important nutrients are listed as a percentage of the recommended daily intakes of those nutrients contained in one serving.

Recommendations for fat, carbohydrates, and sodium (calculated without salt added to the recipes) are based on the National Research Council's *Diet and Health Report*. Protein, calcium, and iron are expressed as percentages of the maximum Recommended Dietary Allowances, also published by the National Research Council. Although not everyone needs this much calcium and iron, using the maximum levels ensures that all needs are covered.

We have chosen 2,000 calories a day as the baseline diet against which you can make appropriate individual adjustments. For example, a small woman might need only 1,400 calories per day, or 70 percent of the fat, carbohydrate, and calorie allowances. A large, physically active man might need 3,000 calories per day, or 50 percent above the allowances.

How do you know how many calories you need? This question is answered in some detail in my book on dieting. However, the short answer is that the average adult man will need between 12 and 15 calories per pound of his body weight and the average adult woman between 10 and 13 calories per pound of her body weight.

Children and adolescents need more calories per pound of body weight to ensure healthy growth. Ask your pediatrician or a registered dietician to estimate your children's calorie needs.

The nutritional information provided with each recipe will help you keep track of your progress in establishing healthier, more balanced eating habits. You will notice that cholesterol is not included; this is because the recipes in this book are extremely low in cholesterol—a natural outcome of their being low in animal fat.

I worked closely with Carl as he developed the recipes for this book; I have even cooked some of them myself. If you use Carl's ground-breaking new approach to microwave cooking, you'll never again need to worry about your diet. And that's as it should be—good, healthy eating should be a pleasure, not a problem.

C. Wayne Callaway, M.D.

Soups

The ease with which the microwave makes soups is astonishing. For most soups, all you do is seal the ingredients in a bowl and let them cook. Some of the soups require pureeing, and a few are more complex and have several steps. But for the most part, microwave soups all but make themselves. And they do it in about a third of the time required for traditional soup making. While I have been quick to point out how fast and easy it is to make soups in a microwave, it does take most soups 45 minutes to an hour to cook, and there is one soup that takes an hour and a half.

These soups take advantage of the special soup-cooking properties of the microwave and would be impossible to adapt to traditional cooking methods. Indeed, it would not make sense to adapt them. They were designed for the microwave. The colors, textures, and fresh tastes in these soups are the result of the special nature of microwave cooking, which cooks ingredients without dulling their color or flavor and without leaving them waterlogged.

There are elegant soups, like the cold fuchsia-colored Summer Beet Soup, the thin, refined Black Bean Consommé, and the sophisticated Lobster Soup with the sweetest, most tender morsels of fresh lobster I have ever tasted.

There are soups with beans, lentils, and peas, such as the thick Many-Bean Soup, the Light Lentil Soup with Carrots, and the Curried Yellow Split Pea Soup. Using the microwave to cook dried beans, as you will see in these recipes and the chapter that follows, eliminates the need for presoaking. And the beans cook to a tender but firm texture without bloating with water. The beans actually retain their individual identities in a new way.

There are seafood soups, like Lots of Tender Seafood in a Light Broth with Ginger, cold summer soups, like Red Pepper Gazpacho, and there's a vibrant Corn Chowder with Mild Green Chilies. There are broths and stocks—which the microwave makes in less than a quarter of the time it would take with traditional simmering. And there is a new technique for making consommés.

There are 15 vegetable soups in this chapter, some elegant, such as the Vegetable Consommé, some thick and hearty, such as the Fragrant Carrot and Sweet Potato Soup, some that are light bisques made without cream but that do not sacrifice the velvety texture of traditional bisques, such as the Carrot Bisque with Tomatoes, and some chunky soups, such as the Kale and Potato Soup with Saffron.

The most important new discovery in this chapter is that the microwave can make its own broth while it is cooking the other ingredients in the soup. In the Mushroom Soup with Barley, for example, the normal ingredients for a beef broth (beef, onion, carrot, celery, etc.) are placed in the bowl with the mushrooms and barley. After the soup is cooked, the broth ingredients are removed and discarded, just as they would be in normal stock making, and it is as though the soup was made by cooking the mushrooms and barley in a beef broth. Similarly, chicken or turkey broths are generated by adding chicken or turkey and aromatic vegetables (onion, carrot, celery, etc.) to the bowl before cooking and by removing them when the soup comes out of the oven. This discovery has eliminated the need for canned broths and stocks, which have no place in good cooking.

Virtually all of the recipes in this chapter use this new technique, and once you have tried it, you will want to adapt traditional soup recipes to this new idea.

Special techniques: All of the soups in this chapter, and many of the recipes in this book, are made in a very large bowl, which replaces the traditional stockpot. The bowl should be microwave-safe, made of china or ceramic, with no metal parts and no precious metals (such as gold or silver) used to decorate it. Bowls this large will just barely fit into most microwave ovens, with only a couple of inches of clearance around them. The fact that the bowl virtually fills the entire cavity of the microwave oven will not interfere with the cooking process.

In order for the soups to cook properly, the bowl must be sealed airtight with microwave-safe plastic wrap. Because the top of the bowl is so large, and because it is critical that the bowl remain sealed to prevent loss of liquid during cooking (a lid will not suffice here), the recipes direct you to seal the bowl with a double layer of plastic wrap. If you are not sure of your ability to seal the bowl properly with just two pieces of plastic wrap, use three or four overlapping pieces. If the seal is airtight, the plastic wrap will inflate like a balloon during the cooking. But even with the best of seals, there will be some seepage, so you may want to place a plate under the bowl to catch the drippings, which can then be poured back into the bowl when the cooking is complete. This will also ease cleanup.

I love soups. Soups are an important part of the way I entertain. I have even made an entire meal for company of just soups, starting with a clear consommé, going on to a chunky vegetable soup in broth, and finishing with the thick bean soup.

It has been 20 years since I created my first soup recipe, but in all that time I have never made soups that looked and tasted as good as these new ones that come from the microwave.

VEGETABLE SOUPS

Fragrant Carrot and
Sweet Potato Soup

This pale orange-colored soup has a medium-thick, textured consistency and heady aromas rising from its surface—the scents of cinnamon and ginger and orange, all of which leave a lingering flavor in the mouth.

Some of the orange peel and spices are cooked with the soup to give depth of flavor; the rest are stirred into the soup after it is pureed so that the fragrances remain fresh. The aroma is best about half an hour after the soup is pureed.

Serves 6

1 small (about ½ pound) sweet potato, scrubbed and quartered

½ pound (2 to 3 medium-size) carrots, trimmed and scrubbed

1 small onion, peeled

1 small celery rib

2 teaspoons dried grated orange peel *or* 2 tablespoons freshly grated orange zest

2-inch piece of cinnamon stick

1½ quarts skim milk

1 whole chicken breast, bone in, skin and all visible fat removed

½ teaspoon ground ginger

¼ teaspoon ground cinnamon

a little freshly ground white pepper to taste

For Garnish (optional)

2 oil-packed sun-dried tomatoes, drained, patted dry, and finely chopped

In a very large bowl, combine the sweet potato, carrots, onion, celery, 1 teaspoon of the orange peel, the cinnamon stick, milk, and chicken breast. Seal airtight with a double layer of plastic wrap and microwave on HIGH for 45 minutes.

Carefully uncover; remove and discard the cinnamon stick and chicken breast. Puree the soup in a food processor. Stir in the remaining orange peel, the ginger, ground cinnamon, and pepper. Cover and set aside for 30 minutes.

Reheat, ladle into soup bowls, garnish with sun-dried tomatoes if desired, and serve.

Nutritional Information
(as a percentage of daily intake)

8% (164) calories
5% (3 g) fat
33% (25 g) carbohydrates
16% (12 g) protein

8% (202 mg) sodium
41% (327 mg) calcium
7% (1 mg) iron

Corn Chowder
with Mild Green Chilies

This is a lively flavored, crisply textured corn chowder that uses tomatoes, like a Manhattan clam chowder. It takes less than 10 minutes of preparation time, though it does need almost an hour to cook in the microwave.

Serve as a meal in itself, with some large chunks of fresh whole wheat or mixed grain bread, as a first course before roast beef, rack of lamb, or a roast chicken. It's also a good starter before all kinds of game.

Serves 8

1 whole chicken breast, bone in, skin and all visible fat removed
1 very large onion, peeled, quartered lengthwise, and thinly sliced
¾ pound red potatoes, scrubbed and cut into ¼-inch dice
1 very large ripe tomato, cored and diced
3 large ears corn, shucked and kernels cut off the cob with a sharp knife
1 4-ounce can chopped mild green chilies
½ teaspoon crushed dried thyme
1½ quarts skim milk
a little salt and freshly ground black pepper to taste

In a very large bowl, combine all ingredients except the salt and pepper and seal airtight with a double layer of plastic wrap. Microwave on HIGH for 50 minutes. Carefully uncover; remove and discard the chicken (which is used only to flavor the soup), season the soup with salt and pepper, and serve.

Variations

Manhattan-Style Corn Chowder: Eliminate the chilies.

Saffron Corn Chowder with Mild Green Chilies: Add ¼ teaspoon saffron threads along with the thyme.

Nutritional Information
(as a percentage of daily intake)

7% (141) calories
2% (1 g) fat
9% (26 g) carbohydrates
12% (9 g) protein
4% (103 mg) sodium
30% (240 mg) calcium
7% (1 mg) iron

Kale and Potato Soup with Saffron

This golden broth with dark green, tender shreds of kale and diced red potatoes is a jamboree of colors. The saffron, in addition to coloring the broth, lends a lively Mediterranean flavor to the soup.

If you make the soup a day ahead, the saffron will color the potatoes bright gold.

Serves 6

1 large whole chicken breast, bone in, skin and all visible fat removed
1 medium-size carrot, trimmed and scrubbed
2 large onions, trimmed but unpeeled
1 celery rib, cut in half
½ teaspoon crushed dried rosemary
1 teaspoon crushed dried oregano
¼ teaspoon crushed saffron threads

6 garlic cloves, peeled
1½ pounds red potatoes, scrubbed and cut into ¼-inch dice
½ pound kale, stems removed, shredded or coarsely chopped
1½ quarts water
juice of ½ lemon
a little salt and freshly ground black pepper to taste

In a very large bowl, combine all ingredients except the lemon juice, salt, and pepper. Seal airtight with a double layer of plastic wrap and microwave on HIGH for 45 minutes. Carefully uncover; remove and discard the chicken, carrot, onions, and celery. Just before serving, stir in the lemon juice and season with salt and pepper.

Nutritional Information
(as a percentage of daily intake)

9% (177) calories
3% (2 g) fat
13% (35 g) carbohydrates
8% (6 g) protein

3% (83 mg) sodium
8% (66 mg) calcium
13% (2 mg) iron

This full-bodied, easier-than-ever-to-make mushroom beef soup uses barley to give it a comforting taste, rather than making the barley the dominant flavor. A bowl or two of this (most guests will want seconds) and a large slice of fresh homemade bread make a perfect impromptu winter meal.

The real magic of this recipe is, however, not in the flavor but in the simplicity of preparation. Everything cooks at once in the same bowl—the beef base, the vegetable enrichments, the mushrooms (which with microwaving become tender but not soft and mushy), even the barley.

Serves 8

2 celery ribs, cut into 2-inch pieces
1 medium-size onion, peeled and quartered
3 large garlic cloves, peeled
1 pound lean stewing beef, all visible fat removed
¼ cup pearl barley
¾ pound small, firm wild mushrooms, such as cremini or shiitake, bottoms trimmed, quartered

½ pound small cultivated mushrooms, bottoms trimmed, quartered
½ teaspoon crushed dried marjoram
½ teaspoon crushed dried savory
½ teaspoon crushed dried rosemary
7 cups water
a little salt and freshly ground black pepper to taste

In a food processor, chop the celery, onion, and garlic. Transfer to a very large bowl and add the beef, barley, mushrooms, marjoram, savory, rosemary, and water. Seal airtight with a double layer of plastic wrap and microwave on HIGH for 45 minutes.

Carefully uncover; remove and discard the beef and season with salt and pepper.

Variations

Hearty Barley and Mushroom Soup: Increase the barley to 1 cup.

Barley and Mushroom Soup with Lamb: Substitute 1½ pounds lean lamb, all visible fat and skin removed, for the beef, and increase the barley to ½ cup.

Nutritional Information
(as a percentage of daily intake)

5% (101) calories
2% (1 g) fat
27% (20 g) carbohydrates
2% (5 g) protein

1% (25 mg) sodium
2% (17 mg) calcium
7% (1 mg) iron

Summer Squash Soup with Spinach and Tomatoes

With its colorful confettilike appearance and simple, honest early spring flavors this soup calls for a huge chunk of toasted sourdough bread to accompany it. The flavors of the ingredients never meld into one new flavor (as they would in a classic minestrone, for example), but rather playfully complement each other.

Serve for a family meal, with a sandwich, or as part of an informal dinner for guests.

One friend who asked for this recipe adds cooked orzo (the rice-shaped pasta) to the soup and serves it with a little grated Romano to make a simple "minestrone." I am including her version of the recipe as a variation below.

Serves 8

2 large whole chicken breasts, bone in, skin and all visible fat removed
1 large carrot, trimmed and scrubbed
1 celery rib
2 large garlic cloves, peeled
1 medium-size onion, peeled
¼ teaspoon crushed dried rosemary
¼ teaspoon crushed dried thyme
¼ teaspoon crushed dried marjoram
2 pounds yellow (crookneck) squash, trimmed, scrubbed, and cut into ¼- to ½-inch dice

2 quarts water
2 large tomatoes, cored and diced
½ pound fresh spinach, cleaned, thick stems removed, shredded
1 small bunch of cilantro or basil, stems discarded and leaves chopped
a little salt and freshly ground black pepper to taste

In a very large bowl, combine the chicken, carrot, celery, garlic, onion, rosemary, thyme, marjoram, squash, and water. Seal airtight with a double layer of plastic wrap and microwave on HIGH for 30 minutes.

Carefully uncover; remove and discard the chicken, carrot, celery, and onion. (I leave in the garlic, which has become tender and sweet, but you may want to remove it.)

Add the tomatoes and spinach, stir, and seal airtight with a double layer of plastic wrap. Microwave on HIGH for 10 minutes. Stir in the cilantro or basil, season with a little salt and pepper, and serve.

Variation

A *Simple Minestrone:* Cut the squash and tomatoes into ¼-inch dice and shred the spinach very finely. Add 1½ cups cooked orzo (rice-shaped pasta) just before seasoning. Sprinkle a heaping teaspoon of grated Romano or Parmesan onto each serving.

Nutritional Information
(as a percentage of daily intake)

4% (77) calories
5% (3 g) fat
4% (12 g) carbohydrates
7% (5 g) protein

3% (83 mg) sodium
16% (130 mg) calcium
20% (3 mg) iron

Here a chicken broth, lightly flavored with mustard, becomes the base for just barely cooked watercress and tomatoes. The flavors of the broth offset the slight bitterness of the watercress, with the tomato adding color, texture, and balance.

Serves 8

1 large whole chicken breast, bone in, skin and all visible fat removed
1 medium-size onion, trimmed but unpeeled
1 celery rib
1 medium-size carrot, trimmed and scrubbed
1 teaspoon crushed dried thyme
3 garlic cloves, unpeeled
1-inch piece of fresh ginger, sliced

7 cups water
1 large bunch of watercress, thick stems removed
1 large vine-ripened tomato, cored and cut into ¼-inch dice
2 scallions, coarsely chopped
2 teaspoons Dijon mustard
a little salt and freshly ground black pepper to taste

In a very large bowl, combine the chicken, onion, celery, carrot, thyme, garlic, ginger, and water. Seal airtight with a double layer of plastic wrap and microwave on HIGH for 45 minutes. Carefully uncover; strain into a large bowl and stir in the watercress, tomato, scallions, and mustard. Season with salt and pepper. Seal airtight with a double layer of plastic wrap and microwave on HIGH for 8 minutes.

Nutritional Information
(as a percentage of daily intake)

2% (31) calories
3% (2 g) fat
1% (3 g) carbohydrates
3% (2 g) protein

2% (59 mg) sodium
1% (9 mg) calcium
0% (0 mg) iron

Wild Mushroom and Spinach Soup with Peas

The large chunks of wild mushrooms in this soup make it ideal for people who like chunky, meaty soups, even though there is no meat here. The deeply flavored turkey broth gives this strongly flavored and textured soup added body.

Serves 10

2½ quarts water
3 turkey drumsticks, skin and all visible fat removed
1 medium-size onion, trimmed and unpeeled
1 large carrot, trimmed and scrubbed
1 celery rib
2 garlic cloves, peeled
1 teaspoon crushed dried thyme
½ teaspoon crushed dried rosemary
¼ teaspoon crushed dried sage

¾ pound fresh shiitake mushrooms, bottoms trimmed, mushrooms cut into ¾- to 1-inch dice
¼ pound fresh spinach, thick stems removed, torn into large bite-size pieces
1 cup shelled fresh peas (about 1¼ pounds unshelled)
a little salt and freshly ground black pepper to taste

In a very large bowl, combine the water, turkey, onion, carrot, celery, garlic, thyme, rosemary, and sage. Seal airtight with a double layer of plastic wrap and microwave on HIGH for 40 minutes. Carefully uncover; add the mushrooms, spinach, and peas. Seal airtight with a double layer of plastic wrap and microwave on HIGH for 8 minutes. Carefully uncover; remove the turkey, onion, carrot, and celery. Taste and season with salt and pepper.

Nutritional Information
(as a percentage of daily intake)

3% (55) calories
3% (2 g) fat
3% (8 g) carbohydrates
4% (3 g) protein

2% (53 mg) sodium
2% (16 mg) calcium
7% (1 mg) iron

Tomato Beef Soup

The utter simplicity of the tomato flavor in this soup will amaze the cook, who knows the secret: canned tomatoes enriched with red peppers and a beef broth and flavored ever so lightly with chili powder, just so the full flavor of the tomato appears. The texture is medium-thin, perfect for a midwinter bowl of soup. And midwinter is the time when I crave this kind of tomato soup, after four or five months without a tomato, a real vine-ripened summer tomato.

Although I serve this at family meals and to friends from mugs, it is a soup worthy of a sit-down dinner.

Serves 10

2 28-ounce cans peeled Italian-style
   plum tomatoes, undrained
2 medium-size sweet red bell peppers,
   cored and quartered
1 quart water
1½ pounds lean stewing beef, all
   visible fat removed, cut into 2-inch
   cubes

1 teaspoon chili powder
a little salt and freshly ground black
   pepper to taste

In a very large bowl, combine all ingredients except salt and pepper. Seal airtight with a double layer of plastic wrap and microwave on HIGH for 45 minutes. Carefully uncover; remove the beef and discard. Puree the soup, in small batches, in a blender, holding the top of the blender jar securely in place to prevent soup from spewing all over the kitchen. Season with salt and pepper and reheat until very hot before serving.

Variation

Lightly Sweet and Sour Tomato Soup: Stir 1 tablespoon of sugar and the juice of ½ lemon into the soup before seasoning with salt and pepper.

Nutritional Information
(as a percentage of daily intake)

3% (63) calories

2% (1 g) fat

4% (11 g) carbohydrates

4% (3 g) protein

12% (287 mg) sodium

6% (46 mg) calcium

7% (1 mg) iron

With more vegetables than liquid, all tender but retaining their individual identities, this is a fine microwave version of a hearty old-fashioned vegetable soup. In a traditional vegetable soup made on the stove top, the flavors and textures would have stewed, melted, and dissolved into each other, which is not the case with this microwave version.

Serves 12

1 medium-size carrot, trimmed, scrubbed, and cut into 1-inch lengths

1 celery rib, cut into 1-inch pieces

1 small onion, peeled and cut into 1-inch chunks

1 small sweet green bell pepper, cored and cut into 1-inch pieces

4 large garlic cloves, peeled and coarsely chopped

½ pound (¼ small head) cabbage, finely shredded

½ pound cauliflower, cut into small pieces

½ pound red or new potatoes, cut into ½-inch dice

1 28-ounce can peeled Italian-style plum tomatoes, undrained

½ teaspoon crushed dried rosemary

½ teaspoon crushed dried thyme

¼ teaspoon fennel seeds

2 quarts Chicken Broth (page 42)

a little salt and freshly ground black pepper to taste

In a food processor, finely chop the carrot, celery, onion, green pepper, and garlic. Transfer to a very large bowl and mix with the cabbage, cauliflower, potatoes, tomatoes and their liquid, rosemary, thyme, and fennel seeds. Stir in the broth and seal airtight with a double layer of plastic wrap. Microwave on HIGH for 60 minutes. Carefully uncover, season with salt and pepper, and serve.

Nutritional Information
(as a percentage of daily intake)

4% (70) calories

2% (1 g) fat

4% (12 g) carbohydrates

4% (3 g) protein

6% (151 mg) sodium

5% (40 mg) calcium

7% (1 mg) iron

Gingered Yellow Pepper Soup
with White Beans

This thinly textured soup is gently perfumed with ginger and has the sweet flavor of yellow peppers. The white beans, which hide on the bottom of the plate, add their own complementary flavor and texture. The fresh herbs add contrast and give the soup a crisp edge.

The color of this soup is an astonishing brilliant yellow; serve it when you want all the guests to talk of nothing else when the plate is set in front of them.

Serves 8

2½ pounds sweet yellow bell peppers, cored and cut into eighths

1 medium-size onion, peeled and cut into eighths

3 large garlic cloves, peeled

1½-inch piece of fresh ginger, peeled and thinly sliced

1 quart Chicken Broth (page 42)

a little salt and freshly ground black pepper to taste

2 cups white beans cooked in water (page 69)

For Garnish

1 tablespoon very finely chopped fresh chives

1 tablespoon very finely chopped fresh parsley

In a very large bowl, combine the yellow peppers, onion, garlic, and ginger. Cover and microwave on HIGH for 15 minutes. Stir in the broth, seal airtight with a double layer of plastic wrap, and microwave on HIGH for 10 minutes. Puree in a blender in small batches, pressing securely on the lid of the blender jar with a kitchen towel to prevent the soup from spewing all over the kitchen. Season with salt and pepper, stir in the beans, return the soup to the bowl, and microwave on HIGH, uncovered, until very hot, about 5 minutes. Mix the chives and parsley together and sprinkle lightly over each serving of the soup.

Nutritional Information
(as a percentage of daily intake)

5% (93) calories

3% (2 g) fat

6% (16 g) carbohydrates

7% (5 g) protein

1% (33 mg) sodium

4% (33 mg) calcium

13% (2 mg) iron

LIGHT BISQUES

Light Tomato Bisque

Serve this soup cold or hot, depending on the weather; it is delicious both ways. The creamy texture rolls around in your mouth, and the hint of cayenne in the back of the throat that you discover after a few swallows balances the slight acidity of the tomatoes.

Serves 7

1 small onion, peeled and quartered
1 small carrot, trimmed, scrubbed, and quartered
1 small celery rib, cut into 1-inch lengths
1 28-ounce can crushed tomatoes in puree

⅛ teaspoon crushed dried thyme
⅛ teaspoon crushed dried rosemary
3½ cups milk
⅛ to ¼ teaspoon cayenne pepper (to taste)
a little salt to taste

In a food processor, finely chop the onion, carrot, and celery. Transfer to a large bowl, seal airtight with plastic wrap, and microwave on HIGH for 6 minutes. Add the tomatoes, thyme, and rosemary, seal airtight with plastic wrap, and microwave on HIGH for 15 minutes, stirring once midway through the cooking to prevent scorching. Puree in small batches in a blender, holding the top of the blender jar securely in place to prevent the soup from gushing all over the kitchen. Stir in the milk and season with cayenne (you should just barely taste it in the back of the throat) and a little salt. Reheat by microwaving on HIGH, uncovered, until very hot but not boiling, about 4 minutes.

Nutritional Information
(as a percentage of daily intake)

5% (104) calories
6% (4 g) fat
4% (12 g) carbohydrates
7% (5 g) protein

10% (247 mg) sodium
23% (181 mg) calcium
0% (0 mg) iron

MICROWAVE NOTE

Because the microwave will curdle whole milk if the cooking time is extended, the milk here is added at the end of the cooking and is microwaved just long enough to reheat the soup.

This lush, emerald green asparagus soup has a medium-thick texture and the fresh scent of rosemary.

Serves 6

1½ pounds fresh pencil-thin asparagus, bottoms trimmed and discarded, cut into 1-inch pieces
2 cups Chicken Broth (page 42)
¼ cup flour
2 cups skim milk

2 teaspoons very finely chopped fresh
rosemary *or* 1 teaspoon crushed
dried rosemary
a little salt and freshly ground black
pepper to taste

Place the asparagus in a medium bowl, seal airtight with plastic wrap, and microwave on HIGH for 6½ minutes. While asparagus is cooking, place the broth and flour in a blender and blend until smooth.

Cool asparagus under cold running water to set the color. Cut 6 of the asparagus tips lengthwise and reserve for garnish.

Place the broth in a large bowl and microwave on HIGH, uncovered, until bubbly and thickened, about 10 minutes, whisking until smooth midway through the cooking and again when the broth is finished cooking. Stir in the milk.

In a blender, in small batches with the lid held securely in place to prevent the soup from spewing all over the kitchen, puree the broth with the cooked asparagus. Mix in the rosemary and season with a little salt and pepper. Reheat, uncovered, in the microwave on HIGH until very hot, about 4 minutes. Whisk until smooth, ladle into bowls, and garnish with the reserved asparagus tips.

Variations

Quick Broccoli Bisque: Substitute broccoli flowerets for the asparagus.

Quick Carrot Bisque: Substitute carrots, scrubbed and sliced, for the asparagus and extend the microwaving time to 9 minutes. Substitute chives for the rosemary.

Nutritional Information
(as a percentage of daily intake)

4% (82) calories

2% (1 g) fat

4% (12 g) carbohydrates

11% (8 g) protein

3% (62 mg) sodium

16% (128 mg) calcium

7% (1 mg) iron

Carrot Bisque with Tomatoes

With its velvety texture and small chunks of diced tomato, this sweet, pale orange soup, scented lightly with the earthy aroma of chili powder and paprika, is at once warm and familiar-tasting, yet full of surprises. No salt or pepper is needed with all these heady flavors.

Serves 8

1 pound carrots, trimmed, scrubbed, and cut into 2-inch pieces
1 medium-size onion, peeled and quartered
2 large garlic cloves, peeled
1 teaspoon chili powder

1 teaspoon paprika
1 quart Chicken Broth (page 42)
3 tablespoons flour
2 cups skim milk
1 large tomato, cored, seeded, and finely diced

Place the carrots, onion, garlic, chili powder, and paprika in a very large bowl. Combine 1 to 2 cups of the chicken broth with the flour in a blender and blend until smooth. Pour over the vegetables with the remaining broth and skim milk and mix. Seal airtight with a double layer of plastic wrap and microwave on HIGH for 30 minutes. Puree in a blender, in small batches, holding the cover securely in place to prevent the soup from exploding out of the jar. Stir in the tomato, then reheat and serve.

Nutritional Information
(as a percentage of daily intake)

4% (87) calories
2% (1 g) fat
5% (15 g) carbohydrates
5% (4 g) protein

4% (85 mg) sodium
13% (100 mg) calcium
0% (0 mg) iron

With its velvety texture and full sweet flavor, this medium-bodied winter bisque is a warmhearted soup that will befriend all your guests. The ordinary parsnip, which we all too often dismiss as unworthy of importance at our table, here shows its valuable character.

The soup is lightly flavored and scented with cardamom and a hint of ginger, though for a sweeter, earthier, purer flavor, both spices can be eliminated.

Serves 8

2 large whole chicken breasts, bone in, skin and all visible fat removed
1 large onion, trimmed but unpeeled
1 medium-size carrot, trimmed and scrubbed
1 celery rib
1½ pounds parsnips, trimmed, peeled, and cut into 2-inch lengths

2 quarts skim milk
1 teaspoon ground cardamom
½ teaspoon ground ginger
1 heaped tablespoon finely chopped fresh chives

In a very large bowl, combine the chicken, onion, carrot, celery, parsnips, and skim milk. Seal airtight with a double layer of plastic wrap and microwave on HIGH for 55 minutes. Carefully uncover; remove and discard the chicken, onion, carrot, and celery. In a blender, in small batches, holding the top securely in place to prevent the soup from spewing all over the kitchen, puree the soup with the cardamom and ginger. Stir in the chives, reheat, and serve.

Nutritional Information
(as a percentage of daily intake)

8% (154) calories
5% (3 g) fat
8% (23 g) carbohydrates
15% (11 g) protein

8% (184 mg) sodium
40% (320 mg) calcium
0% (0 mg) iron

Broccoli and Potato Bisque

This pale green broccoli soup is gently flavored with hints of tarragon and is thickened with potato. As the broccoli cooks, the flavor becomes quite delicate, to some unidentifiable, so a garnish of small broccoli flowerets is added at the last moment. This is a versatile soup, good for company fare or family meals.

The recipe begins by making a chicken essence using milk instead of water, then the broccoli is cooked until tender, thus preserving its delicate flavor and color, and finally, the soup is pureed. If the broccoli were added at the beginning of the cooking, it would have discolored and turned the soup an unattractive khaki color.

Serves 6

1 whole chicken breast, bone in, skin and all visible fat removed
1 medium-size onion, trimmed but unpeeled
1 medium-size carrot, trimmed and scrubbed
1 celery rib
1 small *or* ½ large baking potato, scrubbed and peeled

3 garlic cloves, unpeeled
1 teaspoon crushed dried marjoram
2 teaspoons crushed dried tarragon
7 cups skim milk
1 large bunch of broccoli (about 1¾ pounds)
a little salt and freshly ground black pepper to taste

Combine all ingredients except broccoli, salt, and pepper in a very large bowl. Seal airtight with a double layer of plastic wrap and microwave on HIGH for 40 minutes.

Meanwhile, cut 1 cup of tiny flowerets from the broccoli. Place in a small bowl and cover. Have ready a bowl of ice water. Microwave flowerets on HIGH for 35 seconds. Immediately plunge into ice water to cool and set the color. Drain and set aside until serving time.

Carefully uncover soup; remove and discard the chicken, onion, carrot, and celery. Add the remaining uncooked broccoli to the bowl, seal airtight again, and microwave on HIGH for 10 minutes. Puree the soup in a blender, holding the lid securely in place to prevent the soup from exploding out of the jar, then strain. Taste and season with salt and pepper.

Reheat just before serving. Stir the prepared flowerets into the hot soup and ladle into bowls.

Nutritional Information
(as a percentage of daily intake)

9% (187) calories

5% (3 g) fat

10% (27 g) carbohydrates

21% (16 g) protein

10% (238 mg) sodium

50% (402 mg) calcium

7% (1 mg) iron

BEAN AND LENTIL SOUPS

Many-Bean Soup

All the beans in this highly textured soup cook simultaneously in the microwave—some become soft, some tender, and some stay firm. This gives this soup character, and the final dash of balsamic vinegar brings all the flavors together.

Often I just toss the garlic cloves, whole and peeled, into the soup, rather than chopping them with the other vegetables. This leaves half the servings with a sweet, tender surprise hidden among all the different-colored beans.

Serves 12

2 cups (about 12 ounces) 15-bean or other many-bean combination

2 turkey drumsticks *or* 1 large whole chicken breast, bone in, skin and all visible fat removed

2 quarts water

1 28-ounce can crushed tomatoes in puree

1 teaspoon crushed dried basil

1 teaspoon crushed dried oregano

1 teaspoon crushed dried thyme

1 medium-size carrot, trimmed, scrubbed, and cut into 1-inch pieces

1 celery rib, cut into 2-inch pieces

1 medium-size onion, peeled and quartered

1 sweet red bell pepper, cored, seeded, and cut into 2-inch pieces

8 large garlic cloves, peeled (see note above)

2 tablespoons balsamic vinegar

freshly ground black pepper to taste

In a very large bowl, combine the beans, turkey, water, tomatoes, basil, oregano, and thyme.

In a food processor, finely chop the carrot, celery, onion, red pepper, and garlic and add to the bowl with the other ingredients.

Seal airtight with a double layer of plastic wrap and microwave on HIGH for 99 minutes. Carefully uncover; remove and discard the turkey. Stir in the vinegar and season with pepper.

Nutritional Information
(as a percentage of daily intake)

6% (120) calories
3% (2 g) fat
7% (20 g) carbohydrates
9% (7 g) protein

6% (145 mg) sodium
6% (45 mg) calcium
20% (3 mg) iron

This is a sumptuous, thin, elegant black bean–flavored consommé that belongs at a formal dinner.

What I like best about this soup is that you can taste every flavor—every herb and spice, the turkey, even the onion, celery, and carrot. There are more wonderful subtleties in this soup than you'd expect from a traditional black bean soup.

Crabmeat is used here as a luxury; if not available, use the herbs alone.

Serves 7

½ pound (1¼ cups) black turtle beans
2 turkey drumsticks, skin removed
1 cup canned crushed tomatoes in puree *or* 1 cup canned peeled and drained Italian-style plum tomatoes, tightly packed
1 medium-size onion, peeled
1 celery rib

1 carrot, trimmed and scrubbed
5 large garlic cloves, peeled
1 bay leaf
1½ teaspoons crushed dried thyme
1½ teaspoons crushed dried oregano
1 teaspoon crushed dried rosemary
1½ teaspoons anise seeds
4 generous grinds of black pepper
1½ quarts water

For Garnish
½ cup finest-quality crabmeat
1 tablespoon very finely chopped fresh chives or cilantro

Combine all the soup ingredients in a very large bowl. Seal airtight with a double layer of plastic wrap and microwave on HIGH for 60 minutes.

Carefully uncover; remove and discard the drumsticks. Puree soup in a blender, in small batches, holding a towel securely over the top of the blender to prevent it from spewing soup all over the kitchen. Strain, pressing to extract all the soup, then discard the uncooked bits of bean.

Reheat before serving. Drop a tablespoon of crabmeat into the center of each serving and sprinkle with some of the chopped herbs.

Nutritional Information
(as a percentage of daily intake)

6% (119) calories

3% (2 g) fat

7% (18 g) carbohydrates

12% (9 g) protein

10% (228 mg) sodium

6% (48 mg) calcium

13% (2 mg) iron

Light Lentil Soup with Carrots

There is no reason for lentil soups to be as thick as mud. They can be light in texture and still full-flavored, as in this recipe. Diced carrots are cooked in apple juice for the garnish, and the apple juice adds a little sweetness to the soup. With some herbs sprinkled over each portion, this is a soup worthy of a company meal, but easy enough to make for a family dinner.

Serves 6

½ pound (1¼ cups) green or brown lentils
2 turkey drumsticks, skin and all visible fat removed
1 medium-size onion, peeled
1 large carrot, trimmed, scrubbed, and cut in half
1 celery rib, cut in half
4 garlic cloves, peeled

1 teaspoon crushed dried thyme
½ teaspoon crushed dried rosemary
3 quarts hottest possible tap water
2 medium-size carrots, trimmed, scrubbed, and cut into ¼-inch dice
1 cup apple juice
a little salt and freshly ground black pepper to taste

For Garnish
1 tablespoon chopped fresh parsley or fresh chives

In a very large bowl, combine the lentils, turkey, onion, halved carrot, celery, garlic, thyme, rosemary, and water. Seal airtight with a double layer of plastic wrap and microwave on HIGH for 99 minutes. Carefully uncover; remove and discard the turkey, onion, carrot, and celery. Puree soup in a blender, holding the cover of the blender securely in place with a kitchen towel to prevent it from erupting. Place in a large bowl and set aside.

Combine the diced carrots and apple juice in a medium bowl, cover, and microwave on HIGH for 6 minutes. Add to the pureed soup and season with salt and pepper. Cover and microwave on HIGH until very hot, about 6 minutes, then ladle into soup mugs or plates and sprinkle with parsley or chives.

Fresh Lima Bean Soup with Tomatoes and Herbs

With its tomato-flavored broth and tender but not mushy fresh limas, and the flavors of thyme and cilantro, this is soup with a lively play of flavors and textures. For lima bean lovers, this recipe will become a new friend, and it's easy to make.

Serves 10

2 cups shelled fresh lima beans
1½ quarts Chicken Broth (page 42)
½ teaspoon crushed dried thyme
3 large vine-ripened tomatoes, cored and cut into ½-inch dice

1 scallion, finely chopped
2 tablespoons finely chopped cilantro
a little salt and freshly ground black pepper to taste

In a very large bowl, combine the limas, broth, and thyme and seal airtight with a double layer of plastic wrap. Microwave on HIGH for 25 minutes. Add the tomatoes. Seal airtight with a double layer of plastic wrap and microwave on HIGH for 10 minutes. Stir in the scallion and cilantro, season with salt and pepper, and serve.

Nutritional Information
(as a percentage of daily intake)

3% (6) calories   2% (38 mg) sodium
3% (2 g) fat   2% (16 mg) calcium
3% (9 g) carbohydrates   7% (1 mg) iron
5% (4 g) protein

This thick, bold, golden-colored curried soup, made with yellow split peas rather than the earthier green or brown varieties, makes an audacious beginning to a winter meal. Serve it for a family meal without any garnish, just ladled into mugs or bowls. With chopped cilantro and yogurt as a garnish, the soup becomes a little more formal, ready for a company dinner. For a rustic version, serve the soup in terra-cotta bowls, streaked with Sweet Red Pepper Puree (page 41) and sprinkled with chopped chives or scallions.

Serves 8

1 pound (2¼ cups) dried yellow split peas, rinsed under cold water and drained
1 large whole chicken breast, bone in, skin and all visible fat removed
1 carrot, trimmed and scrubbed
1 small celery rib
1 medium-size onion, trimmed but unpeeled

2 garlic cloves, peeled
2 tablespoons curry powder
5 or 6 generous grinds of black pepper
juice of ½ lemon
1½ quarts water

Combine all ingredients in a very large bowl. Seal airtight with a double layer of plastic wrap and microwave on HIGH for 55 minutes. Carefully uncover; remove and discard the chicken, carrot, celery, and onion.

In small batches, puree soup in a blender, holding the top securely in place to prevent it from exploding all over the kitchen. Reheat and serve, garnished as you wish (see note above).

Nutritional Information
(as a percentage of daily intake)

10% (207) calories
3% (2 g) fat
13% (35 g) carbohydrates
19% (14 g) protein

3% (62 mg) sodium
2% (18 mg) calcium
20% (3 mg) iron

FISH SOUPS

Lots of Tender Seafood in a Light Broth with Ginger

This is an elegant fish soup, a soup of distinction. The delicate but complex flavor comes from combining chicken and fish broths and then gently flavoring them with ginger and cilantro. But all chicken or all fish broth can be used if you prefer.

After the broth is heated, squid, shrimp, and scallops are added and microwaved for three minutes to just cook the seafood so that it remains moist, tender, and sweet. Cilantro and scallions are added as a counterpoint to the sweet fish flavors.

Serves 6

1 cup Chicken Broth (page 42)
2 cups Fish Stock, (page 46)
1 cup water
1-inch piece of young fresh ginger, peeled, halved lengthwise, and sliced paper-thin
2 squid (2 to 3 ounces each), cleaned, tentacles cut into pieces, body split in half lengthwise and then cut into 1-inch-wide bands

6 ounces small shrimp, peeled of all but the tail segment
6 ounces bay scallops
2 scallions, green part only, coarsely chopped
1 tablespoon finely chopped cilantro

In a very large bowl, combine the chicken broth, fish stock, water, and ginger. Microwave on HIGH, uncovered, for 10 minutes. Add the remaining ingredients and microwave on HIGH, uncovered, for 3 minutes. Serve at once.

Nutritional Information
(as a percentage of daily intake)

5% (92) calories
2% (1 g) fat
2% (5 g) carbohydrates
21% (16 g) protein

9% (209 mg) sodium
4% (33 mg) calcium
7% (1 mg) iron

Without a doubt, these are the lightest and easiest-ever quenelles. These delicately textured and flavored small fish dumplings float buoyantly in a light broth with delicate strands of enoki mushrooms.

Quenelles are a good starter for a formal, elegant meal. You might want to follow with Duck with Cherry Sauce (page 210), some couscous (page 64), a green vegetable, and a sorbet (pages 260–264) for dessert if you are daring enough to try an all-microwave meal.

Serves 4

4 pounds fish heads (see note in Fish
    Stock, page 46), gills removed
    and all blood washed away under
    cold running water
2 quarts hottest possible tap water
¼ pound bay scallops
1 egg white
3 tablespoons skim milk

1 3½-ounce package enoki mush-
    rooms, cut 2 inches below the top,
    bottoms discarded
1 teaspoon very finely chopped fresh
    chives
a little salt and freshly ground black
    pepper to taste

In a very large bowl, combine the fish heads and water, seal airtight with a double layer of plastic wrap, and microwave on HIGH for 50 minutes. Strain and pour into an 8-cup glass measure. Microwave, uncovered, on HIGH until reduced to 1 quart, about 30 minutes.

While broth is cooking, place the scallops in a food processor and process until very well pureed, scraping the bottom and sides of the bowl as needed, for about 1 minute. In a small bowl, lightly beat the egg white, then measure out 1 tablespoon of the egg white and add it to the scallops. Puree for 10 seconds, again scraping the bowl to obtain a smooth texture. With the food processor still spinning, slowly drizzle the milk through the feed tube to make a smooth, well-blended quenelle batter.

When broth has reduced, set on the counter and, with 2 tablespoons, scoop about ½ tablespoon of the quenelle mixture onto one spoon, then reverse onto the other to form a lozenge shape. Use the empty spoon to drop the quenelle into the hot broth. At first the quenelle will sink, then it will rise to the surface. Make 12 quenelles in this way. Add the mushrooms to the broth with the quenelles and microwave on HIGH, uncovered, for 2 minutes. Stir in the chives, season with salt and pepper, and serve.

Nutritional Information
(as a percentage of daily intake)

4% (83) calories

2% (1 g) fat

3% (7 g) carbohydrates

16% (12 g) protein

14% (333 mg) sodium

3% (22 mg) calcium

0% (0 mg) iron

Lobster Soup

The champagne-colored lobster broth in this recipe is richly flavored. The lobster meat is tender, fresh, and sweet. The tomato and parsley accents add freshness to the soup as a whole.

This recipe is formal, elegant, and exquisite. It deserves to be the *pièce de résistance* at a formal dinner party. It is too grand and too expensive to serve casually.

This is not a recipe for the squeamish—two whole live lobsters are cut up during the preparation.

Serves 6

2 1¼- to 1½-pound live lobsters
1 medium-size carrot, trimmed and scrubbed
1 small onion, trimmed but unpeeled
1 small celery rib

2 garlic cloves, unpeeled
5 fresh parsley sprigs
5 cups water
½ cup finely diced, cored, and seeded tomato

For Garnish
1 teaspoon very finely chopped fresh parsley

Cut the tails off the lobsters and split the tails lengthwise down the back with a large cook's knife. Bend open the shells and remove the meat with a small spoon, scraping against the inside of the shell. Save shells. Cut meat into 1-inch chunks and reserve. Cover and refrigerate.

Break the claws off the lobsters and arrange on a plate like spokes of a wheel. Microwave on HIGH, uncovered, for 2 minutes to loosen the meat from the shells. Crack with a small hammer or nutcracker and remove the meat from the claws. Save the shells and any juices that accumulate under them. Add the claw meat to the tail meat, cover and refrigerate.

In a very large bowl, combine the lobster heads and all the shells and juices that have accumulated with the carrot, onion, celery, garlic, parsley, and water. Seal airtight with a double layer of plastic wrap and microwave on HIGH for 45 minutes. Carefully uncover, strain into an 8-cup glass measure, and microwave on HIGH, uncovered, until reduced to 1 quart, about 25 minutes.

Add the tomato and reserved lobster meat to the broth and cover. Microwave on HIGH for 5 minutes or until soup is very hot. Lobster will cook while broth is heating.

Ladle into soup bowls or plates and sprinkle the top of each serving with a little parsley. Serve at once.

Nutritional Information
(as a percentage of daily intake)

4% (71) calories   12% (277 mg) sodium
2% (1 g) fat   2% (13 mg) calcium
1% (4 g) carbohydrates   0% (0 mg) iron
11% (15 g) protein

COLD SOUPS

Summer Beet Soup

This brilliant, fuchsia-colored soup is my favorite cold soup. I have made it, with only slight variations, for almost 10 years, but never has it been so good as with the microwave. Microwaving pulls all the flavor and color out of the beets, resulting in a brilliantly colored and sweet, intensely flavored soup.

Serves 8

1 pound beef stewing meat, trimmed
   of all visible fat
1 large tomato
1 large carrot, trimmed, scrubbed, and
   quartered
1 celery rib, cut into 3 pieces
1 large onion, trimmed but unpeeled
1 bay leaf

½ teaspoon crushed dried thyme
2 large garlic cloves, unpeeled
1 whole clove
1½ quarts water
juice of ½ lemon
3 medium-size bunches (12 medium-
   size) of beets, peeled and shredded
1 quart nonfat buttermilk

For Garnish
1 tablespoon finely chopped fresh dill
   or cilantro

Combine all ingredients except the buttermilk in a very large bowl. Seal airtight with a double layer of plastic wrap and microwave on HIGH for 55 minutes. Carefully uncover and strain. Cover and refrigerate until cold. Stir in the buttermilk.

    Serve very cold, each serving garnished with a little chopped dill or cilantro.

Variation

Hot Beet Essence (serves 2): To serve hot as a clear beet soup, reheat the soup after straining and garnish each serving with a teaspoon of light sour cream, if you wish.

Nutritional Information
(as a percentage of daily intake)

5% (93) calories

3% (2 g) fat

5% (13 g) carbohydrates

8% (6 g) protein

7% (176 mg) sodium

19% (150 mg) calcium

0% (0 mg) iron

Red Pepper Gazpacho

Our infatuation with gazpacho in the last decade led restaurants to produce gazpachos in an array of traditional and nontraditional colors, such as green and white; I have even seen a borscht called purple gazpacho.

This version is true to the classic in color but inverts two ingredients: red peppers are used as the base, not the accent flavor, and tomatoes are used as the accent flavor, not the base. Sweeter than a traditional gazpacho, this highly textured summer soup can be given an extra fillip by adding enough cayenne to gently surprise the back of your throat.

There are enough cool flavors and textures and enough colors in this soup that bowls of garnishes are unnecessary.

Serves 4

1 recipe Sweet Red Pepper Puree
  (page 41)
1½ cups plain nonfat yogurt
juice of 1 lemon
1 large pickling cucumber, scrubbed
  and finely diced
1 scallion, finely chopped
1 small vine-ripened tomato, cored,
  seeded, and finely diced

2 teaspoons finely chopped fresh parsley
2 teaspoons finely chopped fresh dill
2 teaspoons finely chopped cilantro
½ teaspoon cayenne pepper, or to taste
  (optional)
freshly ground black pepper to taste

Stir all the ingredients together. Refrigerate until serving time. Serve chilled.

Nutritional Information
(as a percentage of daily intake)

5% (96) calories
2% (1 g) fat
6% (17 g) carbohydrates
9% (7 g) protein

3% (74 mg) sodium
25% (197 mg) calcium
13% (2 mg) iron

================================

Sweet Red Pepper Puree

The fire engine red color and intensely sweet pepper flavor in this recipe are an outstanding example of how the microwave intensifies the colors and flavors of the foods it cooks.

Use this recipe or one of its variations as a dip or as a sauce for vegetables, chicken, or fish.

Makes about 1 ½ cups

2 large sweet red bell peppers, cored
2 large garlic cloves, peeled
juice of ½ lemon

1 teaspoon paprika (preferably Hungarian)
freshly ground black pepper to taste

Combine the peppers and garlic in a large bowl. Cover and microwave on HIGH for 10 minutes. Puree peppers and garlic in a food processor with the lemon juice and paprika, then season with black pepper.

Variations

Sweet and Hot Red Pepper Puree: Add ¼ teaspoon cayenne pepper to the puree with the paprika.

Red Pepper Sauce with Herbs: To either the Sweet Red Pepper Puree recipe or the Sweet and Hot Red Pepper Puree variation, add 1 tablespoon each of finely chopped fresh parsley, chives, and cilantro.

Nutritional Information
(as a percentage of daily intake),
per ¼-cup serving

1% (16) calories
0% (0 g) fat
1% (4 g) carbohydrates
0% (0 g) protein

0% (3 mg) sodium
1% (4 mg) calcium
7% (1 mg) iron

BROTH, CONSOMMÉS, AND STOCK

Chicken Broth

Making chicken broth in the microwave is simpler, easier, and four times faster than making it conventionally. All you do is combine the ingredients, cover, and microwave for 45 minutes.

In the variation below for chicken consommé, the broth is reduced to intensify the flavor, then it is clarified (strained through beaten egg whites to remove the impurities) to make a crystal-clear soup. Although the reduction takes longer in the microwave than it would ordinarily, there is no watching or stirring, so it is easier. I have also developed a quick way to clarify the soup, a variant on the traditional procedure, which speeds up and simplifies the process.

Serves 6

2 large whole chicken breasts, bone in, skin and all visible fat removed
1 medium-size onion, trimmed but unpeeled
1 celery rib
1 medium-size carrot, trimmed and scrubbed
1 teaspoon crushed dried thyme
3 garlic cloves, unpeeled
7 cups water
a little salt and freshly ground black pepper to taste (optional)

In a very large bowl, combine all ingredients except salt and pepper. Seal airtight with a double layer of plastic wrap and microwave on HIGH for 45 minutes. Carefully uncover and strain; then season with pepper only if it's being served on its own as a broth; otherwise, season when it is used in another recipe. Skim fat from the surface of the broth or refrigerate and remove the fat when congealed. Store for 2 days in the refrigerator or freeze for up to 3 months.

Variation

Chicken Consommé (makes 1 quart): Use 3 pounds chicken breasts. Reduce the cooked broth to 4½ cups by microwaving on HIGH, uncovered, for about 40 minutes. Beat 2 egg whites in an electric mixer until they form soft peaks. Continue beating as you slowly pour the boiling reduced soup onto the egg whites. Strain through a large sieve lined with a thin towel that has been dampened with water and squeezed dry. Season. Bring back to a boil before serving.

Nutritional Information
(as a percentage of daily intake)

2% (30) calories   2% (53 mg) sodium
3% (2 g) fat   0% (0 mg) calcium
1% (2 g) carbohydrates 0% (0 mg) iron
3% (2 g) protein

With its deep coral color, rich vegetable flavor, and crystal clarity, this soup rivals the most elegant and labor-intensive classic beef or chicken consommé, yet it takes only a couple of minutes to prepare—though it does cook for an hour.

The recipe can be adapted to the time of year and seasonal availability. Add or substitute shallots, yellow bell peppers, parsnips, celeriac (celery root), leeks, pale-colored cabbages, shredded lettuces, and green or yellow squash, as you like. Carrots, tomatoes, and red bell peppers give the consommé its brilliant color, so be sure to use them.

You should have 6 to 7 cups of chopped vegetables to 7 cups of water.

Serves 6

3 medium-size carrots, trimmed, scrubbed, and quartered

2 medium-size onions, trimmed but unpeeled, quartered

2 medium-size tomatoes, cored and halved

2 celery ribs, quartered

4 parsley sprigs

2 garlic cloves, unpeeled

1 bay leaf

1 sweet red bell pepper, cored, seeded, and quartered

1 medium-size turnip, ends trimmed off, thickly peeled, and quartered

½-inch piece of fresh ginger, unpeeled

7 cups water

a little salt and freshly ground black pepper to taste

For Garnish

1 teaspoon very finely chopped cilantro

1 teaspoon very finely chopped fresh parsley

1 teaspoon very finely chopped fresh chives

In several small batches, using a food processor, finely chop all ingredients except water, salt, and pepper.

Combine with the water in a very large bowl, seal airtight with a double layer of plastic wrap, and microwave on HIGH for 60 minutes.

Carefully uncover and strain through a sieve lined with cheesecloth, pressing gently on the vegetables to release all their liquid. Taste and season with salt and pepper.

Just before serving, mix together the cilantro, parsley, and chives. Reheat soup to very hot, then sprinkle each serving with the chopped herbs.

Variation

Vegetable Stock: Use 9 cups of water to produce 2 quarts of vegetable stock. Vegetable stock can be stored in the refrigerator for 2 days or frozen for 3 months.

Nutritional Information
(as a percentage of daily intake)

1% (28) calories
0% (0 g) fat
2% (6 g) carbohydrates
1% (1 g) protein

0% (7 mg) sodium
0% (0 mg) calcium
0% (0 mg) iron

Fish Stock

Making fish stock, if you don't mind washing and cleaning the fish bones, is as easy as combining two ingredients and microwaving them for half an hour.

About Bones for Fish Stock: For the best flavor, use the heads of large white fish, such as grouper or halibut. Use the bones and tails of white fish if enough heads aren't available. Avoid the heads, tails, or bones of oily fish such as salmon and swordfish, which will make too delicately flavored a stock and will sometimes leave the stock oily and color it an unwanted pale yellow. To prevent bitterness, wash thoroughly to remove all blood and remove the gills.

Serves 3 (3 cups)

**3 pounds fish heads, bones, and tails
(see note above), washed clean
of all blood and chopped or broken into 2- to 3-inch pieces**

1 quart hottest possible tap water

Combine everything in a very large bowl. Seal airtight with a double layer of plastic wrap and microwave on HIGH for 30 minutes. Carefully uncover and strain.

Fish stock can be refrigerated for 2 days or frozen for 3 months.

*Nutritional Information
(as a percentage of daily intake)*

2% (46) calories
0% (0 g) fat
2% (5 g) carbohydrates
8% (6 g) protein

5% (120 mg) sodium
0% (0 mg) calcium
0% (0 mg) iron

Rice, Grains, Beans, and Pasta

The microwave cooks rice better, although not necessarily faster, than ordinary methods. Because the microwave cooks rice on the inside at the same time the water or broth cooks it on the outside, each grain remains separate and distinct. No swollen, watery surfaces to become gummy, just firm but tender grains. With brown rice, the bran (the brown outer covering of the rice) becomes soft without becoming gooey. The grains of white rice never stick together from the starch on their surface. And when you're cooking the fragrant rices, like basmati and tex-mati, the microwave enhances the popcornlike aroma that rises from the rice.

There are more than 15 rice recipes and variations in this chapter. There is a simple microwave pilaf with variations using saffron, curry, herbs, and brown rice. There are brown rice recipes, plain and flavored with orange, and a spicy brown rice casserole with lentils that is a personal favorite. There is an elegantly fragrant recipe for basmati rice with fresh herbs. There are five risotto recipes (see page 47), making this classic rice dish of northern Italy so simple to prepare that it can become part of your everyday cooking. And there is a wild rice casserole with barley and wild mushrooms filled with chewy textures and nutty flavors.

Grains cook magnificently in the microwave. Mix them with flavorings and broth, cover, and pop into the oven. In less than half an hour, uncover and serve. It's that simple. There are two casseroles in this chapter made with barley, the most comforting of all grains. There is a polenta recipe that has taken the grueling hour of stirring out of polenta making, reducing it to one simple stir. There is a recipe that makes couscous, which once took hours of steaming to prepare, in less than a fifth of the normal time. And there is a recipe for millet with lemon and herbs and a recipe for a fresh summer salad made with bulgur.

No other cooking method or technique can touch the microwave for preparing dried beans. Microwaved beans retain their individual identities, tastes, and textures perfectly as they cook to tenderness. And with the microwave, beans can be prepared in one simple step from dry to perfectly cooked. Just combine the beans with water in a very large bowl, seal airtight with plastic wrap (see directions in the introduction to the soup chapter), and microwave until done.

It will take about an hour and 45 minutes to cook most beans, and as much as 2 hours for some very dry beans. The first time I set the timer for 99 minutes on HIGH to cook beans, I confess to being a little uneasy. That was, after all, the longest setting allowed by the oven, and it contradicted all I had read about food cooking quickly in the microwave. But it worked. And the beans tasted better than if they had been boiled. A million times better than canned. No soft mushy textures, no water-saturated surfaces. Just perfect, tender beans.

Contrary to what you've heard, you can cook pasta in the microwave. But certain types of pasta—small individual shapes like bowties and ziti—are best. Except within the context of the recipes here, I do not recommend cooking pasta in the microwave. All too often the result is a gummy, almost unpalatable noodle. If you plan to experiment with pasta in the microwave, don't do it for a company dinner. Try it out on yourself first. The recipe on page 82 will provide you with the details of cooking pasta in the microwave.

Rice Pilaf

Virtually every cook has, at one time or another, made one form or another of rice pilaf, which has become a foundation for home cooking. The gently flavored rice, with each grain separate, has become the standard foil for Western cooking. Although I rarely serve a pilaf, making it in the microwave has revived my interest in this classic.

Serves 4

1 small onion, peeled and quartered
1 large garlic clove, peeled
¼ cup skim milk
1 cup long-grain white rice
2 cups Chicken Broth (page 42),
   Vegetable Consommé (page 44), or
   water

2 teaspoons unsalted butter or fruity
   olive oil (optional)
a little salt and freshly ground black
   pepper to taste

In a food processor, finely chop the onion and garlic and transfer to a large bowl. Add the milk, cover, and microwave on HIGH for 3 minutes. Stir in the rice and stock, cover, and microwave on HIGH until all the broth is absorbed, about 17 minutes. With a fork, stir in the butter or oil, if desired, season with salt and pepper, and serve.

Variations

Yellow (Saffron) Pilaf: Substitute 3 large peeled shallots for the onion and increase the garlic to 2 cloves. Mix ¼ teaspoon crushed saffron with the stock.

Curried Pilaf: Stir in 2 to 3 teaspoons curry powder and 2 tablespoons dried currants or golden raisins with the stock. Add 2 tablespoons toasted almond slices to the pilaf just before seasoning it with salt and pepper.

Herbed Pilaf: Add 2 tablespoons finely chopped fresh parsley, 1 tablespoon finely chopped fresh chives, and 1 tablespoon finely chopped fresh basil, tarragon, or cilantro; or ¼ cup finely chopped fresh herbs of your choice to the cooked rice.

Brown Rice Pilaf: Substitute long-grain brown rice for the white rice and extend the cooking time to 22 minutes. If rice is parboiled (see note, page 54), extend the cooking time to 27 minutes. Add ½ cup chopped toasted hazelnuts or walnuts just before seasoning with salt and pepper, if you wish. Neither curry nor saffron works well with brown rice pilaf, though you might want to add some herbs, perhaps 2 tablespoons of finely chopped fresh parsley, 1 tablespoon finely chopped fresh chives, and 1½ teaspoons finely chopped fresh rosemary or oregano.

Nutritional Information
(as a percentage of daily intake)

11% (214) calories
5% (3 g) fat
15% (41 g) carbohydrates
7% (5 g) protein

2% (54 mg) sodium
5% (38 mg) calcium
13% (2 mg) iron

Herbed Basmati Rice

Using the microwave, the rice is cooked in just over half the normal time, and the grains remain separate without being coated and cooked in oil or fat.

The variation for basmati rice with toasted hazelnuts can be made with water and served for breakfast, with a little honey or maple syrup, or it can be made with broth and used as an accompaniment for chicken or game.

Serves 6

1 cup brown basmati rice
2 cups Chicken Broth (page 42) or water
1 tablespoon finely chopped fresh parsley

1 tablespoon finely chopped cilantro
a little salt and freshly ground black pepper to taste

Combine the rice and broth or water in a large bowl. Seal airtight with plastic wrap and microwave on HIGH for 20 minutes. Carefully uncover, stir in the herbs, season with salt and pepper, and serve.

Variations

Basmati Rice with Toasted Hazelnuts: Place ¼ cup hazelnuts in a large shallow dish and microwave on HIGH, uncovered, for 5 minutes. Remove and rub off the skins (unlike traditional blanching, the skins will slip off easily). Chop nuts coarsely. Cook the rice as directed above and substitute the roasted hazelnuts for the herbs.

Buttered Basmati Rice: Add 1 tablespoon unsalted butter to the rice, then taste and season with salt and pepper.

Nutritional Information
(as a percentage of daily intake)

9% (181) calories
3% (2 g) fat
16% (37 g) carbohydrates
7% (5 g) protein

1% (31 mg) sodium
3% (15 mg) calcium
7% (1 mg) iron

Most people associate brown rice with the gummy, dense concoctions of the sixties' health food movement and don't realize that brown rice is simple, aromatic, and delicious.

Here the rice is cooked with a little orange rind, for flavor and aroma, and some butter can be added if you wish. Use this anytime you would normally serve a pilaf.

Topped with poached fruits or berries and lightly sweetened, this makes a fine breakfast cereal.

Serves 4

1 cup long-grain rice
2¾ cups water or broth (page 42)
1 tablespoon dried grated orange peel
  or the finely grated zest of 1 orange

a little salt and freshly ground black
  pepper to taste
1 tablespoon unsalted butter
  (optional)

Combine the rice, water, or broth, and orange peel in a large bowl, cover, and microwave on HIGH for 22 minutes if parboiled (see note below), for 27 minutes if not. Season with salt and pepper and stir in the butter, if desired.

Variation

Plain Brown Rice: Omit the orange peel.

Nutritional Information
(as a percentage of daily intake)

11% (212) calories
8% (5 g) fat
13% (37 g) carbohydrates
7% (5 g) protein

2% (39 mg) sodium
2% (19 mg) calcium
7% (1 mg) iron

NOTE ON BROWN RICE

Brown rice is processed to remove the tough outer hull but not the bran. It is sometimes parboiled, a process that hardens the grains, ensuring that they remain separated when cooked; parboiling slightly increases the cooking time. Check the package when buying brown rice to determine if it has been parboiled.

With the soft texture of the lentils added to the nutty, slightly chewy brown rice and the deeply colored and flavored seasonings, this is particularly appropriate on winter days when you want food that leaves you feeling warm and cozy inside.

Serves 8

1 cup long-grain brown rice
¼ cup green lentils
3 cups water
2 teaspoons paprika
½ teaspoon onion powder
½ teaspoon garlic powder
½ teaspoon chili powder

¼ teaspoon cayenne pepper
½ cup tomato-vegetable drink
1 tablespoon tomato paste
1 large ripe tomato, cored and cut
  into ¼-inch dice
a little salt and freshly ground black
  pepper to taste

Combine the rice, lentils, water, paprika, onion powder, garlic powder, chili powder, and cayenne in a large bowl and mix well to dissolve the spices. Cover and microwave on HIGH for 25 minutes if rice is parboiled, 35 minutes if not.

Stir in the tomato-vegetable drink, tomato paste, and tomato. Season with salt and pepper to taste and serve immediately.

Nutritional Information
(as a percentage of daily intake)

6% (113) calories
2% (1 g) fat
9% (24 g) carbohydrates
4% (3 g) protein

3% (61 mg) sodium
2% (15 mg) calcium
7% (1 mg) iron

Cold Rice Salad with White Beans and Raspberry Vinegar

I make this colorful rice salad, which is lightly perfumed with raspberry vinegar, for large parties and buffets. The combination of different colors, flavors, and textures makes it as popular as it is festive.

Serves 10

½ small sweet yellow (or orange) bell pepper, cut into 4 pieces
½ small sweet red bell pepper, cut into 4 pieces
½ small sweet green bell pepper, cut into 4 pieces
½ large onion, peeled
2 garlic cloves, peeled
1 quart Chicken Broth (page 42)

2 cups long-grain white or basmati rice
1 cup tightly packed fresh parsley leaves
1 scallion, cut into 4 pieces
2 tablespoons fruity olive oil
2 tablespoons raspberry vinegar
2 cups cooked white beans (page 69)
a little salt and freshly ground black pepper to taste

In a food processor, finely chop the yellow, red, and green peppers with the onion and garlic. Transfer to a very large bowl, cover, and microwave on HIGH for 6 minutes. Set aside.

In a large bowl, combine the broth and rice, cover, and microwave on HIGH for 22 minutes.

While rice is cooking, in a food processor finely chop the parsley and scallion.

Stir the cooked peppers and onion, parsley and scallion, oil, and vinegar into the rice. Gently stir in the beans and season with salt and pepper.

Serve at room temperature or refrigerate to serve cold.

Variation

Hot Confetti Rice: Cook the peppers, onion, and garlic, and the rice, as directed above. Combine, then mix with 2 tablespoons fruity olive oil or butter and ½ cup finely chopped fresh parsley. Mix well, cover, reheat for 3 minutes on HIGH, and serve.

Nutritional Information
(as a percentage of daily intake)

11% (226) calories
6% (4 g) fat
15% (41 g) carbohydrates
9% (7 g) protein

1% (28 mg) sodium
6% (45 mg) calcium
20% (3 mg) iron

If you are unfamiliar with risotto, the creamy rice dish of northern Italy, you're in for a treat. Unlike pilaf, with its dry and separate grains, risotto has a thick, rich, creamy coating over firm and slightly chewy grains.

The classic risotto preparation requires almost an hour of constant attention and stirring. But microwave risotto takes only 3 minutes of preparation and 18 minutes of unattended cooking, so I am willing to make it even for myself for a quick lunch.

If you are a serious cook familiar with risotto, this recipe will convince you never to make another risotto by hand.

Barbara Kafka discovered that risotto could be made in a microwave, and I remember her joy in preparing a saffron risotto for me and pointing out the glistening sheen on the surface of the rice, one of the signs of a great risotto. I have modified Kafka's original recipe slightly to make this fine, astonishingly easy risotto.

Rice Note: Risotto must be made with a medium-grain rice, such as Italian Arborio.

Serves 4

1 tablespoon fruity olive oil
3 shallots, finely chopped
1 large garlic clove, finely chopped
1 cup medium-grain rice such as
  Arborio

2½ cups Chicken Broth (page 42)
2 tablespoons freshly grated Parmesan
  cheese

Stir together the oil, shallots, garlic, and rice in a medium bowl and microwave on HIGH, uncovered, for 3 minutes. Mix in the broth, cover, and microwave on HIGH for 18 minutes. Stir to see if broth is absorbed and risotto is creamy. If not, microwave for another 2 to 5 minutes, then stir in the Parmesan cheese and serve.

Variations

Saffron Risotto: Add ⅛ teaspoon saffron threads, crushed, with the stock. For a clean saffron flavor, do not add the Parmesan, especially if this risotto is used as a side dish. As a first course, the Parmesan will add needed body to the risotto.

Risotto with Sun-Dried Tomatoes: Add 3 tablespoons finely chopped sun-dried tomatoes and 2 tablespoons finely chopped fresh parsley to the risotto with the Parmesan.

Risotto with Olives: Add 2 tablespoons finely chopped black oil-cured or 3 tablespoons finely chopped Calamata olives to the risotto.

Nutritional Information
(as a percentage of daily intake)

13% (269) calories
14% (9 g) fat
15% (42 g) carbohydrates
 8% (6 g) protein

4% (84 mg) sodium
7% (55 mg) calcium
13% (2 mg) iron

Wild Rice Casserole with Barley and Wild Mushrooms

This easy-to-prepare casserole is full of rich, earthy, nutty flavors and is perfect for cold-weather dinners.

Serves 8

½ cup pearl barley
1 cup wild rice
3½ cups Chicken Broth (page 42)

½ pound fresh shiitake or cremini mushrooms, bottoms of stems trimmed, cut into ¾-inch chunks

In a very large bowl, combine the barley, wild rice, broth, and mushrooms. Seal airtight with a double layer of plastic wrap and microwave on HIGH for 45 minutes, or until all the broth is absorbed.

Nutritional Information
(as a percentage of daily intake)

7% (134) calories
2% (1 g) fat
9% (26 g) carbohydrates
7% (5 g) protein

1% (26 mg) sodium
1% (8 mg) calcium
7% (1 mg) iron

BASIC PREPARATION OF WILD RICE

For 2½ cups cooked wild rice, combine 1 cup wild rice and 2 cups Chicken Broth (page 42) or water in a medium bowl and cover. Microwave on HIGH for 30 minutes or until all the liquid is absorbed.

This salad is filled with the freshness of summer—fresh herbs, mostly parsley, the freshest-tasting of all herbs, with a little mint and grated lemon peel—all lightly dressed with a little olive oil and balsamic vinegar.

Bulgur is made by steaming and drying whole wheat berries and then cracking them into tiny pieces. Bulgur has a soft texture and a nutty flavor.

Serves 12

1 pound (about 2 cups) bulgur (fine, medium, or coarse)

1 quart water

1 small bunch fresh parsley, stems removed

leaves from 4 large mint sprigs

3 small scallions, cut into 2-inch lengths

1 garlic clove, peeled

1 tablespoon crushed dried rosemary

3 tablespoons extra-virgin or virgin olive oil

2 tablespoons balsamic vinegar

grated zest of 1 large lemon

a little salt and freshly ground black pepper to taste

Combine the bulgur and water in a large bowl and microwave on HIGH, uncovered, for 15 minutes. Stir, cover, and allow to stand at room temperature until cooled.

Meanwhile, in a food processor, finely chop the parsley, mint, scallions, and garlic with the rosemary, oil, and vinegar. Mix into the bulgur with the lemon zest and season with salt and pepper.

Nutritional Information
(as a percentage of daily intake)

7% (147) calories

6% (4 g) fat

9% (25 g) carbohydrates

5% (4 g) protein

0% (3 mg) sodium

3% (20 mg) calcium

13% (2 mg) iron

BASIC PREPARATION OF BULGUR

Place 2 cups (1 pound) bulgur in a large bowl with 2 cups water. Microwave on HIGH, uncovered, for 15 minutes. Cover and let cool or serve immediately, seasoned as you wish.

Polenta

Until I discovered that I could cook polenta in a microwave, I made it very rarely—the hour or so of required stirring over a water bath placed it well beyond my cooking tolerance. But with the microwave, and only two stirs, I have polenta in just 10 minutes. That makes it easier to prepare than mashed potatoes, and now I often use polenta as a substitute for mashed potatoes.

Serve it with any roast, spooning some of the pan drippings and juices over the polenta.

Polenta is just another name for cornmeal, though the Italian varieties are more coarsely ground than ours. Either can be used in this recipe.

This polenta can be chilled until solid, then sliced and fried or grilled as is traditional in northern Italy.

Serves 6

3 cups water
1 cup polenta (not instant) or
    cornmeal

1 tablespoon unsalted butter
a little salt and freshly ground black
    pepper to taste

Mix the water and polenta in a large bowl and microwave on HIGH, uncovered, for 10 minutes, whisking hard midway through the cooking to make the polenta smooth. When cooked, whisk again until smooth, stir in the butter, and season with salt and pepper. Serve immediately.

Variation

Polenta with Cheese: Flavor, as you wish, with one of these cheeses: 3 ounces soft goat cheese (chèvre), for a sharp, nontraditional flavor; 3 ounces ripe Gorgonzola (Italian blue cheese), or 3 tablespoons grated Parmesan cheese, for a traditional flavor; eliminate the butter and then season, if necessary, with a little salt and pepper.

*Nutritional Information
(as a percentage of daily intake)*

4% (89) calories
5% (3 g) fat
5% (15 g) carbohydrates
3% (2 g) protein

1% (16 mg) sodium
1% (5 mg) calcium
0% (0 mg) iron

This simple golden-colored, saffron-flavored grain is the staple of northern African cooking, with Moroccans locked into heated battle with Tunisians over which nation may claim couscous exclusively as its own. As Americans, fortunately, we don't have to enter into the debate; we can just enjoy the delights of this simple dish, which I eat almost as often for breakfast as for dinner.

Couscous is made by moistening semolina flour, cutting it into tiny bits, and drying it. It is mistakenly thought of as a grain; it's really an eggless pasta.

One of the hallmarks of good couscous is that each tiny grain be separate. Traditionally this is accomplished by steaming the couscous, rubbing it by hand to separate, then steaming the couscous again. Here the couscous is cooked, cooled, and the grains separated and then reheated. Using the microwave, making couscous takes less than a fifth of the traditional preparation time.

Serve plain couscous anytime you would think of serving a rice pilaf or let this great tiny pasta become a part of your next breakfast, with some chopped dried fruits or raisins and a little honey or maple syrup to sweeten it. Just prepare as directed in the basic preparation below.

For large parties, microwave four or five different winter vegetables, such as broccoli, cauliflower, acorn squash, butternut squash, zucchini, carrots, celery root, and potatoes, and arrange the vegetables on a mound of couscous. Serve with the Moroccan sauce Harissa (page 132), passed separately.

Serves 6

3 cups hottest possible tap water
¼ teaspoon crushed saffron threads
2 cups couscous

a little salt and freshly ground white
 pepper to taste

In a large bowl, stir together the water and saffron. Stir in the couscous. Microwave on HIGH, uncovered, for 5 minutes. Fluff and stir with a fork to break up the big lumps, then season with salt and pepper. Cover and refrigerate until well chilled, at least 2 hours.

Fluff, this time using your fingers to separate the grains. Microwave on HIGH until hot, about 6 minutes, then serve.

Variations

Plain Couscous: Eliminate the saffron.

Couscous with Almonds: Add ½ cup toasted slivered almonds just before reheating the couscous.

Couscous with Butter or Olive Oil: For a more tender couscous flavored with butter or olive oil, stir 2 tablespoons of unsalted butter or full-flavored olive oil into the couscous just before serving.

Nutritional Information
(as a percentage of daily intake)

11% (218) calories   0% (10 mg) sodium
 0% (0 g) fat   0% (0 mg) calcium
17% (48 g) carbohydrates 0% (0 mg) iron
11% (8 g) protein

BASIC PREPARATION OF COUSCOUS

Combine 3 cups water or stock (either chicken or vegetable, pages 42 and 44), with 2 cups couscous in a large bowl and microwave on HIGH, uncovered, for 5 minutes. Fluff with a fork and refrigerate until cold, then separate the grains by rubbing the couscous between your fingers. Microwave on HIGH until very hot, about 6 minutes, then stir in 2 tablespoons unsalted butter or full-flavored olive oil and season with salt and pepper. Makes about 5 cups.

Millet with Lemon and Herbs

Millet is a small, mild-tasting, mustard-colored seed with a slightly crunchy texture when cooked. The beady texture makes it an interesting alternative to rice.

Here the millet is cooked, then flavored with fresh and dried herbs and with garlic and lemon. Serve this with fish, chicken, or wild game from quails to venison.

Don't use pepper in this recipe; it will overwhelm the light, delicate flavor of the millet.

Serves 4

1 cup millet
3 cups Chicken Broth (page 42 or water
½ cup tightly packed fresh parsley leaves

1½ teaspoons crushed dried tarragon
½ teaspoon crushed dried marjoram
1 small garlic clove, peeled
grated zest of ¼ lemon
a little salt to taste (optional)

Combine the millet and broth or water in a very large bowl. Microwave on HIGH, uncovered, for 18 minutes. Meanwhile, combine the parsley, tarragon, marjoram, garlic, and lemon zest in a food processor and process until very finely chopped.

Drain the millet and mix with the herbs and lemon zest. Season with salt, if desired, and serve.

Nutritional Information
(as a percentage of daily intake)

7% (135) calories
3% (2 g) fat
9% (24 g) carbohydrates
5% (4 g) protein

2% (45 mg) sodium
2% (18 mg) calcium
20% (3 mg) iron

MICROWAVE NOTE

Millet needs to be microwaved uncovered in an extra-large bowl. If covered or cooked in a smaller bowl, the fibrous particles of the millet bubble up and spew out.

Quinoa with Herbs

Quinoa has recently arrived in America as an exotic grain. It was originally grown high in the Andes Mountains of South America, where it was prized by the ancient Incas. With its firm but tender texture and mild grasslike flavor, quinoa makes an excellent accompaniment to chicken and fish, and it can be used in place of rice in cold salads. In this recipe the quinoa is flavored with onion and garlic, a little mustard, and some fresh herbs.

Serves 6

1 medium-size onion, peeled and quartered
1 large garlic clove, peeled
1 cup quinoa, rinsed under cold running water
2 cups Chicken Broth (page 42)
2 teaspoons Dijon mustard

2 teaspoons olive oil or unsalted butter
juice of ½ lemon
2 tablespoons finely chopped fresh parsley or dill
a little freshly ground black pepper to taste

In a food processor, finely chop the onion and garlic. Transfer to a large bowl, cover, and microwave on HIGH for 5 minutes. Stir in the quinoa and broth and microwave on HIGH, uncovered, until all the broth is absorbed, about 13 minutes.

Stir in the mustard, oil or butter, lemon juice, and herbs. Season with pepper, microwave on HIGH for 2 minutes to reheat, and serve.

Nutritional Information
(as a percentage of daily intake)

9% (178) calories
8% (5 g) fat
8% (29 g) carbohydrates
8% (6 g) protein

3% (63 mg) sodium
3% (29 mg) calcium
20% (3 mg) iron

This recipe is a basic preparation of dried beans, which need no presoaking to cook in the microwave. Most dried beans will cook to tenderness without becoming mushy in about 99 minutes. Small or very well dehydrated beans will take as long as 115 minutes (which requires you to reset the microwave at some point during the cooking—or if you have a microwave that can be programmed sequentially for two settings on HIGH, it can be set for two different times to total 115 minutes).

Makes 6 cups

1 pound (2½ cups) dried beans   **3 quarts hottest possible tap water**

In a very large bowl, combine the beans and water. Seal airtight with a double layer of plastic wrap and microwave on HIGH until tender, 99 to 115 minutes (see note above). Carefully uncover, drain, and serve.

Variation

For 3 cups of cooked beans: Use ½ pound (1¼ cups) dried beans and microwave until tender, about 99 minutes.

*Nutritional Information
(as a percentage of daily intake)
per ½-cup serving*

6% (118) calories   0% (2 mg) sodium
2% (1 g) fat   5% (36 mg) calcium
8% (21 g) carbohydrates   13% (2 mg) iron
11% (8 g) protein

White Bean Puree with Garlic and Chives

This elegant, hearty white puree can be served with grilled or broiled chops, as you would mashed potatoes, or with any roast, the juices of which should be spooned over the puree. Even if you are not a buttermilk lover, you'll find its flavor adds a perfect balance to the earthiness of the beans.

Serves 4

½ pound (1¼ cups) dried Great
   Northern beans
2 quarts water
1 large onion, peeled
3 large garlic cloves, peeled

1 leek, white part only, washed
   thoroughly
¾ cup nonfat buttermilk
a little salt and freshly ground white
   pepper to taste

For Garnish
2 teaspoons finely chopped fresh chives

Combine the beans, water, onion, garlic, and leek in a large bowl and seal airtight with a double layer of plastic wrap. Microwave on HIGH until tender, about 99 minutes. Test for doneness; beans may need another 10 to 15 minutes of cooking.

Carefully uncover and drain. Puree the beans and vegetables in a food processor with the buttermilk. Press through a sieve, then season with salt and pepper and reheat on HIGH, covered, until very hot, about 4 minutes. Stir well.

To serve, scoop ½ cup of the puree onto each plate and sprinkle each serving with ½ teaspoon of the chives.

Nutritional Information
(as a percentage of daily intake)

12% (245) calories
 2% (1 g) fat
16% (44 g) carbohydrates
21% (16 g) protein

3% (63 mg) sodium
20% (160 mg) calcium
33% (5 mg) iron

BASIC PREPARATION OF WHITE BEANS
Cooked in Stock

Combine 2 quarts water, a large whole chicken breast, bone in and skin and all visible fat removed, a small carrot, trimmed and scrubbed, and a celery rib with ½ pound (1¼ cups) dried white beans. Seal airtight with a double layer of plastic wrap and microwave on HIGH until tender, about 99 minutes. Carefully uncover; drain and discard all the vegetables and chicken. Mix with 1 tablespoon unsalted butter or fruity olive oil and season with a little salt and freshly ground white pepper.

Cooked in Water

Combine 2 quarts hottest possible tap water with ½ pound (1¼ cups) dried white beans in a very large bowl, seal airtight with a double layer of plastic wrap, and microwave on HIGH until tender, about 99 minutes.

Chilled Red Kidney Beans

The rich, almost nutty flavor of red kidney beans blends perfectly with a thick coating of tomato sauce flavored with chili powder. Because of the way a microwave cooks, all of the flavors remain distinct, so there is an unexpected complexity to the taste of this recipe.

Serve with grilled, roasted, or broiled red meats or to accompany a roast chicken or poached chicken breast, page 189 (in which case the beans can be spooned over the chicken).

Serves 6

3 quarts hottest possible tap water
½ pound (1¼ cups) dried red kidney beans
1 cup Chunky Tomato Sauce (page 107)

2 teaspoons chili powder
½ teaspoon crushed dried oregano

Combine the water and beans in a very large bowl. Seal airtight with a double layer of plastic wrap and microwave on HIGH for 80 minutes. Carefully uncover, drain, and return to the bowl. Mix with the tomato sauce, chili powder, and oregano, cover, and microwave on HIGH for 12 minutes.

Variation

Red Beans in Tomato Sauce: For a mild version, eliminate the chili powder and oregano and proceed as directed above.

Nutritional Information
(as a percentage of daily intake)

8% (152) calories
3% (2 g) fat
9% (24 g) carbohydrates
12% (9 g) protein

6% (151 mg) sodium
6% (49 mg) calcium
20% (3 mg) iron

BASIC PREPARATION OF KIDNEY BEANS

For ½ to 1 pound of beans, combine beans with 3 quarts hottest possible tap water in a very large bowl. Seal airtight with a double layer of plastic wrap and microwave on HIGH for 95 minutes. Carefully uncover, drain, and serve.

Brilliant colors and a northern African combination of spices and flavors combine here to make ordinary white beans into a radiant bean side dish.

Serve this sun-drenched, spicy, tomato-flavored recipe to accompany roasts of beef or lamb, instead of potatoes, or to enliven grilled or roasted chicken or game. This is also a great substitute for potato salad at picnics.

Serves 6

1 large sweet red bell pepper, cored
2 teaspoons tomato paste
1 tablespoon balsamic vinegar
1 small garlic clove, peeled
¼ teaspoon ground cinnamon
¼ teaspoon ground cumin
¼ teaspoon ground caraway seeds

¼ teaspoon cayenne pepper
⅛ teaspoon freshly ground black pepper
leaves from 3 small parsley sprigs
leaves from 4 large cilantro sprigs
3 cups cooked Great Northern beans (page 69)

Place the red pepper in a medium bowl, cover, and microwave on HIGH for 6 minutes. Puree, without the liquid that has accumulated under the pepper, in a food processor with the tomato paste, vinegar, garlic, cinnamon, cumin, caraway, cayenne, and black pepper. Add the parsley and cilantro and process until herbs are finely chopped. Mix with the beans. Serve cold or at room temperature.

Nutritional Information
(as a percentage of daily intake)

6% (115) calories
2% (1 g) fat
8% (21 g) carbohydrates
9% (7 g) protein

0% (9 mg) sodium
7% (53 mg) calcium
20% (3 mg) iron

Lentils, perhaps because of their association with thick, heavy lentil soups, are generally thought of as a winter food. But here they are used to make a rich, intensely flavored cold salad with walnuts that is tantalizing as an appetizer before a summer meal.

To serve, arrange the lentil salad on small plates with a few slices of an ice-cold, luscious, vine-ripened tomato.

Serves 6

1 recipe Winter Lentils (page 74)
2 tablespoons fruity olive oil
2 tablespoons balsamic vinegar
½ cup (about ¼ pound) chopped walnuts

2 tablespoons finely chopped fresh chives or scallions
2 tablespoons finely chopped fresh parsley

Mix the lentils with the remaining ingredients. Taste and adjust the seasonings if necessary. Transfer to a container, cover tightly, and refrigerate until needed. Serve chilled or at room temperature.

Nutritional Information
(as a percentage of daily intake)

10% (190) calories
9% (6 g) fat
10% (28 g) carbohydrates
13% (10 g) protein

2% (50 mg) sodium
7% (53 mg) calcium
27% (4 mg) iron

Winter Lentils

Earthy green or brown lentils, one of the great winter legumes, are flavored here with leeks, carrots, and celery. Serve with roasted chicken or lamb.

Serves 8

2 leeks, white part only, split length-
    wise, washed thoroughly, and cut
    into 1-inch lengths
2 carrots, trimmed, scrubbed, and cut
    into 1-inch lengths
2 celery ribs, cut into 1-inch lengths
1 medium-size onion, peeled and cut
    into eighths

3 garlic cloves, peeled
1 cup green or brown lentils
2½ cups Chicken Broth (page 42)
a little salt and freshly ground black
    pepper to taste

In a food processor, finely chop the leeks, carrots, celery, onion, and garlic. Transfer to a very large bowl, cover, and microwave on HIGH for 6 minutes. Add the lentils and broth, cover, and microwave on HIGH for 35 minutes. Season with salt and pepper and serve.

Nutritional Information
(as a pecentage of daily intake)

9% (188) calories
2% (1 g) fat
13% (35 g) carbohydrates
17% (13 g) protein

2% (38 mg) sodium
6% (50 mg) calcium
33% (5 mg) iron

Here bold Mediterranean flavors—garlic, lemon, parsley, anchovies, and olive oil—make a dressing for baby limas. Serve this as a cold summer salad or to accompany a garlic-studded leg of lamb or a roasted prime rib.

Serves 4 to 6

1½ cups (about ¾ pound) dried baby
   lima beans
1½ quarts water
3 tablespoons full-flavored olive oil
6 canned anchovy fillets, drained

1 cup tightly packed fresh parsley leaves
1 large garlic clove, peeled
juice of 1 large lemon
freshly ground black pepper to taste

Combine the beans and water in a very large bowl. Seal airtight with a double layer of plastic wrap and microwave on HIGH until tender, about 90 minutes. Carefully uncover, drain, and rinse.

Combine the oil, anchovies, parsley, garlic, and lemon juice in a food processor and process until finely chopped. Pour over the beans and stir well. Season with pepper to taste. Serve cold or at room temperature.

Nutritional Information
(as a percentage of daily intake)

10% (204) calories
17% (11 g) fat
 7% (20 g) carbohydrates
11% (8 g) protein

0% (8 mg) sodium
7% (52 mg) calcium
20% (3 mg) iron

BASIC PREPARATION OF DRIED BABY LIMA BEANS

Combine 1 cup dried baby limas with 1½ quarts water in a very large bowl. Seal airtight with a double layer of plastic wrap and microwave on HIGH until tender, about 90 minutes. Carefully uncover and drain. Toss with 1 tablespoon unsalted butter, 2 tablespoons finely chopped fresh parsley or tarragon, and a little salt and freshly ground pepper to taste.

Black-Eyed Pea Salad
with Cilantro

Black-eyed peas have assumed a modest, almost menial position in the world of legumes; but here they are made into a cold salad with red onions and lots of cilantro that can be served with dignity in place of potato salad, as an accompaniment to roasted or grilled red meats, barbecued poultry, or game, or as part of a vegetarian meal.

The sauce here also can be used to dress vegetables or pasta salads.

Serves 6

½ pound (1¼ cups) black-eyed peas   1½ quarts hottest possible tap water

For the Sauce

½ cup plain nonfat yogurt

3 tablespoons balsamic vinegar

1 small red onion, peeled and quartered

1 garlic clove, peeled

1 small bunch (1 cup tightly packed) cilantro

a little freshly ground black pepper to taste

Combine the peas and water in a large bowl and seal airtight with a double layer of plastic wrap. Microwave on HIGH until tender, about 90 minutes. Carefully uncover and drain.

While peas are cooking, make the sauce by combining the remaining ingredients in a food processor. Pulse until everything is finely chopped. Toss with the cooked peas and serve cold or at room temperature.

Nutritional Information
(as a percentage of daily intake)

7% (138) calories

0% (0 g) fat

9% (25 g) carbohydrates

12% (9 g) protein

1% (24 mg) sodium

9% (72 mg) calcium

20% (3 mg) iron

Chick-peas cook in one easy step in the microwave. Add chick-peas to salads or rice dishes or use them in your favorite recipe.

Makes 3 cups

½ pound (1¼ cups) dried chick-peas

2½ quarts hottest possible tap water, Chicken Broth (page 42), or Vegetable Consommé (page 44)

Combine the chick-peas and water or stock in a very large bowl, seal airtight with a double layer of plastic wrap, and microwave on HIGH until tender, about 99 minutes. Carefully uncover, drain, and cool. Then store in the refrigerator in a covered container.

Nutritional Information
(as a percentage of daily intake)
per ½-cup serving

7% (141) calories
3% (2 g) fat
8% (23 g) carbohydrates
11% (8 g) protein

0% (8 mg) sodium
7% (56 mg) calcium
20% (3 mg) iron

This light version of hummus, with less tahini than usual, allows all the Mediterranean flavors of the chick-peas and herbs to assert themselves, thus giving it a bright taste not usually found in hummus.

Serve cold from the refrigerator, bring to room temperature before serving, or microwave on HIGH until warm, about 2 minutes. The hummus can be stuffed into hollowed-out cherry tomato halves, if you wish, to make it easy to handle as an hors d'oeuvre.

This recipe also makes an excellent summer appetizer, served with three or four slices of a large, vine-ripened tomato, crisp slices of sourdough whole wheat bread, and a tender young scallion set on the plate with some soft leaves of Boston or Bibb lettuce

Serves 16

½ pound (1¼ cups) dried chick-peas	juice of 1½ large lemons
2½ quarts water	3 large garlic cloves, peeled
1 whole chicken breast, bone in, skin and all visible fat removed	½ cup fresh parsley leaves
	¼ cup fresh mint leaves
½ pound tahini (sesame seed paste)	¼ teaspoon cayenne pepper

For Garnish
fresh mint leaves   **Toasted Pita Triangles (recipe follows)**

Place the chick-peas, water, and chicken in a very large bowl and seal airtight with a double layer of plastic wrap. Microwave on HIGH until chick-peas are tender, about 99 minutes. Carefully uncover and drain, reserving ¾ cup of the cooking liquid. Discard the chicken.

In a food processor, puree until smooth the chick-peas, reserved cooking liquid, tahini, lemon juice, and garlic. Add the parsley, mint, and cayenne and pulse until the herbs are finely chopped. Refrigerate until needed.

To serve, mound in a serving bowl, garnish with mint, and serve with toasted pita triangles.

Nutritional Information
(as a percentage of daily intake)

8% (156) calories
15% (10 g) fat
4% (12 g) carbohydrates
8% (6 g) protein

1% (26 mg) sodium
6% (44 mg) calcium
13% (2 mg) iron

You'll find a dozen ways to use these microwave-toasted whole wheat pita triangles, which are as crisp as crackers. Of course, you can use regular white flour pita breads if you prefer.

Makes 72 pieces

**3 medium-size whole wheat pita
  breads**

Place each loaf of pita flat on a cutting board and cut in half (across the diameter) to form 2 pockets. Separate the halves of each pocket, forming 12 semicircles. Cut each semicircle like a pie into 6 triangles.

Place a paper towel on a large plate and arrange 12 pieces of the pita in a circle, tips toward the center. Microwave on HIGH until crisp, about 1½ minutes. Test the first batch for crispness after 1¼ minutes, then again after another 15 and 30 seconds if more time was needed. Set aside to cool and repeat with the remaining pita triangles.

Variation
  Pita Melba Toast: Use regular white flour pitas instead of whole wheat.

*Nutritional Information
(as a percentage of daily intake)
per 4-piece serving*

1% (27) calories   2% (56 mg) sodium
0% (0 g) fat   1% (8 mg) calcium
2% (5 g) carbohydrates   0% (0 mg) iron
1% (1 g) protein

The delicate, sweet flavor of Egyptian lentils is combined with similarly colored and flavored carrots in this recipe to make a brilliant orange grain dish with the feeling of the northern African desert sun. The almonds, again sweet in flavor, add to the mixture of textures in this dish. And the lime juice and herbs finish the flavor balance. This is one of my favorite recipes in this chapter.

Serves 8

2 medium-size carrots, trimmed, scrubbed, and cut into 1-inch lengths

1 medium-size onion, peeled and cut into eighths

1 teaspoon dried marjoram

½ teaspoon dried tarragon

1½ cups (about ¾ pound) red lentils

2½ cups Chicken Broth (page 42)

⅓ cup (2 ounces) finely chopped almonds

1 tablespoon fruity olive oil

juice of 1 lime

½ cup finely chopped fresh parsley

a little salt and freshly ground black pepper to taste

In a food processor, very finely chop the carrots, onion, marjoram, and tarragon. Transfer to a large bowl, cover, and microwave on HIGH for 3 minutes. Stir in the lentils and broth, cover, and microwave on HIGH for 18 minutes. Drain if any of the broth has not been absorbed. Stir in the remaining ingredients. Serve hot.

Nutritional Information
(as a percentage of daily intake)

9% (191) calories

9% (6 g) fat

10% (27 g) carbohydrates

15% (11 g) protein

1% (27 mg) sodium

6% (50 mg) calcium

27% (4 mg) iron

Pasta cooked in the microwave retains its texture and identity better than when it's boiled. Each piece of pasta remains separate. The noodles do not become waterlogged, but stay firm and tender throughout. Also, pasta doesn't stick together during microwave cooking, so there's no need for stirring. However, not all pasta cooks well in the microwave, which led many food writers to believe that *no* pasta cooks well in the microwave. The best pastas for microwaving are the medium-size individual shapes, such as penne, ziti, rigatoni, bow ties, and sea shells.

Very small dried pasta, such as the rice-shaped orzo and alphabets, becomes very soft and gummy. The same happens with most of the better brands of long, thin pastas, such as linguine and spaghetti.

Most dried pasta cooks in 10 to 11 minutes. After you have cooked your first bowl of pasta in the microwave, note the texture and time and use it as a guide for all future pasta cooking.

Serves 4 to 5

2 quarts hottest possible tap water   **1 pound fresh or dried pasta (see note above)**

Place the water in a very large bowl and microwave on HIGH, uncovered, for 15 minutes. Very carefully remove the bowl from the oven or simply slide it forward and add the pasta to the nearly boiling water. Return to the center of the oven and microwave for 2 minutes if fresh, 10 to 11 minutes if dried. Drain and serve.

Variation

For ½ pound pasta (serves 2 to 3): Prepare as directed above, reducing the cooking time to 8 to 9 minutes.

Nutritional Information
(as a percentage of daily intake)
per 1-cup serving

10% (200) calories   0% (3 mg) sodium
3% (2 g) fat   2% (16 mg) calcium
13% (37 g) carbohydrates   20% (3 mg) iron
9% (7 g) protein

Barley and Sea Shells, the Perfect Winter Pasta

Comforting earthy flavors and textures make this the perfect winter pasta. The small, tender but still slightly chewy sea shells are cooked with barley and are accented with ground walnuts. Thus soft, chewy, and crunchy elements combine to make this a textural playground in the mouth.

This was the first pasta recipe I tested in the microwave, and so I thank food writer and friend Karen MacNeil for telling me that I could actually do it.

Serve the pasta as an accompaniment to large roasts or broiled chops, with a simple green vegetable, or as part of a winter vegetarian meal.

Serves 6

1 medium-size onion, peeled and thinly sliced
1 small leek, white part only, split lengthwise, washed thoroughly, and thinly sliced
1 large garlic clove, finely chopped
⅓ cup skim milk
1 large whole chicken breast, bone in, skin and all visible fat removed

½ cup medium pearl barley
1½ quarts water
½ pound dried sea shell pasta
⅔ cup walnut pieces, finely chopped
a little salt and freshly ground white pepper to taste

In a medium bowl, combine the onion, leek, garlic, and milk. Cover and microwave on HIGH for 7 minutes. Set aside.

Combine the chicken, barley, and water in a very large bowl. Seal airtight with a double layer of plastic wrap and microwave on HIGH for 30 minutes. Carefully uncover and add the sea shells. Seal again and microwave on HIGH for 10 minutes. Carefully uncover and drain well in a colander, shaking and tossing the shells to remove excess water. Discard the chicken and transfer barley and shells to a large serving bowl. Stir in the walnuts and cooked onion mixture and season with salt and pepper. Serve immediately.

Nutritional Information
(as a percentage of daily intake)

16% (325) calories
18% (12 g) fat
16% (45 g) carbohydrates

15% (11 g) protein
3% (66 mg) sodium

7% (58 mg) calcium
20% (3 mg) iron

Rotini with Tomatoes and Cilantro Pesto

This is a vibrantly colored summer pasta with an emerald green herb sauce and small chunks of intensely red tomatoes. This sauce has become my response to the ubiquitous and extremely fattening pesto. With more herbs and flavors, more interest and complexity, this sauce will soon win the hearts of your favorite pesto lovers.

Substitute basil for the cilantro, if you wish, or for the chives for a more subtle variation. Use lemon juice instead of lime juice. Use tarragon instead of the cilantro. Add some mint (not too much, or it will overwhelm the sauce). Or just play with the sauce using whatever herbs are on hand—a little lemon thyme or young rosemary is a perfect accent instead of the jalapeño pepper flavor.

Serves 4

2 quarts hottest possible tap water
1 small bunch (1 cup tightly packed leaves) of cilantro
1 small bunch of fresh chives
a large handful of fresh parsley leaves
2 garlic cloves, peeled
½ jalapeño pepper, seeded (optional)

¾ cup plain nonfat yogurt
juice of ½ lime
¼ cup freshly grated Parmesan cheese
freshly ground black pepper to taste
1 pound dried rotini
2 large vine-ripened tomatoes, cored and diced

Place the water in a very large bowl and microwave on HIGH, uncovered, for 15 minutes.

While water is heating, in a food processor puree the cilantro, chives, parsley, garlic, jalapeño, yogurt, lime juice, and Parmesan. Season to taste with freshly ground black pepper.

Very carefully remove the bowl of water from the microwave and add the pasta. Microwave on HIGH, uncovered, for 10 minutes.

Drain the cooked pasta and toss with the tomatoes and sauce. Serve at once.

Variation

Chicken and Tomatoes with Herbed Pasta: Toss 1 cup diced cooked chicken (page 189) with the pasta.

Nutritional Information
(as a percentage of daily intake)

13% (267) calories
6% (4 g) fat
16% (45 g) carbohydrates
16% (12 g) protein

6% (148 mg) sodium
24% (195 mg) calcium
27% (4 mg) iron

Here eggplant, which cooks sublimely in the microwave, becomes a lively Mediterranean-style ragoût, full of bouncy flavors and textures, that turns into a chunky sauce for microwave-cooked rigatoni.

This is a great one-dish summer meal, with just a loaf of whole wheat bread and some juicy fresh fruit for dessert.

Serves 6

1 1-pound eggplant, trimmed and cut into ½-inch dice

½ pound fresh spinach, washed, thick stems removed, roughly chopped

juice of 1 large lemon

leaves from 1 small bunch of fresh basil (about 1 cup tightly packed), coarsely chopped

2 tablespoons very finely chopped red onion

1 garlic clove, very finely chopped

2 large (¾-pound) vine-ripened tomatoes, cored and cut into ½-inch dice

2 tablespoons drained capers, rinsed

freshly ground black pepper to taste

2 quarts hottest possible tap water

½ pound dried rigatoni

In a large bowl, stir together the eggplant, spinach, and lemon juice. Cover and microwave on HIGH for 12 minutes. Add the basil, red onion, garlic, tomatoes, and capers and mix well. Season with pepper to taste. Set aside, uncovered, to mellow while the rigatoni is cooking.

Place the water in a very large bowl and microwave on HIGH, uncovered, for 15 minutes. Very carefully remove from the oven and add the rigatoni to the nearly boiling water. Microwave on HIGH, uncovered, for 10 minutes, drain, and toss with the vegetable ragoût.

Serve warm as it is, refrigerate and serve cool (not cold, which would mask the flavors), or cover and reheat in the microwave, 2 to 3 minutes on HIGH if you want the pasta hot.

Variation

Eggplant Ragoût: Omit the pasta, place the ragoût in a strainer to drain off the excess liquid, and serve hot or cold as a vegetable.

9% (177) calories

3% (2 g) fat

12% (34 g) carbohydrates

11% (8 g) protein

7% (159 mg) sodium

15% (123 mg) calcium

33% (5 mg) iron

As the story goes, and as the name indicates, this was the dish that the prostitutes of Italy threw together when the police were knocking at their door and they needed to prove they were just having dinner with a friend. That bit of gastronomic mythology aside, the balance of brash flavors in this recipe has made it popular on this side of the Atlantic.

The only time-consuming preparation is the pitting of the olives, and that is more tedious than time-consuming. When I order puttanesca in restaurants, if the olives are not pitted, I know there is a lazy chef, and I don't expect much from the rest of the food. It's also dangerous to serve pits in unexpected places, like a pasta sauce.

Serves 6

1 35-ounce can peeled Italian-style plum tomatoes, drained and cut in half
1 2-ounce can anchovies rolled around capers
1 tablespoon drained capers, rinsed
3 tablespoons tomato paste
4 large garlic cloves, peeled and roughly chopped

½ cup imported black (preferably Greek or Moroccan) or Calamata olives, pitted and broken into 4 or 5 pieces each
¼ teaspoon hot red pepper flakes
a little freshly ground black pepper to taste
2 quarts hottest possible tap water
1½ pounds fresh penne

In a large bowl, stir together the tomatoes, anchovies, capers, tomato paste, garlic, olives, hot red pepper flakes, and black pepper. Cover and microwave on HIGH for 12 minutes. Set aside.

Pour the water into a very large bowl and microwave on HIGH, uncovered, for 15 minutes. Carefully remove from the oven, place the penne in the nearly boiling water, and microwave on HIGH, uncovered, for 2 minutes. Drain and toss with the sauce. Place back in the bowl, cover, and microwave on HIGH to reheat, about 3 minutes.

Nutritional Information
(as a percentage of daily intake)

15% (300) calories
6% (4 g) fat
20% (54 g) carbohydrates

15% (11 g) protein
24% (587 mg) sodium

10% (76 mg) calcium
27% (4 mg) iron

Vegetables

From artichokes to zucchini, the microwave cooks vegetables superlatively. There is in fact no *better* way to cook vegetables than in the microwave. Because a variety of fresh vegetables is so important a part of a well-balanced diet, this chapter is the largest in the book, with over 70 recipes and variations.

The microwave makes green vegetables greener, orange vegetables even more orange, and imbues the muddy color of vegetables like eggplant with a pastel hue. Yellow peppers become electric yellow in color. Butternut squash becomes burnt sienna. Red peppers become fire engine red. Broccoli becomes kelly green. No more khaki-colored Brussels sprouts. No more camouflage-colored snow peas. No more dull gray artichokes. The microwave enhances and amplifies the natural colors of the vegetables it cooks.

The microwave coaxes vegetables into tenderness without destroying their natural texture. The leaves of a Brussels sprout separate into a thousand tiny layers that break apart in your mouth rather than turning into a wad. Broccoli becomes tender without becoming soft, and the tiny buds at the top of each floweret retain their individual identities. Asparagus tips stay tight rather than becoming waterlogged and disintegrating while the stalks cook. Waxy potatoes retain their mildly waxy texture and hold together, even when diced before cooking. Green beans stay firm without being squeaky. Whole or cut up, diced or julienned, vegetables retain their varied and fragile textures perfectly when cooked in a microwave oven.

The subtle scents and fragrances of vegetables, their sweetness, their earthiness, their nuttiness, their spiciness become obvious when vegetables are cooked in a microwave. No other way of cooking brings out the aromas and perfumes of vegetables like microwaving.

The flavors of microwaved vegetables are clean and crisp and fresh, brisk and pure. Microwaved vegetables taste more natural, more intense, more complex. Carrots are sweeter. Broccoli is astonishingly fresh. Acorn squash develops a nuttiness. Spinach tastes bold and audacious. Parsnips lose their humility and become sweeter and fuller-bodied than ever before. Mushrooms taste rustic and natural, woodsy.

If you want to taste the full, natural flavor of a vegetable, forget steaming, stewing, poaching, baking, boiling, sautéing, and frying. For a vegetable to retain its full, natural flavor, it must be cooked in a microwave.

A Special Note on the Texture of Microwaved Vegetables: In some of the recipes in this chapter, particularly those for six to eight servings, there will be some differences in the texture of individual pieces of the vegetable. Some pieces will be a bit firmer than others. None, however, will be undercooked.

In traditional methods of cooking, part of the vegetable is often overcooked—the outsides of diced potatoes become a little mushy or the tips of the asparagus become softer than the stalks. In microwaving there is some variation, but the variations are only in the degree of firmness. If you haven't cooked vegetables in a microwave before, you may notice this difference.

Curried Acorn Squash

With acorn squash, bigger is better. Buy acorn squashes that weigh between 2 and 2½ pounds and serve each person a quarter, which will look attractive and fit neatly on a plate, instead of those oversized halves.

Here the squash are very lightly glazed with a mustard-colored coating that brushes a light curry flavor onto the sweet squash.

Serves 4

1 2- to 2¼-pound acorn squash   **2 tablespoons curry powder**
2 tablespoons honey

Place the whole acorn squash in the center of the oven and microwave on HIGH for 1 minute to soften and make cutting easy. Trim off the stem and cut lengthwise into quarters. Scoop out the seeds and fiber.

Blend together the honey and curry powder. Smear on the inside of each piece of squash.

Arrange the squash like spokes on a large plate or platter, the narrower ends meeting at the center of the plate. Drape with plastic wrap (use several layers if necessary) and seal under the plate. Microwave on HIGH for 10 minutes. Immediately puncture the plastic wrap to prevent it from shrinking and crushing the squash, then uncover and serve.

Variations

Chilied Acorn Squash: Substitute chili powder for the curry powder.

Acorn Squash with Harissa: Cook the acorn squash as directed on page 93, with or without the butter, then spoon a heaping tablespoon of *Harissa* (page 132) onto each piece.

Nutritional Information
(as a percentage of daily intake)

9% (178) calories   1% (14 mg) sodium
2% (1 g) fat   16% (124 mg) calcium
17% (46 g) carbohydrates   20% (3 mg) iron
4% (3 g) protein

BASIC PREPARATION OF ACORN SQUASH

To make the squash easy to cut, place the whole squash in the center of the oven and microwave on HIGH for 1 minute, then halve small (1- to 1¼-pound) squash or quarter large (2- to 2½-pound) squash. Place ½ teaspoon unsalted butter in the center of each piece and wrap in plastic wrap (either by wrapping each piece or by arranging the squash like spokes in a large shallow dish or on a very large plate and then covering with plastic wrap). Microwave on HIGH for 7 minutes for small squash, 10 minutes for large squash. Immediately after microwaving, puncture the plastic wrap to prevent it from shrinking and crushing the squash.

An artichoke appetizer is perfect for socializing, especially when you are having company you expect to engage in spirited conversation. Here the artichoke is served with two tantalizing sauces, one acidic and the other sweet.

The microwave makes it very easy to cook artichokes. Four artichokes, arranged in a shallow dish, cook in less than 15 minutes, a quarter of the time it would take in ordinary cooking, and with none of the fuss.

Serves 4

1½ cups light sour cream
1 tablespoon Dijon mustard
2 teaspoons coarse mustard
3 tablespoons honey
3 tablespoons finely chopped fresh dill
6 oil-packed sun-dried tomatoes, drained and patted dry

1 large garlic clove, peeled
2 teaspoons drained capers, rinsed
2 tablespoons tightly packed parsley leaves
4 medium-size (½-pound) artichokes
½ lemon

To Make the Honey Mustard Dill Sauce: Mix ¾ cup sour cream with the mustards, honey, and dill.

To Make the Sun-Dried Tomato and Caper Sauce: Finely chop the tomatoes, garlic, capers, and parsley in a food processor. Mix with the remaining ¾ cup sour cream.

With a sharp cook's knife, cut the top 1 to 1½ inches off the artichokes. Next, clip the thorny ends off the remaining leaves with a pair of scissors. Tear any discolored or damaged leaves off at the bottom. Cut the bottom flush so the artichoke will stand level on a plate. Rub the cut edges with lemon as you work to prevent discoloration.

Arrange the trimmed artichokes in the corners of a large shallow dish. Seal airtight with a double layer of plastic wrap (this seal prevents the outside leaves from drying and discoloring) and microwave on HIGH for 13 minutes.

Immediately puncture the plastic wrap to stop it from shrinking and crushing the artichokes. Unwrap and, when cool enough to handle, loosen the outer leaves from the top, then pinch together and pull out the spike-tipped leaves inside the artichoke. With the tip of a spoon, scrape out the fuzz, called the *choke,* that is attached to the artichoke bottom. Press the leaves back together and serve, at room temperature or chilled, accompanied by the two sauces.

Nutritional Information
(as a percentage of daily intake)

13% (263) calories

14% (9 g) fat

17% (46 g) carbohydrates

8% (6 g) protein

14% (328 mg) sodium

15% (117 mg) calcium

20% (3 mg) iron

BASIC PREPARATION OF ARTICHOKES

For 1 Artichoke:

Prepare the artichoke as directed in the recipe above, place in a medium bowl, seal airtight with plastic wrap, and microwave on HIGH for 6 minutes.

For 2 Artichokes:

Prepare the artichokes as directed in the recipe above, place in the diagonally opposite corners of a large shallow dish, seal airtight with plastic wrap, and microwave on HIGH for 9 minutes.

For 3 Artichokes:

Prepare the artichokes as directed in the recipe above, place in the corners of a very large shallow dish, seal airtight with plastic wrap, and microwave on HIGH for 11 minutes.

Artichoke Puree

This elegant vegetable puree is perfect for a special dinner. Its pale pastel green color and sweet, delicate artichoke flavor are the result of the special way microwaving enhances the flavor and color of vegetables. Unfortunately, it does look a bit like baby food.

Several things are done in this recipe to save time: the artichokes are cooked whole, without trimming, and the leaves are discarded, not scraped.

I make this recipe when artichokes are in peak season, in April and May. I am a bit wasteful here, in that I buy huge 1-pound artichokes and use only the stems and bottoms for the puree. I do not bother, though you could if you wish, to churn the leaves through a food mill to extract the extra artichoke meat attached to them.

Serves 4

8 huge (1-pound) artichokes, stems cut off flush with the bottom of the artichokes, peeled, and rubbed with lemon juice to prevent discoloration
1 very small onion, peeled and quartered

2 large garlic cloves, peeled
¼ teaspoon crushed dried thyme
juice of 1 lemon
a little salt and freshly ground black pepper to taste

Arrange 4 artichokes on a large plate. Drape loosely with plastic wrap, sealing under the plate. Microwave on HIGH for 20 minutes. Uncover immediately to prevent the plastic wrap from shrinking and crushing the artichokes. Repeat with the remaining artichokes. Place the stems in a medium bowl, cover, and microwave on HIGH for 8 minutes. Peel stems and set aside.

When artichokes are cool enough to handle, gently remove all leaves so that only the large fleshy bottoms remain. With a spoon, scoop the fuzzy choke off the artichoke bottoms.

In a food processor, puree the artichoke bottoms and stems, onion, garlic, thyme, and lemon juice. Process for a full 5 minutes to lighten the texture and color.

Transfer to a bowl, cover, and microwave on HIGH for 4 minutes. Serve.

Variation

Artichoke Puree with Cilantro or Parsley: Add the leaves from 3 to 4 stems of cilantro or parsley to the fully pureed artichokes and pulse until finely chopped.

Nutritional Information
(as a percentage of daily intake)

3% (58) calories   3% (80 mg) sodium
0% (0 g) fat   7% (52 mg) calcium
5% (13 g) carbohydrates   13% (2 mg) iron
4% (3 g) protein

Asparagus with Emerald Sauce

This emerald sauce has a lively, vibrant flavor and an enticing color that adds sparkle to the rich natural flavor of asparagus. And it is quick and easy to make.

Serves 4

1 pound pencil-thin asparagus, bottoms trimmed

½ cup plain, nonfat yogurt

1 tablespoon balsamic vinegar

½ cup tightly packed cilantro leaves

½ cup tightly packed fresh parsley leaves

a little salt and freshly ground black pepper to taste

Place the asparagus in a dish large enough to hold them. Cover and microwave on HIGH for 4 minutes.

While asparagus is cooking, combine the yogurt, vinegar, cilantro, and parsley in a food processor and process to form a speckled emerald-colored sauce. Season with salt and pepper.

Arrange the asparagus on a platter or on serving plates and spoon sauce over.

Nutritional Information
(as a percentage of daily intake)

3% (51) calories

0% (0 g) fat

3% (8 g) carbohydrates

8% (6 g) protein

1% (30 mg) sodium

13% (105 mg) calcium

13% (2 mg) iron

BASIC PREPARATION OF ASPARAGUS

I generally prefer to cook pencil-thin asparagus—they're the easiest to clean and they stack neatly and attractively. But thicker asparagus stalks can be used if you wish; just trim the bottoms and peel the lower half of each spear.

Place 1 pound asparagus, dotted with 1 teaspoon unsalted butter, in a meat loaf pan or shallow dish. Cover and microwave on HIGH for 4 minutes. Cook 1½ pounds with 1½ teaspoons unsalted butter for 6 minutes, 2 pounds with 2 teaspoons unsalted butter for 7 minutes. Toss and season with a little salt and freshly ground black pepper.

Sesame-Flavored Asparagus

Here the asparagus is lightly coated in a deeply colored, nutty-flavored sauce made with dark sesame oil, Chinese oyster sauce, and sesame seeds. The heady flavors and aromas of the sauce give the asparagus an assertive Asian taste.

Serves 6

1½ pounds pencil-thin asparagus, bottom ends trimmed
juice of ½ lemon
1 tablespoon dark sesame oil

1 tablespoon oyster sauce
2 teaspoons sesame seeds
a little freshly ground black pepper to taste

Place the asparagus in a large shallow dish. Mix together the remaining ingredients and pour over the asparagus. Toss until all the asparagus are lightly coated. Seal airtight and microwave on HIGH for 6½ minutes. Carefully uncover, toss, and serve.

Nutritional Information
(as a percentage of daily intake)

4% (77) calories
8% (5 g) fat
2% (5 g) carbohydrates
5% (4 g) protein

4% (91 mg) sodium
4% (32 mg) calcium
7% (1 mg) iron

TO TOAST SESAME SEEDS IN THE MICROWAVE

In traditional toasting of sesame seeds, the seeds turn a deep mahogany color as they cook. In the microwave they do not color on the outside because they toast on the inside. The flavor is the same, however.

Spread 2 teaspoons to ¼ cup sesame seeds evenly over a large plate. Microwave on HIGH, uncovered, for 6 to 8 minutes, until slightly toasted. (Test by tasting a cooled seed.)

Extravagantly expensive fresh white asparagus are considered by some gourmets to be the greatest of all asparagus—though not by me. I generally prefer young green asparagus from California.

White asparagus are stronger in flavor than green, sometimes a little bitter, and can be very fibrous. They must be peeled, even those as thin as a pencil, for the microwave emphasizes the corky, fibrous nature of the asparagus and will cook the spears tender on the inside but will not soften the wood-hard outside.

These spears are so expensive that I serve them as a cold appetizer, not a casual vegetable side dish, accompanied by the Hot and Sour Red Onion Chutney from the recipe on page 152.

Serves 4 as an appetizer

¾ pound fresh white asparagus, gently scrubbed, peeled, and bottoms trimmed

1 recipe Hot and Sour Red Onion Chutney (page 152)

Place the asparagus in a large shallow dish, cover, and microwave on HIGH for 3 minutes. Plunge into ice water to cool. Arrange on plates and spoon some chutney over each serving.

Nutritional Information
(as a percentage of daily intake)

2% (42) calories
0% (0 g) fat
3% (8 g) carbohydrates
5% (4 g) protein

0% (9 mg) sodium
7% (53 mg) calcium
13% (2 mg) iron

BASIC PREPARATION OF WHITE ASPARAGUS

Trim the bottoms and peel from just below the tip 1 pound fresh white asparagus. Arrange in a large shallow dish, dot with 1½ teaspoons unsalted butter, cover, and microwave on HIGH for 4 minutes. Season with a little salt and freshly ground black pepper, toss, and serve.

Gigantic Asparagus with Fresh Tomato Salsa

Sometimes, when I want the asparagus to be the center of attention at a meal, I buy huge spears, as thick as my thumb, and serve them as an appetizer with fresh tomato salsa or Golden Onion Relish (page 155).

Serves 6 as an appetizer

2 pounds very thick (almost nickel-size at the base) asparagus, ends trimmed and lower half of each spear peeled

1 recipe Fresh Tomato Salsa (recipe follows)

Place the asparagus in a shallow dish large enough to hold them below the rim, seal airtight, and microwave on HIGH for 5 minutes. Carefully uncover and serve.

Nutritional Information
(as a percentage of daily intake)

3% (55) calories
0% (0 g) fat
4% (10 g) carbohydrates
8% (6 g) protein

1% (16 mg) sodium
6% (48 mg) calcium
13% (2 mg) iron

Fresh Tomato Salsa

Here's a quick, uncooked salsa that is richly flavored with ripe tomatoes and mildly spiced with green chilies.

Makes 2 cups

2 very large vine-ripened tomatoes, cored and quartered
1 large garlic clove, peeled
5 scallions, white part and 2 inches of the green, cut in half
1 cup tightly packed cilantro leaves

2 teaspoons chili powder
juice of 1 lime
1 4-ounce can chopped mild green chilies, undrained
freshly ground black pepper to taste

In a food processor, combine tomatoes, garlic, scallions, cilantro, chili powder, and lime juice. Pulse on and off quickly to form a finely chopped sauce. Stir in the chilies and season with pepper. Cover and refrigerate until needed.

Nutritional Information
(as a percentage of daily intake)
per ½-cup serving

2% (30) calories

0% (0 g) fat

3% (7 g) carbohydrates

3% (2 g) protein

1% (20 mg) sodium

3% (22 mg) calcium

7% (1 mg) iron

Golden Beets with Dried Peaches and Pecans

I number among my friends a dedicated beet lover like myself, for whose fortieth birthday I created this recipe. The delicate, flowery fragrance and sweet fruitiness of the golden beets are combined with chunks of moist peaches and are strewn with small pieces of pecans—one of the best combinations of flavors and textures.

Serve hot with chicken, pork, or game or add the juice of half a lemon to the cooked beets, refrigerate, and serve as a cold salad.

Serves 4

½ cup coarsely chopped moist dried peaches *or* ¼ cup each dried apricots and dried peaches

¼ cup apple juice

4 bunches of baby golden beets, trimmed, scrubbed, peeled, and halved, *or* ½ pound golden beets, cleaned and cut into ½-inch dice

¼ cup coarsely chopped pecans

Combine peaches and apple juice in a small bowl, cover, and microwave on HIGH for 2 minutes. Set aside.

Place beets in a medium bowl and cover. Microwave on HIGH for 7 minutes. Stir in the peaches and nuts, cover, and reheat on HIGH for 1 minute.

Nutritional Information
(as a percentage of daily intake)

12% (231) calories

9% (6 g) fat

17% (47 g) carbohydrates

5% (4 g) protein

2% (36 mg) sodium

4% (29 mg) calcium

20% (3 mg) iron

BASIC PREPARATION OF BEETS

Use either golden beets or regular beets. Four small beets will weigh about ½ pound, 4 large beets about 1 pound. Scrub, peel, and slice or dice the beets, place in a large bowl, cover, and microwave on HIGH for 7 minutes for ½ pound, 11 minutes for 1 pound. Toss ½ pound beets with ½ teaspoon unsalted butter and season with a little salt and pepper; 1 pound of beets should be tossed with ¾ teaspoon unsalted butter and then seasoned.

Here is a simple, quick family recipe.

Serves 3

**1 medium-size (about 1¼-pound)
bunch broccoli, cut into flowerets,
stems peeled and cut into ¾-inch
lengths on the bias, *or* 1¼ pound
ready-cut flowerets**

**1 cup Chunky Tomato Sauce (page
107)**

Mix broccoli flowerets and tomato sauce in a large bowl. Cover and microwave on HIGH for 8 minutes.

*Nutritional Information
(as a percentage of daily intake)*

6% (113) calories
2% (1 g) fat
9% (25 g) carbohydrates
8% (6 g) protein

19% (456 mg) sodium
15% (120 mg) calcium
20% (3 mg) iron

BASIC PREPARATION OF BROCCOLI

For plain broccoli, cut a medium-size bunch (about 1¼ pounds) into
flowerets, peel the thick stems and cut into inch-long pieces (halve
lengthwise if very thick). Place in a large bowl or shallow dish, cover,
and microwave on HIGH for 6 minutes.

Chunky Tomato Sauce

This is a particularly flavorful, highly seasoned chunky tomato sauce that has been part of my cooking for 20 years, but is now easier to make than ever before thanks to the microwave.

The upper edge of the bowl will crust and brown, so be careful not to stir it into the sauce. If you're preparing the Thick and Chunky Tomato Sauce variation, expect the sauce on the edge of the bowl to burn slightly.

This tomato sauce can be stored in the refrigerator for 1 week or in the freezer for up to 4 months.

Makes 2½ quarts

1 large celery rib, cut into 2-inch lengths
2 medium-size carrots, trimmed, scrubbed and cut into 3 pieces each
1 large onion, peeled and cut into 6 wedges
4 to 5 large garlic cloves, peeled
2 28-ounce cans crushed tomatoes in puree

1 28-ounce can peeled Italian-style plum tomatoes, undrained
2 6-ounce cans tomato paste
2 teaspoons crushed dried basil
1 teaspoon crushed dried oregano
½ teaspoon crushed dried thyme
½ teaspoon crushed dried rosemary
2 bay leaves
freshly ground black pepper to taste

In a food processor, chop the celery, carrots, onion, and garlic. Transfer to a very large bowl and mix with the crushed tomatoes, peeled tomatoes, and tomato paste. Microwave on HIGH for 60 minutes, uncovered, stirring 2 or 3 times to minimize crusting around the edge of the bowl. Stir in the herbs and microwave on HIGH, uncovered, until a thick, chunky sauce forms, about 30 minutes. Stir 2 or 3 times to prevent scorching. Season with pepper.

Variation

Thick and Chunky Tomato Sauce (makes 2 quarts): This makes a very thick, rich tomato sauce with a spreadable consistency. Prepare as directed, stirring well after the total 90 minutes of cooking, and microwave on HIGH, uncovered, until very thick, another 20 to 30 minutes, stirring occasionally.

Nutritional Information
(as a percentage of daily intake)
per 1-cup serving

5% (96) calories
2% (1 g) fat
8% (21 g) carbohydrates

5% (4 g) protein
18% (440 mg) sodium

11% (91 mg) calcium
20% (3 mg) iron

Here broccoli is coated in an Asian-style soy-based sauce redolent with ginger and garlic. Even those tired of broccoli will enjoy this recipe. The sauce competes with, but doesn't overpower, the broccoli.

Serves 4

¼ cup **Chinese oyster sauce**
¼ cup **Chicken Broth (page 42)**
½-inch piece of **fresh ginger, peeled and quartered**
1 large **garlic clove, peeled**
1 teaspoon **soy sauce**
2 teaspoons **cornstarch**
a little **freshly ground black pepper to taste**

1 large (1½-pound) bunch of **broccoli, cut into flowerets, stems peeled and cut on the bias into ¾-inch lengths,** *or* 1½ pounds **ready-cut broccoli flowerets**
1 **scallion, finely chopped**

In a blender, combine the oyster sauce, broth, ginger, garlic, soy sauce, cornstarch, and pepper and blend until smooth. Strain into a small bowl and microwave on HIGH, uncovered, for 1½ minutes. Stir together.

Place the broccoli in a large shallow dish or large bowl. Pour sauce over broccoli and mix well. Cover and microwave on HIGH for 7 minutes. Sprinkle with the chopped scallion, mix, and serve, spooning sauce from the bottom of the dish over the broccoli.

Variations

Cauliflower with Oyster Sauce: Substitute a medium head (1½ pounds) cauliflower, cored and cut into flowerets, for the broccoli, microwaving for 6 minutes.

Green Beans with Oyster Sauce: Prepare the sauce and combine with 1 pound, snapped and strung green beans, in a large bowl or large shallow dish. Mix well, cover, and microwave on HIGH for 7 minutes. Stir and serve, spooning extra sauce from the bottom of the bowl over the beans.

Snow Peas with Oyster Sauce: Prepare the sauce and combine with 1 pound snapped and strung snow peas, in a large bowl or shallow dish. Cover and microwave on HIGH for 5 minutes. Mix well and serve with extra sauce from the bottom of the dish spooned over the snow peas.

Nutritional Information
(as a percentage of daily intake)

4% (74) calories
2% (1 g) fat
5% (14 g) carbohydrates
9% (7 g) protein

12% (283 mg) sodium
14% (114 mg) calcium
13% (2 mg) iron

Broccoli and Cauliflower with Red Peppers

This festive combination of broccoli and cauliflower laced with ginger-flavored chopped red peppers is a quick (especially if you buy the broccoli and cauliflower ready-cut into flowerets) and colorful vegetable good for large parties or dinners or to take to a potluck meal or party.

Serves 8

2 large sweet red bell peppers, cored and cut into 2-inch pieces
1 small onion, peeled and quartered
2 large garlic cloves, peeled
1-inch piece of fresh ginger, peeled

¾ pound ready-cut broccoli flowerets *or* the flowerets from a very large (2-pound) bunch of broccoli
¾ pound ready-cut cauliflower flowerets *or* the flowerets from a large (2-pound) head of cauliflower

In a food processor, finely chop the red peppers, onion, garlic, and ginger. Transfer to a very large bowl, cover, and microwave on HIGH for 5 minutes.

Add the broccoli and cauliflower, toss well, cover, and microwave on HIGH for 7 minutes. Stir and serve.

Variations

Broccoli with Red Peppers: Increase the broccoli to 1½ pounds and eliminate the cauliflower.

Cauliflower with Red Peppers: Increase the cauliflower to 1½ pounds and eliminate the broccoli.

Nutritional Information
(as a percentage of daily intake)

3% (63) calories
2% (1 g) fat
5% (13 g) carbohydrates
8% (6 g) protein

2% (46 mg) sodium
11% (87 mg) calcium
13% (2 mg) iron

This recipe uses only broccoli stems, which are julienned—easy if you have a mandoline or gadget made for julienning. If you don't mind the julienning, you'll love this recipe, which is a play of textures and flavors that will do cartwheels in your mouth.

The 4 broccoli stems called for in this recipe come from about 2 pounds of broccoli.

Serves 4

4 broccoli stems, about 1 inch by 6 inches, peeled, bottom ends trimmed, and julienned (about 3 cups)

½ to ¾ cup Winter Green Salsa (recipe follows) or a variation

Place the broccoli in a medium bowl, cover, and microwave on HIGH for 3 minutes. Mix with the salsa and either serve hot or refrigerate to serve cold.

Variation

Simple Julienne of Broccoli Stems: Prepare as directed, substituting 1 teaspoon unsalted butter or fruity olive oil for the salsa.

Nutritional Information
(as a percentage of daily intake)

3% (64) calories

2% (1 g) fat

5% (13 g) carbohydrates

7% (5 g) protein

1% (25 mg) sodium

23% (186 mg) calcium

20% (3 mg) iron

Winter Green Salsa

This salsa can be made any time of the year and is especially good as a winter substitute for fresh tomato salsa when flavorful tomatoes are not available. The spicy flavor and the scent added by the celery seeds make this sauce particularly lively with green vegetables—not only broccoli but also green beans, peas, asparagus, and artichokes.

Makes about 1½ cups

2 4-ounce cans chopped mild green chilies
2 scallions
1 large *or* 2 small bunches cilantro
1 large garlic clove, peeled
¾ teaspoon celery seeds
juice of 1 lime

Combine all the ingredients in a food processor and process until a sauce forms, with only small bits visible in it.

Variations

Light Green Salsa: Add a medium-size unpeeled cucumber, scrubbed, halved, and seeded, to the food processor with the other ingredients.

Green Salsa Dip: Mix the Winter Green Salsa with an equal amount of plain nonfat yogurt.

Nutritional Information
(as a percentage of daily intake)
per ¼-cup serving

1% (14) calories
0% (0 g) fat
1% (3 g) carbohydrates
1% (1 g) protein

3% (68 mg) sodium
3% (23 mg) calcium
7% (1 mg) iron

You'll be astonished by how well Brussels sprouts cook in the microwave. The leaves actually separate as the sprouts cook, leaving a flaky texture reminiscent of puff paste, rather than the traditional soggy mush that has given Brussels sprouts a bad name. And amazingly the color doesn't change; cooked sprouts keep their pale green raw appearance.

Brussels sprouts need a sauce, such as Winter Green Salsa (page 112) or Fresh Tomato Salsa (page 102) or, as indicated here, a little butter to balance their flavor with their texture.

Serves 6

2 pints Brussels sprouts, bottoms trimmed, any damaged outer leaves removed

1 tablespoon unsalted butter
a little salt and freshly ground black pepper to taste

Place the Brussels sprouts in a large bowl or a large shallow dish. Cover and microwave on HIGH for 7 minutes. Toss with the butter and season with salt and pepper.

Nutritional Information
(as a percentage of daily intake)

3% (57) calories
3% (2 g) fat
3% (9 g) carbohydrates
5% (4 g) protein

0% (11 mg) sodium
5% (38 mg) calcium
7% (1 mg) iron

Brussels Sprouts with Sweet Red Pepper Puree

Brussels sprouts develop a delicate flavor and leafy texture in the microwave. Here they are company fare, with a sauce of pureed sweet red peppers.

Serves 3

1 pint Brussels sprouts, bottoms trimmed and any damaged outer leaves removed

¾ cup Sweet Red Pepper Puree (page 41)

Mix Brussels sprouts and red pepper puree in a large bowl. Cover and microwave on HIGH for 8 minutes.

Variations

Brussels Sprouts with Tomato Sauce: Substitute 1 cup Chunky Tomato Sauce (page 107) for the red pepper puree.

Brussels Sprouts with Harissa: Substitute Harissa (page 132) for the tomato sauce.

Nutritional Information
(as a percentage of daily intake)

5% (109) calories
2% (1 g) fat
9% (24 g) carbohydrates
8% (6 g) protein

1% (21 mg) sodium
7% (56 mg) calcium
33% (5 mg) iron

In late summer I serve this recipe as a cold salad or side dish. Where the weather gets cold, I serve it hot from the microwave to enliven a meal with its fragrance, bold, spicy taste and, contrasting vegetable sweetness. In winter the squash accompanies roasted chicken, simply cooked tuna or salmon, or steaks.

The combination of nine spices and two herbs produces a complex, unified chili flavor with a single taste that has a discreet elegance. And using onion powder and garlic powder, instead of fresh onions and garlic, makes this recipe simple to prepare without sacrificing those two flavors to expedience. The slight tartness of the lemon juice brings together the spiciness and the sweetness without the need for salt.

Confession: When I prepare this at the beach, where the spice rack is somewhat limited, I just mix 3 tablespoons of chili powder into the lemon juice, and the final dish is still quite good.

Serves 6

2 tablespoons chili powder
1 teaspoon paprika
1 teaspoon ground cumin
½ teaspoon ground cinnamon
⅛ teaspoon cayenne pepper
⅛ teaspoon freshly ground white
  pepper
⅛ teaspoon freshly ground black
  pepper

½ teaspoon onion powder
½ teaspoon garlic powder
½ teaspoon crushed dried thyme
1 teaspoon crushed dried oregano
juice of 1 lemon
1 3-pound butternut squash, split
  lengthwise, fibrous center and
  seeds removed, peeled, and cut into
  ¾-inch dice

Stir the spices and herbs into the lemon juice, then toss with the squash in a very large bowl. Cover and microwave on HIGH for 14 minutes.

To serve hot, just uncover and send to the table; to serve cold, refrigerate until needed.

5% (96) calories   2% (45 mg) sodium
2% (1 g) fat   12% (95 mg) calcium
9% (24 g) carbohydrates   13% (2 mg) iron
3% (2 g) protein

BASIC PREPARATION OF BUTTERNUT SQUASH

Split a 3-pound butternut squash in half lengthwise. Scoop out the fibrous center. Peel and cut into ¼- to 1-inch dice. Place in a very large bowl, cover, and microwave on HIGH for 14 minutes. Toss with 2 teaspoons unsalted butter and season with a little lemon juice or salt and freshly ground black pepper.

Sweet and Sour Red Cabbage with Hidden Shiitakes

The cabbage here has a mild sweet-and-sour taste and a firm but tender texture. Soft slivers of shiitake mushrooms are hidden in the red cabbage shreds. It is essential to the final texture of this recipe that the vegetables be shredded very finely and that they all be the same size.

Serves 4

4 cups (about ½ medium-size head, core removed) finely shredded red cabbage

1 small red onion, peeled and finely shredded

6 ounces fresh shiitake mushrooms, caps only, cut into fine slivers

½ cup red wine vinegar

2 tablespoons sugar

freshly ground black pepper to taste

In a very large bowl, mix together the cabbage, onion, shiitakes, vinegar, and sugar. Cover and microwave on HIGH for 11 minutes. Season with pepper.

Variation

Sweet and Sour Red Cabbage: Omit the shiitakes. When the cabbage is cooked, toss with 1½ teaspoons unsalted butter and then season with freshly ground black pepper.

Nutritional Information
(as a percentage of daily intake)

4% (82) calories

0% (0 g) fat

8% (21 g) carbohydrates

3% (2 g) protein

0% (11 mg) sodium

6% (46 mg) calcium

7% (1 mg) iron

BASIC PREPARATION OF RED OR GREEN CABBAGE

Place 4 cups finely shredded cabbage in a very large bowl, cover, and microwave on HIGH for 11 minutes. Toss with 1 tablespoon unsalted butter and season with a little salt and freshly ground black pepper.

There's a liveliness to this curry that enhances the tender but not soft cabbage. And because microwaving emphasizes the aromas of spices better than other cooking techniques, this is a very fragrant dish, more fragrant than spicy.

Serve this with roasted poultry or game or with pork and another simply flavored vegetable.

Serves 6

1 tablespoon curry powder
1 teaspoon ground ginger
½ teaspoon garlic powder
½ teaspoon onion powder
½ teaspoon ground cumin
½ teaspoon ground coriander

juice of 1 lime
1 small (2¼-pound) head of green cabbage, cored and shredded
1 medium-size onion, peeled, halved lengthwise, and thinly sliced

In a small bowl, mix together the spices. Place the lime juice, cabbage, and onion in a very large bowl and toss with the spices until spices are evenly distributed. Cover and microwave on HIGH for 16 minutes. Stir well and serve.

Variation

Chilied Cabbage: Substitute 1 tablespoon chili powder, ½ teaspoon paprika, ½ teaspoon ground cumin, ¼ teaspoon ground cinnamon, ¼ teaspoon onion powder, ¼ teaspoon garlic powder, a pinch cayenne, a pinch freshly ground white pepper, and a pinch freshly ground black pepper for the spices.

Nutritional Information
(as a percentage of daily intake)

3% (52) calories
2% (1 g) fat
4% (12 g) carbohydrates
3% (2 g) protein

1% (27 mg) sodium
11% (86 mg) calcium
13% (2 mg) iron

BASIC PREPARATION OF CABBAGE

Core and shred a 2-pound head of cabbage. Place in a very large bowl, cover, and microwave on HIGH for 15 minutes, then stir in 2 teaspoons unsalted butter and season to taste with a little salt and some freshly ground black or white pepper.

To Prepare Whole Cooked Cabbage Leaves

The microwave works like magic to cook whole cabbage leaves for stuffing. Just core the cabbage, place on a plate or directly on the floor in the center of the oven, and microwave on HIGH for 6 minutes. Remove and let cool slightly, then peel off the whole cooked leaves as needed.

Glazed Carrots

Better than carrots glazed with butter and brown sugar is this dish of radiant orange-colored carrots, sliced or julienned (I generally prefer julienned), glazed with a reduction of apple juice flavored with a little rosemary or some fresh chives.

Serves 4

2 cups apple juice
1 teaspoons crushed dried rosemary
1 tablespoon cornstarch
1 pound carrots, trimmed, scrubbed, and either sliced ¼ inch thick or julienned

1 teaspoon finely chopped fresh rosemary *or* finely chopped fresh chives

Combine the apple juice and dried rosemary in a medium bowl and microwave on HIGH, uncovered, for 30 minutes, or until reduced to about ⅔ cup. Pour into a blender and add the cornstarch. Blend for 10 seconds.

Place the carrots in a large shallow dish or bowl and strain the apple juice over them. Mix well, cover, and microwave on HIGH for 9 minutes. Toss well with the fresh rosemary. Serve at once.

Variations

Glazed Carrots with Oregano: Substitute dried oregano for the dried rosemary and fresh oregano for the fresh rosemary.

Carrots with Oyster Sauce Glaze: Prepare the sauce as directed in Broccoli with Oyster Sauce (page 108) and substitute that for the apple juice glaze. Substitute 1 tablespoon chopped cilantro for the fresh rosemary.

Nutritional Information
(as a percentage of daily intake)

6% (119) calories
0% (0 g) fat
11% (29 g) carbohydrates
1% (1 g) protein

2% (48 mg) sodium
5% (42 mg) calcium
7% (1 mg) iron

BASIC PREPARATION OF CARROTS

To prepare 1 pound carrots, either cut into ¼-inch slices or julienne, place in a large bowl, cover, and microwave on HIGH for 9 minutes. Mix with 1 teaspoon fruity olive oil or unsalted butter and season with a little salt and freshly ground black pepper.

For 2 pounds (serves 8) prepare as directed above, but extend the cooking time to 13 minutes, toss with 1½ teaspoons unsalted butter or fruity olive oil, and season with a little salt and freshly ground pepper.

As with so many vegetables, cauliflower can be cooked plain in the microwave with spectacular results. The natural, delicate cabbage flavor and flowery aroma of cauliflower is intensified with microwave cooking.

Serves 4

1 small (1½-pound) head of cauliflower, cored, leaves discarded, cut into flowerets, *or* 1¼ pounds ready-cut flowerets

1 recipe Emerald Sauce (page 98)

Place the cauliflower in a large shallow dish or large bowl, cover, and microwave on HIGH for 6 minutes. Toss with the sauce and serve.

Nutritional Information
(as a percentage of daily intake)

2% (45) calories
0% (0 g) fat
3% (8 g) carbohydrates
5% (4 g) protein

2% (42 mg) sodium
13% (103 mg) calcium
7% (1 mg) iron

BASIC PREPARATION OF CAULIFLOWER

Core a small head (about 1½ pounds) of cauliflower and discard the outer leaves. Cut into flowerets and place in a large shallow dish or large bowl. Cover and microwave on HIGH for 6 minutes. Toss with 2 teaspoons unsalted butter and season with a little salt and freshly ground black pepper.

Here's a simple family recipe for firm but tender flowerets of cauliflower in a rich, chunky tomato sauce.

Serves 3

1 medium-size (1¾-pound) head of cauliflower, cored and cut into flowerets with about 1 inch of stem

1 cup Chunky Tomato Sauce (page 107)

Mix cauliflower and tomato sauce in a large bowl. Cover and microwave on HIGH for 8 minutes.

Variation

Cauliflower with Harissa: Substitute Harissa (page 132) for the tomato sauce.

Nutritional Information
(as a percentage of daily intake)

6% (120) calories
2% (1 g) fat
9% (26 g) carbohydrates
8% (6 g) protein

19% (454 mg) sodium
15% (119 mg) calcium
20% (3 mg) iron

Celery Root and Potato Puree

With its slightly sweet flavor and delicate overtones of celery, I prefer this elegant puree to mashed potatoes anytime.

Celery root, also called *celeriac*, is a thick, crusty root vegetable with the texture of a parsnip, tender but not mealy when cooked. It has a delicate, sweet flavor scented with the aroma of celery seeds.

Serve as a winter vegetable, with a little of the juice or pan gravy from a roast, or anytime as a substitute for mashed potatoes.

Serves 6

1 ¾-pound baking potato, peeled and cut into 2-inch chunks

1 1-pound celery root, peeled and cut into 2-inch chunks

¼ cup skim milk

1 tablespoon fruity olive oil or unsalted butter

a little salt and freshly ground white pepper to taste

Combine the potato and celery root in a large bowl. Cover and microwave on HIGH for 15 minutes. With a potato ricer or an electric beater, puree the potatoes and celery root until smooth with the milk and oil or butter. Season with a little salt and pepper. Serve very hot.

Nutritional Information
(as a percentage of daily intake)

7% (135) calories

3% (2 g) fat

9% (26 g) carbohydrates

4% (3 g) protein

2% (59 mg) sodium

5% (41 mg) calcium

7% (1 mg) iron

Swiss Chard
with Rosemary and Garlic

This dark, leafy green with thick, hard white stems has a sweet, only ever so slightly bitter, earthy flavor that makes it a rich accompaniment to cold-weather meals, to roasts and grilled meats. When cooked, it develops a silken texture and sensual appeal.

Because the stems take longer to cook than the leaves, they are cooked first, then the leaves are added and the cooking is completed. Microwaving chard takes only half the time of ordinary cooking.

Serves 6

2 tablespoons olive oil
2 very large garlic cloves, peeled and finely chopped
2 pounds Swiss chard, washed, leaves and stems separated

2 teaspoons fresh rosemary leaves *or* 1 teaspoon dried rosemary
a little salt and freshly ground black pepper to taste

Place the oil and garlic in a large bowl and microwave on HIGH, uncovered, for 1 minute and 15 seconds.

While garlic is cooking, cut the chard stems into 2-inch lengths and chop very finely, almost to a puree, in a food processor. Add to the garlic and oil and cover. Microwave on HIGH for 10 minutes.

While stems are cooking, coarsely chop the chard leaves. Add the leaves to the stems, cover, and microwave on HIGH for 10 minutes.

In a food processor, puree the cooked chard and stems with the rosemary until silken. Season with a little salt and pepper. The chard will be soupy, so serve it in small bowls or ramekins.

Nutritional Information
(as a percentage of daily intake)

3% (59) calories
8% (5 g) fat
1% (4 g) carbohydrates
3% (2 g) protein

8% (192 mg) sodium
6% (47 mg) calcium
13% (2 mg) iron

MICROWAVE NOTE

Here is one of the very few instances in this book when garlic is cooked in oil, mimicking the traditional sauté of garlic that starts so many recipes. This is so that the garlic flavor will remain sharp. Normal cooking of garlic in the microwave leaves the cloves tender and sweet.

Light Caponata
(Sicilian Eggplant Spread)

This enlightened caponata is made without its usual cup of olive oil. Nonetheless, it remains true to the sun-baked flavors in the original. Unlike traditional caponata, which can be served refrigerator cold, this spread needs to be warmed before serving.

In addition to serving it mounded in a bowl surrounded by crackers or Toasted Pita Triangles (page 80), this spread can also be used in place of mayonnaise on sandwiches or as a vegetable to accompany other somewhat blandly seasoned foods.

I sometimes spread this caponata on large slices of sourdough bread, lightly toasted, and serve it with a bowl of soup in place of the ubiquitous salad for a quick lunch.

Serves 8 as an appetizer

1½ pounds eggplant, trimmed but unpeeled and cut into 2-inch chunks
1 scallion, cut into 4 pieces
⅓ cup green French or Spanish olives, pitted
2 large garlic cloves, peeled
2 tablespoons drained capers, rinsed

juice of 1 lemon
½ cup tightly packed fresh parsley leaves
¼ cup tightly packed fresh basil leaves
½ teaspoon dried oregano
a little freshly ground black pepper to taste

Place the eggplant in a very large bowl, cover, and microwave on HIGH for 15 minutes. Puree with the remaining ingredients in a food processor, pulsing until everything is well mixed and finely chopped. Refrigerate until cold. Serve warm or at least at room temperature.

To heat from the refrigerator, cover and microwave on HIGH for 5 minutes. Stir well and serve.

Nutritional Information
(as a percentage of daily intake)
per ¼-cup serving

2% (36) calories
2% (1 g) fat
3% (7 g) carbohydrates
1% (1 g) protein

8% (189 mg) sodium
6% (49 mg) calcium
7% (1 mg) iron

Corn on the cob cooks magnificently in the microwave. The corn steams in its husk, becoming tender, even sweeter, and more flavorful than if poached in water or milk. But there is a drawback. Because the corn is cooked in its husk, the husk must be removed when the corn is very hot. Even with a thick towel to protect your hands, this is awkward.

Because the microwave heats deeply into the cob, not just on the surface as with traditional cooking, you may want to warn your guests that the cob itself may be very hot, even when the outer surface of the kernels seems cool.

Serving Notes: A little salt and a peppermill can be served with the corn, or you could serve a little curry or chili powder instead of salt and pepper, perhaps placing those spices in little formal salt cellars. Instead of butter, rub with a small wedge of lemon or lime. Or try serving the corn with Red Pepper Sauce (page 166) or with some commercially prepared red or green pepper jelly.

Serves 4

4 ears of fresh corn

Arrange the corn like spokes of a wheel on the floor of the oven, small ends meeting at the center, thick ends pointing toward the corners of the oven. Microwave on HIGH for 10 minutes. Carefully remove from the oven and, using a thick clean towel or pot holders, pull off the husk and silk (both will come off easily). Serve immediately as the kernels cool quickly.

Nutritional Information
(as a percentage of daily intake)
per ear of corn

3% (59) calories	0% (3 mg) sodium
0% (0 g) fat	0% (2 mg) calcium
5% (14 g) carbohydrates	0% (0 mg) iron
3% (2 g) protein	

DIRECTIONS FOR COOKING CORN
(COOK NO MORE
THAN FOUR EARS AT A TIME)

For 1 Ear:

Place in the center of the oven and microwave on HIGH for 3 minutes, then carefully remove husk and silk as directed in the recipe above.

For 2 Ears:

Place the corn, evenly spaced, on the floor of the oven and microwave on HIGH for 6 minutes, then carefully remove husks and silk as directed in the recipe above.

For 3 Ears:

Arrange the corn like spokes of a wheel, as directed in the recipe above, then microwave on HIGH for 9 minutes. Remove the husks and silk as directed in the recipe above.

This is one of the best green bean dishes ever. The microwave brightens the beans, leaving them more vibrantly colored than would be possible with ordinary cooking techniques. And the green sauce enlivens the sweetness of the beans with an unexpected but gentle piquancy.

Serve hot during the winter or cold in summer.

Serves 4

1 pound fresh green beans, snapped and strung
1 4-ounce can mild green chilies
leaves from 1 small bunch of fresh parsley
2 tablespoons plain nonfat yogurt

1 scallion
1 large garlic clove, peeled
juice of ½ lime
a little freshly ground black pepper to taste

Place the beans in a large bowl or shallow dish, cover, and microwave on HIGH for 7 minutes. While beans are cooking, combine the remaining ingredients in a food processor and puree. Pour dressing over the cooked beans, mix well, and serve; or refrigerate to serve cold.

Nutritional Information
(as a percentage of daily intake)

2% (48) calories
2% (1 g) fat
3% (9 g) carbohydrates
3% (2 g) protein

2% (42 mg) sodium
9% (74 mg) calcium
13% (2 mg) iron

BASIC PREPARATION OF GREEN BEANS

Snap and string 1 pound beans, place in a large bowl or shallow dish, cover, microwave on HIGH for 7 minutes, then toss with 1 teaspoon fruity olive oil or unsalted butter and season with a little salt and freshly ground black pepper.

Here's a simple company recipe for green beans cooked in harissa, a spicy Moroccan sauce flavored with sweet red pepper and tomato.

Serves 4

**1 pound fresh green beans, snapped
    and strung**

1 cup Harissa (recipe follows)

Mix green beans and harissa in a large bowl. Cover and microwave on HIGH for 11 minutes.

Variation

Green Beans with Tomato Sauce: Substitute Chunky Tomato Sauce (page 107) for the harissa.

*Nutritional Information
(as a percentage of daily intake)*

3% (63) calories

0% (11 mg) sodium

2% (1 g) fat

5% (40 mg) calcium

5% (14 g) carbohydrates

20% (3 mg) iron

4% (3 g) protein

Harissa

This classic Moroccan sauce has as many variations as its companion dish, couscous. In this version the soft, sweet flavor of the red peppers is supported by a burst of tomato flavor and a gentle mix of traditional harissa spices. This is a moderately hot sauce. For a milder version, simply use half as much cayenne as suggested below.

This unusual sauce will become a good friend to you. Try it with broccoli or Brussels sprouts (pages 106 and 113), with acorn squash (page 92), or use it as a topping for potatoes or sweet potatoes instead of butter or sour cream. Harissa is an excellent accompaniment to grilled and roasted poultry and meats.

Makes 1 cup

2 large sweet red bell peppers, cored
1 tablespoon tomato paste
juice of ½ small lemon
1 garlic clove, peeled
¼ teaspoon ground cinnamon

¼ teaspoon ground cumin
¼ teaspoon ground caraway seeds
¼ teaspoon cayenne pepper
freshly ground black pepper to taste

Place the red peppers in a large bowl, cover, and microwave on HIGH for 10 minutes. Puree (without the liquid that has accumulated under the peppers) in a food processor with the remaining ingredients.

Variation

For 2 Cups Harissa: Double all the ingredients, microwaving the peppers, covered, in a very large bowl for 15 minutes.

Nutritional Information
(as a percentage of daily intake)
per ¼-cup serving

5% (104) calories
2% (1 g) fat
9% (24 g) carbohydrates
5% (4 g) protein

1% (20 mg) sodium
6% (51 mg) calcium
33% (5 mg) iron

Kale, with its earthy, slightly bitter flavor, softens without becoming limp when cooked in the microwave. Here a bunch of cilantro is cooked with the kale to give it an unexpected new dimension.

I am fond of cooking greens of all kinds with a bunch of some herb, such as parsley or dill, in the bowl; you might want to try it.

Serves 6

1½ pounds tender kale, such as red kale, washed, stems removed, and leaves torn into pieces no larger than about 2 inches
1 large bunch of cilantro, washed and thick stems removed

1 cup Chicken Broth (page 42)
juice of ½ lime
a little salt and freshly ground black pepper to taste

Combine the kale, cilantro, and broth in a very large bowl, cover, and microwave on HIGH for 15 minutes, stirring once midway through the cooking. Transfer, with the liquid in the bowl, to a food processor and add the lime juice. Chop coarsely and season with salt and pepper.

*Nutritional Information
(as a percentage of daily intake)*

3% (69) calories
2% (1 g) fat
5% (13 g) carbohydrates
7% (5 g) protein

3% (66 mg) sodium
21% (167 mg) calcium
13% (2 mg) iron

BASIC PREPARATION OF KALE

Wash, remove the stems, and finely chop 1½ pounds kale. Place in a very large bowl with ¾ cup Chicken Broth (page 42) or water, cover, and microwave on HIGH for 15 minutes, stirring once midway through the cooking. Drain and mix with 1 tablespoon unsalted butter. Season with a little salt and freshly ground black pepper.

Okra with Tomatoes

For me, this is the ultimate okra recipe—okra is stewed with tomatoes and onions; a little fresh basil and a small piece of a jalapeño are added for support, and everything is improved by the microwave. The okra is a brighter green after cooking than it was before cooking and is crisp but tender and soft-centered, not slimy.

To keep the texture of the okra at its finest, use small okra, about 2 inches long, and when trimming the tops, do not cut into the pod.

Serves 6

3 garlic cloves, peeled
1 medium-size onion, peeled and
   quartered
½ jalapeño pepper, seeded
1 tablespoon olive oil
1 pound okra, trimmed (see note
   above)

1 cup canned crushed tomatoes in
   puree
juice of 1 lemon
a little freshly ground black pepper to
   taste
leaves from 1 small bunch of fresh
   basil, finely chopped

In a food processor, chop the garlic, onion, pepper, and oil. Transfer to a large bowl, cover, and microwave on HIGH for 3 minutes. Add the okra, tomatoes, lemon juice, and black pepper and mix well. Cover and microwave on HIGH for 9 minutes. Stir in the basil and serve hot or refrigerate to serve cold.

Nutritional Information
(as a percentage of daily intake)

3% (50) calories
3% (2 g) fat
2% (6 g) carbohydrates
1% (1 g) protein

3% (71 mg) sodium
4% (35 mg) calcium
7% (1 mg) iron

Parsnip Puree

With their sweet, mild flavor hinting of coconut, parsnips make one of winter's most satisfying purees, so sweet and fragrant.

Serves 8

2 pounds parsnips, peeled, trimmed, and cut into 2-inch pieces
1 large onion, peeled and quartered
2 large garlic cloves, peeled

1 medium-size leek, white part only, split lengthwise, washed thoroughly, and cut in half
1½ cups skim milk

In a food processor, in several batches, finely chop the parsnips, onion, garlic, and leek. Transfer to a very large bowl, cover, and microwave on HIGH for 12 minutes.

In a food processor, puree the parsnips and milk until smooth (it may take a minute or 2). Reheat before serving.

Variations

Curried Parsnip Puree: Add 1 to 2 tablespoons curry powder to the parsnips before cooking.

Saffron Parsnip Puree: Add ¼ teaspoon saffron threads to the parsnips when pureeing.

Nutritional Information
(as a percentage of daily intake)

3% (69) calories
0% (0 g) fat
5% (15 g) carbohydrates
4% (3 g) protein

1% (31 mg) sodium
11% (85 mg) calcium
0% (0 mg) iron

BASIC PREPARATION OF PARSNIPS

Trim, peel, and cut 2 pounds parsnips into slices or cubes. Place in a very large bowl, cover, and microwave on HIGH for 12 minutes. Toss with 1 tablespoon unsalted butter and season with a little salt and freshly ground black pepper.

Fresh peas are one of the surprises of winter farmer's markets, and with a little seasoning they can be quite a jazzy addition to a meal. When cooked in the microwave, peas become firm but tender, not thick-skinned beads with mushy centers as they do in ordinary cooking.

Here some red onion, sun-dried tomatoes, and basil turn humble winter peas into an energetic, company-worthy vegetable.

Serves 6

2 cups (1 pound) shelled fresh green peas (about 2 pounds in the shell)
1 small red onion, very finely chopped
1 large garlic clove, finely chopped

2 tablespoons finely chopped sun-dried tomatoes
1½ teaspoons crushed dried basil

Mix everything together in a large bowl, cover, and microwave on HIGH for 6 minutes.

Nutritional Information
(as a percentage of daily intake)

2% (49) calories
0% (0 g) fat
3% (9 g) carbohydrates
4% (3 g) protein

0% (4 mg) sodium
1% (5 mg) calcium
0% (0 mg) iron

BASIC   PREPARATION   OF   FRESH   PEAS

Place 2 cups fresh peas in a large bowl, cover, and microwave on HIGH for 6 minutes. Toss with 2 teaspoons unsalted butter or 1½ teaspoons fruity olive oil and season with a little salt and freshly ground black pepper to taste. Here the butter not only adds flavor but also softens the texture.

Purple Potato Puree with Tarragon and Parsley

Blue potatoes are starchier than regular potatoes, and sweeter, and when I find them in the market I always buy a few pounds to serve just for the fun of it. The color of the mashed blue potatoes is Play-Doh purple. Adults are amazed by the color of these potatoes; kids giggle and stick their fingers in them.

Serves 4

1½ pounds blue potatoes, peeled and cut into ¾-inch dice
½ cup skim milk
1 tablespoon finely chopped fresh tarragon

1 tablespoon finely chopped fresh parsley
a little salt and freshly ground black pepper to taste

Place the potatoes in a large bowl, cover, and microwave on HIGH for 12 minutes. Mash through a potato ricer or with an electric beater, beating in the milk until mostly smooth (a few small lumps are okay), then mix in the herbs. Season with salt and pepper.

Place in a bowl, cover, and reheat on HIGH for about 4 minutes just before serving.

Nutritional Information
(as a percentage of daily intake)

10% (203) calories
0% (0 g) fat
17% (46 g) carbohydrates
7% (5 g) protein

1% (30 mg) sodium
7% (55 mg) calcium
13% (2 mg) iron

Despite what you've heard, a microwaved "baked" potato is not identical to a traditional baked potato—it's a little creamier, sometimes a little waxier (depending on the potato) and less mealy, and the skin *will* become crisp. Microwaving is a satisfying, delicious way to prepare potatoes. And it takes only a few minutes to microwave potatoes, not the better part of an hour.

Gently slather the potatoes with a little light sour cream and chopped chives or top each potato with a couple of tablespoons of one of the sauces suggested below.

To ensure even cooking, turn the potato over midway through the cooking or place a double layer of paper toweling under the potatoes.

One friend has found that wrapping the potatoes in foil after removing them from the microwave and letting them stand for five minutes makes them creamier. I am not willing to be that fussy, but you might want to try it.

Serves 4

4 ½-pound baking potatoes, scrubbed and pricked in 2 or 3 places with a fork or the tip of a knife

¼ cup light sour cream or one of the following sauces: Emerald Sauce (page 98), Winter Green Salsa (page 112), Cilantro Pesto (page 84), Harissa (page 132), Sweet Red Pepper Puree (page 41)

Arrange the potatoes evenly spaced like spokes of a wheel on the floor of the oven. Microwave on HIGH for 20 minutes, turning the potatoes over once about midway through the cooking or placing a double layer of paper towels under the potatoes to ensure even cooking. Serve with sour cream or one of the recommended sauces.

Variations

For 1 potato: Place in the center of the oven and microwave on HIGH for 7 minutes, turning midway through the cooking or placing a double layer of paper towels under the potatoes to ensure even cooking.

For 2 potatoes: Place in the oven so that they divide the oven floor in thirds. Microwave on HIGH for 11 minutes, turning once midway through the cooking or placing a double layer of paper towels under the potatoes to ensure even cooking.

For 3 potatoes: Arrange like spokes of a wheel and microwave on HIGH for 16 minutes, turning once midway through the cooking or placing a double layer of paper towels under the potatoes to ensure even cooking.

Nutritional Information
(as a percentage of daily intake)

11% (220) calories   1% (16 mg) sodium
0% (0 g) fat   3% (20 mg) calcium
19% (51 g) carbohydrates   20% (3 mg) iron
7% (5 g) protein

QUICK AND EASY MASHED POTATOES (A BASIC PREPARATION)

Arrange 3 or 4 all-purpose or baking potatoes, weighing 1½ pounds, evenly spaced like spokes of a wheel on the floor of the microwave oven. Microwave on HIGH for 18 minutes, either turning the potatoes over (so the side on the floor of the oven becomes the top) midway through the cooking or lining the oven floor with a double layer of paper towels to ensure even cooking. Peel, if you wish, mash, and blend with ½ cup skim milk. Season to taste with a little salt and some freshly ground pepper. Serves 6.

There are times in winter, often around the holidays, when nothing but a rutabaga puree will satisfy me. But I know that rutabagas, also called *yellow turnips*, have a strong taste that is not to everyone's liking.

In this recipe the microwave somehow lightens the texture of the vegetable, leaving a tender, light puree with a golden, glistening appearance and the scent and gentle aftertaste of ginger.

Serves 4

2½ pounds rutabagas, thickly peeled and cut into 2-inch pieces
1½-inch piece of fresh ginger, peeled

a little freshly ground black pepper to taste
a pinch of cayenne pepper

Place the rutabagas in a large bowl and cover. Microwave on HIGH for 12 minutes. In a food processor, puree the rutabagas, and the liquid that accumulated under them during cooking, with the ginger. Season with pepper and cayenne.

Variation

Buttered Rutabagas: Dice the rutabagas and cook as directed, then toss with 2 teaspoons unsalted butter and season with a little salt and freshly ground black pepper to taste. Add a pinch of cayenne if you wish.

Nutritional Information
(as a percentage of daily intake)

5% (92) calories
0% (0 g) fat
7% (20 g) carbohydrates
4% (3 g) protein

2% (49 mg) sodium
14% (114 mg) calcium
7% (1 mg) iron

Snow Peas with Cashews and Black Mushrooms

This is a playful use of Asian flavorings with a highly textured combination of ingredients. Tender but still crunchy snow peas contrast with soft, deeply flavored mushrooms and the crunchy roasted cashews. There is a little acidity, there is a little "hot," and there is a little salt in this recipe. And it all works to create a stunning effect, both visually and in your mouth.

Serves 6

1 ounce dried Chinese black (winter) mushrooms
1 teaspoon chili paste with garlic (available in Asian markets and some large supermarkets)
2 tablespoons soy sauce
1 tablespoon rice wine vinegar
1 large garlic clove
1 pound snow peas, snapped and strung
¾ cup roasted cashews

Soak the mushrooms for 15 minutes in just enough hottest possible tap water to cover, then drain and cut into bite-size pieces, discarding tough stems.

Mix the chili paste, soy sauce, vinegar, and garlic together in a large shallow dish or very large bowl. Add the snow peas, mushrooms, and cashews and toss until coated. Cover and microwave on HIGH for 6½ minutes.

Nutritional Information
(as a percentage of daily intake)

7% (149) calories
12% (8 g) fat
6% (16 g) carbohydrates
8% (6 g) protein

16% (395 mg) sodium
6% (46 mg) calcium
60% (9 mg) iron

BASIC PREPARATION OF SNOW PEAS

Place 1 pound snow peas, snapped and strung, in a large bowl or shallow dish. Cover and microwave on HIGH for 5 minutes. Toss with 1½ teaspoons unsalted butter, then season with a little salt and freshly ground black pepper.

Serve this as a hot vegetable or cold as part of a summer picnic or buffet. The gentle flavors of the squash are enhanced by the tomato and scallion, which contribute to the recipe's festive confetti appearance.

Serves 6

1 pound medium-size yellow summer squash, trimmed and sliced ⅓ inch thick (split lengthwise if thick)
1 pound medium-size zucchini, trimmed and sliced ⅓ inch thick
1 large ripe tomato, cored and cut into ½-inch dice

2 tablespoons finely chopped fresh parsley
1 small scallion, finely chopped
¼ cup plain nonfat yogurt
a little salt and freshly ground black pepper to taste

Mix the squash and zucchini in a large bowl, seal airtight with plastic wrap, and microwave on HIGH for 9 minutes. Carefully uncover and stir in the tomato, parsley, scallion, and yogurt. Season with salt and pepper and serve immediately. Do not reheat after yogurt is added.

*Nutritional Information
(as a percentage of daily intake)*

2% (34) calories
0% (0 g) fat
3% (7 g) carbohydrates
3% (2 g) protein

1% (12 mg) sodium
6% (50 mg) calcium
7% (1 mg) iron

**BASIC PREPARATION OF
YELLOW SQUASH OR ZUCCHINI**

Slice or julienne the squash or zucchini. For 1 pound, 3 servings, place in a medium bowl, cover, and microwave on HIGH for 6 minutes. Mix with ½ teaspoon unsalted butter or fruity olive oil and season with a little salt and freshly ground black pepper. For 2 pounds, 6 servings, place in a very large bowl, cover, and microwave on HIGH for 9 minutes. Mix with 1 teaspoon unsalted butter or fruity oil and season with a little salt and freshly ground black pepper.

This exuberant bright yellow and dark green combination of crookneck (yellow) squash and zucchini has a rich squash flavor because only the very flavorful skins are used. For a lighter flavor, use 3 pounds of crookneck squash; for a very deep flavor, use 3 pounds of zucchini.

Serves 4

2 pounds yellow summer squash
1 pound zucchini
½ cup nonfat buttermilk

a little salt and freshly ground black
pepper to taste

Cut the squash and zucchini into 3-inch lengths; then, with a mandoline or plastic vegetable julienner, cut the skins only into fine julienne.

In a large bowl, mix the julienned skins with the buttermilk, cover, and microwave on HIGH for 5 minutes. Season with salt and pepper.

Variations

Julienne of Summer Squash Skins with Dill and Lemon: Add ½ teaspoon grated lemon zest and 1 tablespoon finely chopped fresh dill to the squash just before seasoning.

Julienne of Summer Squash Skins with Mixed Fresh Herbs: Add 1 teaspoon finely chopped fresh mint and 2 teaspoons finely chopped fresh parsley just before seasoning.

Nutritional Information
(as a percentage of daily intake)

4% (71) calories
2% (1 g) fat
5% (14 g) carbohydrates
5% (4 g) protein

2% (39 mg) sodium
13% (102 mg) calcium
7% (1 mg) iron

Spiced Sweet Potato Puree

Cinnamon, cardamom, ginger, and nutmeg make this fragrant puree of sweet potatoes one of the best sweet potato dishes ever—the spices bringing out the natural sweetness of the potatoes.

Don't puree the sweet potatoes in a food processor or they'll turn gluey.

Serves 4

2 pounds sweet potatoes, scrubbed and pricked in 2 or 3 places with a fork or the tip of a knife
¾ cup skim milk
½ teaspoon ground cinnamon

¼ teaspoon ground cardamom
¼ teaspoon ground ginger
⅛ teaspoon freshly grated nutmeg
a little salt and freshly ground white pepper to taste

If you're cooking 2 large sweet potatoes, arrange them on the oven floor so they are evenly spaced in the oven. If you're using 3 or 4 sweet potatoes, arrange them like spokes of a wheel. Microwave on HIGH for 15 minutes.

Peel, then mash in a potato ricer or beat with an electric mixer. Add the milk and spices and mix or beat until smooth. Season with salt and pepper.

Variation

Sweetened and Spiced Sweet Potato Puree: Add 2 tablespoons honey or brown sugar.

Nutritional Information
(as a percentage of daily intake)

13% (252) calories
0% (0 g) fat
21% (58 g) carbohydrates
8% (6 g) protein

2% (48 mg) sodium
15% (120 mg) calcium
7% (1 mg) iron

Spicy White Turnips

This recipe uses white turnips, those that are half white and half purple in color, not yellow turnips, which are usually called *rutabagas*.

White turnips have a mild, snappy flavor. Here they are cooked with a spicy tomato salsa.

Serves 6

2 pounds turnips, peeled and cut into ¼**-inch dice**

2 cups Fresh Tomato Salsa (page 102), placed in a strainer and drained

In a large bowl, mix the turnips and salsa. Cover and microwave on HIGH for 9 minutes.

Nutritional Information
(as a percentage of daily intake)

3% (61) calories
0% (0 g) fat
5% (14 g) carbohydrates
3% (2 g) protein

5% (116 mg) sodium
7% (58 mg) calcium
7% (1 mg) iron

BASIC PREPARATION OF WHITE TURNIPS

Peel and dice or slice 2 pounds white turnips. Place in a large bowl with 1½ teaspoons unsalted butter, cover, and microwave on HIGH for 9 minutes. Season with a little salt and freshly ground black pepper, stir, and serve.

Gently Candied Yams

Here the yams are cooked in apple juice, which has been reduced and concentrated, giving them a candied flavor.

Yams have a milder flavor and lighter color than sweet potatoes, and a starchier texture with a barklike skin. Small yams, weighing about 6 ounces each, have the best flavor and texture. Sweet potatoes can be substituted for yams in this recipe.

Serves 6

3 cups apple juice

1½ pounds yams, peeled and cut into ½-inch disks

Place the apple juice in a 4- to 8-cup glass measure and microwave on HIGH, uncovered, until juice reduces to 1 cup, about 35 minutes.

Arrange the yams in a single layer in a very large shallow rectangular dish. Pour the reduced juice over the yams, cover, and microwave on HIGH for 12 minutes. Cool to room temperature so the yams can absorb some of the apple juice and develop a candied flavor, then microwave on HIGH, uncovered, for 4 to 6 minutes to reheat.

Nutritional Information
(as a percentage of daily intake)

10% (202) calories
0% (0 g) fat
17% (48 g) carbohydrates
3% (2 g) protein

1% (21 mg) sodium
4% (28 mg) calcium
7% (1 mg) iron

Zucchini with Leeks and Mint

A simple green vegetable with bursts of fresh flavor from the herbs and the lime juice.

Serves 6

4 medium-size leeks, white parts only, split lengthwise, washed thoroughly, and sliced
1 large garlic clove, peeled and finely chopped
juice of ½ lime
1½ pounds zucchini, trimmed and sliced

1 tablespoon finely chopped fresh mint
1 tablespoon finely chopped fresh parsley
a little salt and freshly ground black pepper to taste

Combine the leeks, garlic, and lime juice in a large bowl, cover, and microwave on HIGH for 5 minutes. Add the zucchini and mix well. Cover and microwave on HIGH for 6 minutes. Stir in the herbs and season lightly with salt and generously with pepper.

Nutritional Information
(as a percentage of daily intake)

2% (34) calories
0% (0 g) fat
3% (7 g) carbohydrates
3% (2 g) protein

0% (8 mg) sodium
4% (33 mg) calcium
7% (1 mg) iron

Zucchini and Mushrooms with Fresh Herbs

Cut into chunks, zucchini and mushrooms combine here with the flavors of fresh herbs and a little lime juice to make a fresh-tasting, softly textured vegetable that needs almost no salt and pepper.

Serves 6

1 large onion, peeled and cut into eighths

2 large garlic cloves, peeled

1½ pounds medium-size zucchini, trimmed, split into quarters lengthwise, and sliced ½ inch thick

½ pound mushrooms, trimmed and cut into ½-inch pieces

juice of ½ lime

¼ cup finely chopped fresh parsley

¼ cup finely chopped fresh chives

a little salt and freshly ground black pepper to taste

In a food processor, very finely chop the onion and garlic. Transfer to a very large bowl, cover, and microwave on HIGH for 4 minutes. Stir in the zucchini and mushrooms, cover, and microwave on HIGH for 10 minutes. Drain; the mushrooms will have given off considerable liquid. Stir in the lime juice, parsley, and chives and season with a little salt and pepper.

Nutritional Information
(as a percentage of daily intake)

2% (35) calories

0% (0 g) fat

3% (7 g) carbohydrates

3% (2 g) protein

0% (4 mg) sodium

3% (25 mg) calcium

7% (1 mg) iron

Fish

Everything about fish is getting better. It's getting more attention in markets across the country, so even supermarket fish is fresher and better-tasting. More varieties of fish are now available than ever before—rich fish like mackerel, amberjack, and shad; elegant fish like salmon from the Pacific Northwest; sweet, mild-flavored white fish like sole, cod, and flounder; firm-fleshed fish like tuna and swordfish; and newcomers, like the small shark once called dogfish that is now marketed as snow cod. Where once fish steaks were about all one could find, there are now whole fish, fillets, and even cubes of fish ready for skewering. And thanks to the microwave, there is now a simple way to cook fish perfectly.

Microwaved fish is moist, tender, and succulent, easy to cook perfectly without overcooking. The evenness of the heating, the gentleness of the cooking method, and the way microwave cooking enhances the natural flavors makes microwaving ideal for fish of all kinds. Clams and mussels are coaxed into opening without becoming rubbery. Lobster becomes succulent and sweet without toughening. Scallops melt in your mouth. Rockfish becomes more tender and subtly flavored than with ordinary poaching. Salmon fillets, large and small, microwave magnificently.

Flatfish cook perfectly in the microwave without becoming dry and flaky. Cod microwaves to a buttery tenderness without falling apart. Salmon becomes succulent. Shad retains all its natural richness. Red snapper and rockfish retain their subtle flavors and textures without tightening during microwave cooking. Trout tastes fresher than ever. Flounder, with its mild flavor, develops character as it cooks in the microwave. And squid becomes tender and delicate without becoming rubbery.

Any fish that's floppy—that flaps around when held at one end and waved—will cook perfectly in the microwave. Only firm-fleshed fish like swordfish and tuna, because of their tight muscle fiber, require special attention to cook well in the microwave, as you will see in the directions for the recipes using those fish.

Special Techniques for Cooking Fish: Fish poaches magnificently in the microwave—covered in broth, skim milk (whole or low-fat milk will curdle in the microwave), or water in a shallow dish just large enough to hold it, and covered tightly. When poaching small (4- to 6-ounce) pieces of fish, arrange them like spokes, as evenly spaced as possible, in the shallow dish, the narrower ends pointed toward the center. This ensures even heating.

To microwave larger pieces of fish, arrange them as evenly spaced as possible on a very large plate or in a large shallow dish, and microwave until done.

Testing for Doneness: Fish is fragile, perhaps the most fragile of all the foods we commonly cook. One pound of most varieties of fish microwaves in just 3 minutes. If you're cooking fish fillets without a recipe, use that as your rule of thumb. If you're poaching, add another minute or 2 to allow for the heating of the poaching liquid. Fish is done when it changes from translucent to opaque. And the only test for doneness is to make a small slit in the center of one of the pieces of fish with the tip of a sharp knife to see if the fish has become opaque. Most fish will not flake when microwaved, so forget any testing method that instructs you to check for easy flaking.

Amberjack with Hot and Sour Red Onion Chutney

Amberjack can be described as a cross between grouper and tuna—with a firm texture like grouper and a rich dark color and flavor like tuna, but milder. Here it is mated with a quick red onion chutney that is bold, tart, and crunchy, so good, indeed, that it is worth eating by the spoonful.

The popping you may hear when amberjack cooks indicates that the edge is overcooking slightly; it will appear splintered when the fish comes from the oven. Just trim and serve.

Serves 4

1 pound fillet of amberjack, cut into quarters

1 medium-size red onion, peeled and quartered

1 cup tightly packed fresh dill leaves

½ teaspoon crushed dried marjoram *or* 1 tablespoon finely chopped fresh marjoram

juice of 1 large lemon

a little freshly ground black pepper to taste

In a large shallow dish, arrange the amberjack fillets like spokes of a wheel. Seal airtight with plastic wrap and microwave on HIGH for 3 minutes. You may hear some popping as the fish cooks.

While fish is cooking, combine the remaining ingredients in a food processor and chop finely. Transfer to a medium bowl and seal airtight with plastic wrap.

When fish is removed from the oven, puncture a hole in the plastic wrap and set aside.

Microwave the red onion chutney mixture on HIGH for 3 minutes.

Arrange the fish on plates, stir the red onion chutney well and serve a large dollop with each portion.

Nutritional Information
(as a percentage of daily intake)

8% (169) calories

8% (5 g) fat

1% (4 g) carbohydrates

39% (29 g) protein

0% (7 mg) sodium

6% (48 mg) calcium

20% (3 mg) iron

Clams Posilipo

As a child, this was the only way I would eat clams: cooked in a spicy tomato sauce with lots of garlic. It is still one of my favorite dishes, though it makes for messy eating so I serve it only when I'm making an informal dinner for close friends. I remember the heavy scent of oregano in the sauce, but here it's replaced by today's herb, cilantro. Basil can be substituted if you wish. The tomato sauce mixes with the clam juices that are released during the cooking to make an intensely flavored sauce. Large loaves of Italian bread are a must for soaking up the extra sauce.

Serves 4

2 garlic cloves, peeled and finely chopped
1 teaspoon olive oil
⅔ cup Chunky Tomato Sauce (page 107)
⅓ cup Fish Stock (page 46) or Chicken Broth (page 42)
2 tablespoons finely chopped fresh parsley

2 tablespoons finely chopped cilantro or basil
a little freshly ground black pepper to taste
24 small littleneck clams, shells scrubbed clean under cold running water

In a very large bowl, mix the garlic and oil and microwave on HIGH, uncovered, for 1½ minutes. Mix with the tomato sauce, broth, parsley, and cilantro. Season lightly with pepper. Add the clams, cover, and microwave on HIGH for 7 minutes. Stir the clams so they heat evenly and all open, cover again, and microwave on HIGH for 4 minutes. Discard any unopened clams. Ladle into large plates and serve.

Nutritional Information
(as a percentage of daily intake)

4% (76) calories
3% (2 g) fat
2% (6 g) carbohydrates
12% (9 g) protein

5% (108 mg) sodium
7% (57 mg) calcium
13% (2 mg) iron

Poached Cod with
Golden Onion Relish

This popular, buttery-textured, medium-firm white fish with a slightly musky flavor flakes apart into moist, tender morsels when properly cooked. Overcook it, however, and cod develops the texture of wet balsam chips, all too often the problem with traditionally cooked cod where the exact cooking time is difficult to determine.

Here the cod is poached gently and served with a sweet onion relish.

Alternative Fish: Flounder or catfish.

Serves 4

1 cup Fish Stock (page 46), Chicken Broth (page 42), or skim milk
2 ½-pound cod fillets

½ cup Golden Onion Relish (page 155)

Place the stock in a shallow rectangular dish just large enough to hold the fillets side by side. Microwave on HIGH, uncovered, for 2 minutes. Add the cod to the hot stock, cover, and microwave on HIGH for 3 minutes. Carefully lift fillets out of the stock, cut each in half, and place on plates with 2 heaping tablespoons onion relish next to each serving.

Variation

Salmon with Golden Onion Relish: Substitute a 1-pound salmon fillet, skinned and cut into 4 pieces, for the cod, then prepare as directed.

Nutritional Information
(as a percentage of daily intake)

6% (111) calories
2% (1 g) fat
1% (4 g) carbohydrates
28% (21 g) protein

5% (126 mg) sodium
3% (26 mg) calcium
7% (1 mg) iron

Golden Onion Relish

This champagne-gold-colored, sweet onion and cabbage relish not only makes the perfect accompaniment for microwaved fish, but can be spread on a sandwich or used as a sauce for asparagus or broccoli, or it can be served with a lamb chop or steak or with a piece of poached chicken or a whole roasted bird. It's a handy all-purpose relish, sauce, chutney, or spread, and that's why I make 5 cups at a time. I store a cup or 2 in the refrigerator (for up to 3 weeks) and the rest in the freezer (for up to 3 months).

Makes 5 cups

2 pounds onions, peeled and cut into eighths

¼ small head of cabbage, cut into eighths

2 large sweet yellow bell peppers, cored and cut into eighths

5 garlic cloves, peeled

2-inch piece of fresh ginger, peeled and quartered

2 teaspoons hot red pepper sauce

¾ cup red wine vinegar

½ cup Dijon mustard

½ cup Chicken Broth (page 42)

3 tablespoons cornstarch

In a food processor, in small batches, finely chop the onions, cabbage, peppers, garlic, and ginger. Transfer to a very large bowl and mix with the red pepper sauce, vinegar, and mustard. Blend the broth with the cornstarch and stir into vegetables. Seal airtight with a double layer of plastic wrap and microwave on HIGH for 25 minutes. Carefully uncover and stir well (some of the sauce will have begun to caramelize around the edge of the bowl; just mix it into the relish). Seal airtight with a double layer of plastic wrap and microwave on HIGH for 20 minutes. Carefully uncover, stir well, cool, and refrigerate or freeze.

Variation

Curried Onion Relish: Add 3 to 4 tablespoons curry powder.

Nutritional Information
(as a percentage of daily intake)
per 2-tablespoon serving

1% (18) calories

0% (0 g) fat

1% (4 g) carbohydrates

1% (1 g) protein

2% (42 mg) sodium

2% (13 mg) calcium

0% (0 mg) iron

Deviled Crab

Colorful, mildly hot, alive with flavor, and slightly crunchy in texture, this great deviled crabmeat is made without the gobs of cream and butter traditionally found in deviled crab recipes. The crab flavor is lighter, and the natural sweet subtleties of the crab can be tasted.

Serve this as a crab salad appetizer, as a light entrée, or use for picnics or sandwiches.

Alternative Fish: Cooked shrimp or cooked crayfish tails.

Serves 8 as an entrée, 12 as an appetizer

1 medium-size sweet red bell pepper, cored and cut into eighths
1 small jalapeño pepper, seeded
2 scallions, cut into 2-inch pieces
2 celery ribs, cut into 2-inch pieces
2 garlic cloves, peeled
½ cup tightly packed fresh parsley leaves
½ cup tightly packed fresh dill leaves
juice of 1 lemon
3 cups fresh soft white bread crumbs (from about 7 slices regular commercial bread)

1 tablespoon coarse mustard
1 tablespoon Dijon mustard
1½ to 2 tablespoons hot red pepper sauce
1 pound finest-quality lump crabmeat, gently picked over without crushing the lumps to remove all bone and cartilage
¼ cup skim milk
freshly ground black pepper to taste

In a food processor, finely chop the sweet red pepper, jalapeño, scallions, celery, and garlic. Transfer to a very large bowl. Without cleaning the food processor bowl, finely chop the parsley and dill and add to the other chopped vegetables. Add the lemon juice, bread crumbs, mustards, and hot red pepper sauce and mix well. Add the crabmeat, skim milk, and black pepper and toss with your hands until just mixed. Be careful not to crush the crab. Cover and microwave on HIGH for 8 minutes. Serve.

Nutritional Information
(as a percentage of daily intake)
per entrée serving

6% (128) calories

3% (2 g) fat

5% (15 g) carbohydrates

17% (13 g) protein

27% (648 mg) sodium

9% (75 mg) calcium

13% (2 mg) iron

Finnan Haddie Salad

This cold smoked haddock from Findon (pronounced Finnan), Scotland, has a pale yellow color, a gentle nutty fragrance, and a subtle smoky peat flavor. Poaching it in milk enhances the delicacy of the fish and removes some of the unwanted salt used for the curing.

Unfortunately, finnan haddie has been so overshadowed by the smoked salmon of Scotland that most Americans have never heard of it. Yet it ranks as one of the noblest of smoked fish.

Try serving this next time you think about making a shrimp or scallop salad, or serve it as a first course at a company dinner.

Alternative Fish: Hot-smoked, sometimes called kippered, salmon or tuna.

Serves 6

½ pound boneless and skinless finnan haddie, cut into 4 pieces

1 cup skim milk

1 pound small red potatoes, cut into ¼-inch dice

1 tablespoon finely chopped fresh chives

2 teaspoons finely chopped fresh tarragon

2 teaspoons finely chopped fresh parsley

¼ cup light sour cream

a little freshly ground white or black pepper to taste

Combine the finnan haddie and milk in a medium bowl, cover, and microwave on HIGH for 6 minutes. Drain and flake fish apart with your fingers.

Place the potatoes in a large bowl. Cover and microwave on HIGH for 12 minutes. Toss with the flaked fish, herbs, and sour cream. Season with pepper. Serve at room temperature or refrigerate and serve cold.

Variation

Finnan Haddie Salad with Asparagus (serves 6 as an appetizer, 4 as a lunch entrée): Microwave 1½ pounds fresh asparagus (page 99), then plunge them into cold water to cool. Drain, dry, and arrange on plates in long, neat stacks. Place a mound of finnan haddie salad at the base of the asparagus spears.

Nutritional Information
(as a percentage of daily intake)

7% (143) calories

3% (2 g) fat

7% (20 g) carbohydrates

15% (11 g) protein

20% (488 mg) sodium

4% (35 mg) calcium

7% (1 mg) iron

Flounder with Tomato Salsa

This makes a quick meal for two when you have some salsa, homemade or store-bought, handy. With just a minute of preparation, and 5 minutes cooking, a lively entrée is ready to eat. And there's enough for two portions.

The sweet, bland flavor of flounder, with its semifirm but flaky texture, makes a good foil for the acidic, spicy flavor of the salsa. The two actually enhance each other, rather than the salsa overwhelming the fish as one might suppose.

Alternative Fish: Snapper, bass, hake, haddock, or cod.

Serves 2

½ cup **Fish Stock (page 46)** *or*
  Chicken Broth (page 42)
juice of ½ lemon
½-pound flounder fillet

½ cup **Fresh Tomato Salsa**
  (page 102), or store-bought salsa
  drained

In a large shallow rectangular dish, combine the broth and lemon juice. Slide in the flounder, cover, and microwave on HIGH for 5 minutes.

With a spatula, carefully cut the fish in half lengthwise, lift onto plates, and spoon half the salsa atop each portion.

Variation

Flounder with Salsa for Four: Double the quantities of all ingredients. Place the broth and lemon juice in a very shallow dish that holds the fillets in one layer. Cover and microwave on HIGH for 8 minutes.

Nutritional Information
(as a percentage of daily intake)

6% (127) calories
3% (2 g) fat
3% (7 g) carbohydrates
29% (22 g) protein

5% (118 mg) sodium
5% (41 mg) calcium
7% (1 mg) iron

Golden Halibut and Spinach
with Hidden Herbs

Halibut is one of the most tender of the flat white fishes. The taste is delicate, very fresh, almost sweet. And there are virtually no bones in halibut, which adds further appeal to this favorite from Alaska and the northern Pacific.

Halibuts weigh from 40 to 400 pounds, so a 1-pound piece, as called for in this recipe, can come in different shapes and sizes. But don't worry; any 1-pound piece of halibut, filleted, skinned, and cut into 4 equal pieces, can be used.

The delicate flavor of halibut is emphasized by the light wash of saffron in this recipe, and the spinach, with its earthy flavor and hidden herbs, adds a strong but complementary contrast with lots of subtleties. The colors of this dish vibrate, they are so alive.

Alternative Fish: Snapper or bass.

Serves 4

¾ pound spinach, thick stems removed, washed thoroughly, drained, and coarsely chopped

1 small bunch of fresh parsley, thick stems removed, washed thoroughly, drained, and coarsely chopped

1 small bunch of fresh dill or cilantro, thick stems removed, washed thoroughly, drained, and coarsely chopped

a little salt and freshly ground black pepper to taste

juice of ½ lemon

⅛ teaspoon saffron threads

1-pound skinless halibut fillet *or* 1¼ pounds fresh halibut, spine and skin removed, then cut into 4 equal pieces

Combine spinach, parsley, and dill in a very large bowl, mix well, cover, and microwave on HIGH for 5 minutes to wilt. Season with salt and a little pepper, mix well, and transfer to a large shallow dish.

Combine the lemon juice and saffron in a small bowl or mortar and blend together, either with a pestle or the back of a spoon. Rub lemon juice all over the halibut, then arrange the 4 pieces of fish like spokes of a wheel atop the spinach, the narrowest ends of the fish pointing toward the center. Cover and microwave on HIGH for 3½ minutes. Serve.

Variation

Curried Halibut and Spinach with Hidden Herbs: Substitute ¼ teaspoon curry powder for the saffron.

Nutritional Information
(as a percentage of daily intake)

8% (155) calories

5% (3 g) fat

2% (5 g) carbohydrates

33% (25 g) protein

6% (152 mg) sodium

19% (155 mg) calcium

33% (5 mg) iron

Microwaving has made cooking mussels simple enough to do rather casually. Here the broth and mussels are combined and cooked in only 10 minutes. No messy steamers, no oven top splattered, and no massive kitchen mess. Just one bowl to rinse after the mussels are served.

The recipe requires a fine loaf of bread—French, Italian, or sourdough—to mop up the juices.

Serves 4

1 cup Fish Stock (page 46) or
   Chicken Broth, (page 42)
1 very large vine-ripened tomato,
   cored and cut into ½-inch dice

1 teaspoon crushed dried rosemary
1 teaspoon Dijon mustard
3 pounds mussels, scrubbed and
   bearded

In a very large bowl, mix together the broth, tomatoes, rosemary, and mustard. Add the mussels, cover, and microwave on HIGH for 10 minutes. Stir well, discard any unopened mussels, and arrange the mussels in 4 large bowls or soup plates for serving. Ladle the cooking liquid over the mussels and serve.

Nutritional Information
(as a percentage of daily intake)

5% (100) calories
5% (3 g) fat
2% (6 g) carbohydrates
19% (14 g) protein

17% (409 mg) sodium
13% (104 mg) calcium
47% (7 mg) iron

Mahimahi Teriyaki

Mahimahi is a firm fish that flakes into large chunks when cooked. The flavor is light and the texture slightly chewy, like a good steak. Here the fish is strengthened and enhanced by a light teriyaki marinade. The longer the fish marinates, the deeper the teriyaki flavor will be.

Mahimahi is also called dorado, dolphin, or dolphinfish. But its Hawaiian name, mahimahi, is preferred because of confusion with the other dolphin, which is a mammal, not a fish.

Alternative Fish: Grouper.

Serves 4

¼ cup soy sauce
juice of ½ lemon
1 tablespoon brown sugar
1½-inch piece of fresh ginger, peeled
   and cut into 4 pieces

2 large garlic cloves, peeled
a half dozen or so generous grinds of
   black pepper
1 1-pound skinless mahimahi fillet,
   cut into 4 equal pieces

Combine everything but the fish in a blender and blend very well. Pour over the mahimahi, cover, and marinate in the refrigerator for 2 hours or overnight, turning the fish occasionally.

Drain and arrange the fish like spokes of a wheel around the edge of a large shallow dish or very large plate. Cover and microwave on HIGH for 6 minutes. Immediately uncover and serve with some of the juices that have accumulated under the fish spooned on top.

Nutritional Information
(as a percentage of daily intake)

7% (136) calories
3% (2 g) fat
1% (2 g) carbohydrates
29% (22 g) protein

17% (408 mg) sodium
5% (37 mg) calcium
7% (1 mg) iron

MICROWAVE NOTE

Because the flesh of mahimahi is very dense, it takes almost twice as long to cook as most other fish for example. But that's only 6 minutes for 4 servings.

Orange Roughy
with Red Pepper Sauce

Without a doubt, orange roughy is among the most interesting-tasting members of what I call the floppy white fish family. It's better than sole, a little thicker and firmer with a more complex flavor; it's flaky like flounder, but it doesn't fall apart; and it's sweeter than snapper. Were orange roughy better known, I suspect it would be more in demand than its popular cousins, flounder and sole.

This dish features a fire engine red, gently sweetened, and lightly soured sauce, served over the microwave-poached fillets.

Alternative Fish: Flounder, snapper, halibut, bass, or sole—petrale, rex, Dover, or lemon.

Serves 4

1 very large sweet red bell pepper,
    cored and cut into 8 pieces
1½ tablespoons raspberry vinegar
1 teaspoon hot red pepper sauce
1 tablespoon sugar
1 small garlic clove, peeled

2 teaspoons cornstarch
2 ½-pound orange roughy fillets
½ cup Fish Stock (page 46),
    Chicken Broth (page 42), or skim
    milk

In a food processor, combine the red pepper, vinegar, hot pepper sauce, sugar, garlic, and cornstarch and process until soupy. Transfer to a medium bowl, cover, and microwave on HIGH for 4 minutes. Set aside.

Meanwhile, place the fish in a large rectangular shallow dish large enough to hold both fillets next to each other without touching. Pour in the broth or milk, cover, and microwave on HIGH for 4 minutes. Cut each piece of fish in half and, with a spatula, transfer to plates and top with the red pepper sauce.

Variation

Poached Chicken with Red Pepper Sauce: Prepare the red pepper sauce and serve over poached chicken breasts (page 189).

Nutritional Information
(as a percentage of daily intake)

7% (148) calories
5% (3 g) fat
3% (8 g) carbohydrates
31% (23 g) protein

3% (74 mg) sodium
2% (16 mg) calcium
7% (1 mg) iron

Salmon Puttanesca

The salmon, which will lighten in color as it cooks to a pale pink, is tender and succulent, and the chunky sauce is a sparkling Mediterranean complement to its richness.

Extra sauce can be refrigerated for up to 2 weeks or frozen for up to 3 months. There will be enough for four large pasta servings.

Alternative Fish: Amberjack or yellowtail.

Serves 4

2 8- to 9-ounce salmon steaks, cut in half so spinal column and rib bones can be removed, then skin removed

⅔ cup puttanesca sauce (page 88), held in a strainer until drained of excess liquid

In a large shallow dish, arrange the salmon strips like spokes of a wheel, the thickest ends against the outside edge of the dish, the thin flaps pointing toward the center. Spoon sauce into the center of the dish, cover, and microwave on HIGH for 6 minutes.

Serve immediately with some of the chunky puttanesca sauce spooned onto each serving.

Nutritional Information
(as a percentage of daily intake)

13% (253) calories
15% (10 g) fat
7% (19 g) carbohydrates
33% (25 g) protein

56% (1,355 mg) sodium
23% (186 mg) calcium
20% (3 mg) iron

These succulent, moist, perfectly cooked salmon fillets are coated with the traditional herb and spice mixture of New Orleans's famous blackened redfish. And thanks to the microwave, all the herbs and spices can be tasted, unlike the original, where the surface of the fish is charred to a cinder.

Alternative Fish: Red snapper.

Serves 4

1 tablespoon paprika
1½ teaspoons onion powder
1½ teaspoons garlic powder
½ teaspoon cayenne pepper
½ teaspoon freshly ground white pepper
½ teaspoon freshly ground black pepper

½ teaspoon crushed dried thyme
½ teaspoon crushed dried oregano
½ teaspoon crushed dried marjoram
1 pound salmon fillets, skinned and cut into 4 pieces

Blend together everything but the fish. Evenly coat the salmon fillets on all sides with the spice mixture. Marinate in the refrigerator for 2 hours or overnight, arranged evenly around the edge of a very large plate or shallow dish, covered with plastic wrap.

Microwave—on the same plate and still covered—on HIGH for 3 minutes.

Nutritional Information
(as a percentage of daily intake)

8% (162) calories
11% (7 g) fat
1% (2 g) carbohydrates
31% (23 g) protein

3% (83 mg) sodium
8% (64 mg) calcium
13% (2 mg) iron

This elegant way to serve a large piece of salmon for a party is easier than ever before with the microwave. Not only does the microwave poach better than stove-top poaching in terms of leaving the fish evenly cooked and texturally sound (moist, succulent, just barely opaque throughout without overcooking and drying the edges), but the procedure is clean and neat as well.

Serving Note: Serve the salmon hot or use the variation below for a cold poached fillet. Any of the following sauces can be served with the salmon: Hot and Sour Red Onion Chutney (page 152), Golden Onion Relish (page 155), Winter Green Salsa (page 112), or Harissa (page 132).

Serves 8

2 pounds salmon fillets (have the fish-monger remove the skin and all the small bones before weighing the salmon)

3 cups Fish Stock (page 46), Chicken Broth (page 42), skim milk, or water
sauce (see note above)

Place the fillet, skinned side down, in a large shallow dish and add the liquid. Cover and microwave on HIGH for 7 minutes. Using 2 spatulas, carefully lift the salmon out of the liquid and place on a serving platter. Serve with the sauce passed separately.

Variation

Cold Poached Salmon for a Party: Serving the salmon cold, weather and menu permitting, allows you to poach the fish a day ahead, make the sauce ahead, and have very little work to do when the guests arrive. A large cold fillet of salmon on a handsome platter is one of the most elegant of party dishes. To poach a salmon to serve cold, proceed as directed, but reduce the microwaving time to 6 minutes. When fish is removed from the oven, uncover and place in the refrigerator until cold, then cover and keep refrigerated until serving time. Serve the sauce of your choice with the salmon.

Nutritional Information
(as a percentage of daily intake)

8% (155) calories

11% (7 g) fat

0% (0 g) carbohydrates

31% (23 g) protein

4% (87 mg) sodium

6% (51 mg) calcium

7% (1 mg) iron

Here Chinese fermented black beans are added to what would otherwise be considered a fairly tame scallop recipe typical of the French Riviera, with a play of colors and flavors—the acidic tomatoes and lemon juice, the fresh herbs, the black pepper, and the distinct taste of the fermented beans—that all work together in a bouncy, unexpected way. The scallops are perfectly cooked, sweet, moist, even around the edges, and tender.

Serves 4 as an entrée, 6 as an appetizer

1 medium-size onion, peeled and
 quartered
2 garlic cloves, peeled
1 tablespoon fermented black beans,
 rinsed well under cold running water
juice of ½ lemon
1 large ripe tomato, cored, seeded,
 and diced

¾ pound bay scallops
1 tablespoon finely chopped fresh
 parsley
1 tablespoon finely chopped fresh dill
 or cilantro
a little freshly ground black pepper to
 taste

In a food processor, finely chop the onion and garlic. Add 1 tablespoon of the black beans and pulse just to coarsely chop beans. Transfer to a medium bowl, add the remaining black beans and lemon juice, cover, and microwave on HIGH for 5 minutes. Stir in the tomato, scallops, parsley, and dill or cilantro and season with pepper. Cover and microwave on HIGH for 4 minutes.

*Nutritional Information
(as a percentage of daily intake)
per entrée serving*

5% (97) calories
2% (1 g) fat
3% (7 g) carbohydrates
20% (15 g) protein

13% (323 mg) sodium
5% (40 mg) calcium
7% (1 mg) iron

Shad is one of the heralds of spring—along with asparagus and rhubarb. It is a smooth but firm-textured fish with a distinct but not heavy flavor. It is also incredibly rich. Here it is flavored with a little butter, lemon, and parsley.

Shad is best prepared very simply, served with some potatoes and asparagus. For a highly seasonal meal, serve the Rhubarb and Blackberry Ice Cream with Strawberry Sauce (page 267) for dessert.

Shad are very bony—with several extra, long rows of tiny bones attached to their ribs. Buy only shad that have been professionally boned.

Serves 4

1 pound shad, professionally filleted of all bones but left on the skin
1 teaspoon unsalted butter, melted in a small dish in the microwave on HIGH for 10 seconds

juice of ½ lemon
1½ teaspoons finely chopped fresh parsley
a little salt and freshly ground black pepper to taste

The shad will look like a series of long flaps attached to a piece of skin. Cut the flesh off the skin, leaving the long fillets intact. Mix the butter and lemon juice and rub on the shad. Arrange fish in 4 equal, widely spaced, parallel rows on a very large plate.

Cover and microwave on HIGH for 3 minutes. Transfer to plates, sprinkle with parsley and a little salt and pepper, and serve.

Nutritional Information
(as a percentage of daily intake)

12% (239) calories
21% (14 g) fat
 0% (0 g) carbohydrates
35% (26 g) protein

4% (89 mg) sodium
3% (27 mg) calcium
7% (1 mg) iron

Shrimp Salad

This unusual combination of shrimp and potatoes in a salad, dressed lightly with sour cream and fresh herbs, is great for summer picnics and parties. The dressing is light and the herbs add a fresh taste and color to this gently textured salad.

Serves 4 as an entrée, 6 as an appetizer

1 ½-pound red potato, scrubbed
1¼ pounds medium-size shrimp, shelled and deveined
1 large ripe plum tomato, cut into ¼-inch dice
1 small celery rib, very finely chopped
2 tablespoons very finely chopped red onion
¼ cup light sour cream

juice of ½ lemon
1 tablespoon finely chopped fresh tarragon
1 tablespoon finely chopped fresh parsley
1 tablespoon finely chopped fresh chives
freshly ground black pepper to taste

Place the potato in the center of the oven and microwave on HIGH for 5 minutes. With a pot holder or thick towel, remove the potato and place it in a bowl under cold running water to cool. Place the shrimp in a large bowl, cover, and microwave on HIGH for 3 minutes and 45 seconds. While shrimp are cooking, cut the potato into ¼-inch dice.

Add diced potato to the bowl with the shrimp and toss gently. Stir in the tomato, celery, red onion, sour cream, lemon juice, tarragon, parsley, and chives. Season with pepper. Refrigerate and serve cold.

Nutritional Information
(as a percentage of daily intake)
per entrée serving

11% (219) calories
8% (5 g) fat
7% (19 g) carbohydrates
36% (27 g) protein

10% (250 mg) sodium
13% (105 mg) calcium
20% (3 mg) iron

BASIC PREPARATION OF SHRIMP

For Peeled Shrimp:

Place 1 pound shelled and deveined shrimp in a large bowl. Cover and microwave on HIGH for 3 minutes and 45 seconds. Serve immediately or cool under cold running water.

For Unpeeled Shrimp:

Place 1 pound unpeeled shrimp in a very large bowl, cover, and microwave on HIGH for 3½ minutes. Immediately cool under cold running water and peel.

Squid cooks magnificently in the microwave. Just clean it and cut into strips or circles. The microwave enhances the fragrance and sweet flavor of the squid, and the squid is always tender—never developing the rubber band texture of more traditional cooking methods.

Strips of squid form the base for this Provençal-style ragoût, which is flavored with tomato, onion and garlic, and lots of herbs—some not so Provençal. A cup of cooked white beans can be substituted for the potato if you wish. Serve over rice.

Serves 4

1 large (½-pound) red potato

4 squids (1¼ pounds), tentacles trimmed, heads and quills removed and discarded, bodies split lengthwise into halves, cleaned, and cut crosswise into ¼-inch strips

1 medium-size onion, peeled and quartered

1 large garlic clove, peeled

juice of ½ lemon

1 large ripe tomato, cored and diced

1 tablespoon finely chopped cilantro

1 tablespoon finely chopped fresh basil

1 tablespoon finely chopped fresh parsley

a little salt and freshly ground black pepper to taste

Place the potato in the center of the oven and microwave on HIGH for 7 minutes. Cool and cut into ¼-inch dice.

Place the squid pieces in a large bowl, cover, and microwave on HIGH for 2½ minutes. Uncover and set aside to cool.

In a food processor, combine the onion, garlic, and lemon juice and chop finely. Transfer to a large bowl, cover, and microwave on HIGH for 5 minutes. Mix with the squid, potato, tomato, cilantro, basil, and parsley. Season with salt and pepper, cover, and microwave on HIGH for 1 minute to reheat.

Nutritional Information
(as a percentage of daily intake)

11% (210) calories

2% (3 g) fat

8% (22 g) carbohydrates

33% (25 g) protein

11% (260 mg) sodium

5% (37 mg) calcium

13% (2 mg) iron

Poached Red Snapper with Fresh Tomato and Sorrel Salsa

This firm white fish with its light flavor has become so popular, it's becoming extravagantly expensive, largely as a result of a national fixation in the late 1980s for blackened red snapper.

Here a fresh tomato salsa is made with sorrel. The tart flavor of the sorrel, the fresh taste of the dill, and the tomatoes make an extraordinary chutneylike sauce to complement the snapper.

Alternative Fish: Cod, halibut, hake, or flounder.

Serves 4

1 very large ripe tomato, cored and cut into ¼-inch dice
1 cup finely shredded fresh sorrel leaves
½ cup finely chopped fresh dill
1 scallion, green part only, finely chopped
½ small jalapeño pepper, seeded (optional)
1 1-pound red snapper fillet, skinned and cut into 4 pieces

In a large bowl, mix everything but the fish. Cover and microwave on HIGH for 4 minutes. Uncover and set aside.

While the salsa is cooking, place the fish on a very large plate or a very large shallow dish, evenly spaced like spokes of a wheel, the narrow ends pointed toward the center, cover, and microwave on HIGH for 3 minutes. Transfer to plates, spoon salsa over the fish, and serve.

Nutritional Information
(as a percentage of daily intake)

6% (126) calories
3% (2 g) fat
1% (4 g) carbohydrates
32% (24 g) protein

3% (68 mg) sodium
12% (96 mg) calcium
13% (2 mg) iron

Certainly the most beautifully textured of all fish, striped bass, or rockfish, has a pristine appearance, a moist, tender texture, and a sweet, delicate taste that hints of the open seas. It is among the best fish for cooking in the microwave.

This striped bass is cooked on a bed of onions and tomatoes that form a light, delicate, textured tomato sauce to accompany the fish.

Alternative Fish: Other bass, redfish, snapper, or shark.

Serves 4

1 large onion, peeled and cut into
  2-inch pieces
2 large garlic cloves, peeled
1 large ripe tomato, cored and diced
juice of ½ lemon

2 tablespoons chopped fresh parsley
1 tablespoon chopped fresh dill
1 1-pound striped bass (rockfish) fillet, quartered

In a food processor, finely chop the onion and garlic. Transfer them to a large shallow dish and mix with the tomato and lemon juice. Cover and microwave on HIGH for 5 minutes.

Stir in the parsley and dill and lay the rockfish like spokes of a wheel on top of the mixture. Cover and microwave on HIGH for 3 minutes.

Nutritional Information
(as a percentage of daily intake)

7% (134) calories
5% (3 g) fat
1% (4 g) carbohydrates
31% (23 g) protein

3% (69 mg) sodium
3% (27 mg) calcium
7% (1 mg) iron

SIMPLE POACHED STRIPED BASS

Place a 1-pound fillet in a large shallow dish with 1 cup Fish Stock (page 46) or skim milk, cover, and microwave on HIGH for 3 minutes and 15 seconds. Serve at once with a sauce of your choice.

The swordfish may pop; in fact, sometimes it even sounds like it's exploding as pockets of air or fat in the fish burst, but don't worry. Here the swordfish is slightly undercooked to minimize this problem and is then allowed to rest at room temperature to complete the cooking. The mildly spicy, cilantro- and celery-flavored salsa complements the rich swordfish without detracting from the natural flavor of the fish.

Alternative Fish: Grouper or tuna.

Serves 4

½ cup Fish Stock (page 46), Chicken Broth (page 42), or water
1-pound skinless swordfish fillet, cut into 4 equal pieces

1 cup Winter Green Salsa (page 112)

Place the broth in a large shallow dish and arrange the swordfish in the dish like spokes of a wheel, the narrower ends pointed toward the center. Cover and microwave on HIGH for 4½ minutes. Set aside to rest for 3 minutes, then place on a plate and top each serving with ¼ cup salsa.

Nutritional Information
(as a percentage of daily intake)

7% (146) calories
5% (3 g) fat
3% (5 g) carbohydrates
31% (23 g) protein

4% (86 mg) sodium
7% (56 mg) calcium
13% (2 mg) iron

Swordfish, like tuna, becomes tough and dry if overcooked, even slightly. And in the microwave that problem is exacerbated, so here you are instructed to slightly undercook the fish and then let it complete its cooking by resting for a few minutes at room temperature. I think you'll be satisfied with the results. You may hear a popping noise as the fish cooks; that's normal for swordfish cooking in the microwave.

The swordfish is cooked with a light version of caponata, the Sicilian eggplant specialty that is filled with the flavors of the Mediterranean. Extra caponata can be stored in a covered container in the refrigerator and used as a spread to moisten sandwiches.

Alternative Fish: Tuna.

Serves 4

¾-pound eggplant, trimmed but unpeeled and cut into 2- to 3-inch chunks
½ scallion, cut into 2 pieces
2 tablespoons coarsely chopped French or Spanish green olives
2 large garlic cloves, peeled
1 tablespoon drained capers, rinsed
juice of ½ lemon
2 tablespoons red wine vinegar

½ cup tightly packed fresh dill
¼ teaspoon dried basil
¼ teaspoon dried marjoram
¼ teaspoon dried summer savory
a little freshly ground black pepper to taste
1 pound swordfish (from a steak about ¾ to 1 inch thick), skin removed, cut into 4 pie-shaped pieces

Place the eggplant in a very large bowl, cover, and microwave on HIGH for 15 minutes. In a food processor, puree the cooked eggplant with the scallion, olives, garlic, capers, lemon juice, vinegar, dill, basil, marjoram, and savory, pulsing until everything is well mixed and finely chopped. Season with pepper.

Arrange the swordfish like spokes of a wheel in a large shallow dish, pointed ends toward the center. Place a large dollop (about ¼ cup) of the caponata (eggplant mixture) between the pieces of swordfish, cover, and microwave on HIGH for 5 minutes. Uncover and allow to rest for 3 to 5 minutes before serving.

Uncover and serve a piece of swordfish per person, with a quarter of the caponata spooned over each piece of fish.

Variation

Swordfish Puttanesca: Substitute 1 cup of puttanesca sauce (page 88), held briefly in a strainer to drain off the excess water, for the caponata.

Nutritional Information
(as a percentage of daily intake)

8% (162) calories
6% (4 g) fat
3% (7 g) carbohydrates
31% (23 g) protein

7% (164 mg) sodium
9% (73 mg) calcium
13% (2 mg) iron

Microwaving is the best way to cook tilefish. Tilefish has a very firm, succulent, almost chewy texture and a delicate, sweet taste similar to scallops and lobster. Both the texture and flavor are more evident when tilefish is cooked in the microwave than when it is cooked conventionally. Here the sweetness and texture are accented by lemon and capers in a light parsley sauce that is produced when the fish cooks.

Serves 4

juice of 1 large lemon

2 teaspoons drained capers, rinsed and coarsely chopped

2 tablespoons finely chopped fresh parsley

a little freshly ground black pepper to taste

1 1-pound tilefish fillet, cut into 4 equal pieces

In a large shallow dish, mix together the lemon juice, capers, parsley, and pepper. Arrange the fish like spokes of a wheel, narrower ends pointed toward the center, in the dish. Cover and microwave on HIGH for 4½ minutes. Transfer the fish to plates and spoon some of the juices, capers, and parsley over each serving.

Variation

Halibut with Capers and Parsley: Substitute halibut for the tilefish and reduce the cooking time to 3 minutes.

Nutritional Information
(as a percentage of daily intake)

6% (129) calories

3% (2 g) fat

0% (1 g) carbohydrates

29% (22 g) protein

6% (142 mg) sodium

5% (37 mg) calcium

7% (1 mg) iron

Farmed into a standard size of 10 ounces, most store-bought trout are now sold boned with head and tail in place—looking like a butterfly of flaps in fish's clothing. Although I occasionally enjoy a trout, they are still a little too bony to make good company food.

This trout is prepared quite simply—rubbed with just a smidgen of butter, then sprinkled with fresh herbs and served with a lemon wedge.

Serves 2

10-ounce boned brown trout, head and tail cut off, then split lengthwise and the bony section attached to the fin at the top of the fish cut off

1 teaspoon unsalted butter

½ teaspoon very finely chopped fresh chives

½ teaspoon very finely chopped fresh parsley

2 lemon wedges

Place the trout in a large shallow dish, the 2 pieces separated as much as possible. Cover and microwave on HIGH for 3 minutes. With a large spatula, transfer the trout to plates, rub each piece with half the butter, and sprinkle with half the chives and half the parsley. Place a lemon wedge next to the fish and serve.

Nutritional Information
(as a percentage of daily intake)

15% (292) calories

23% (15 g) fat

0% (0 g) carbohydrates

47% (35 g) protein

4% (96 mg) sodium

5% (43 mg) calcium

13% (2 mg) iron

This tuna is as good served cold as hot from the oven. If you're serving it cold, reduce the cooking time by 30 seconds, uncover, and allow the steak to cool in the broth in the refrigerator for half an hour, then cover until needed.

Tuna has a firm texture and a distinct taste. Here it is served with a lemon-flavored mustard sauce, heady with flavor, that can complement the strong taste of the fresh tuna.

Tuna is not a perfectly textured fish for microwaving, as the edges sometime overcook and need to be trimmed. But microwaving keeps the fish moist and tender.

Alternative Fish: Swordfish.

Serves 4

2 ½-pound tuna steaks, cut in half
  and skin removed if necessary
¼ cup Fish Stock (page 46), Chicken
  Broth (page 42), or water
2 tablespoons Dijon mustard

2 tablespoons coarse mustard
1 tablespoon light sour cream
juice of 1 small lemon
a goodly amount of freshly ground
  black pepper

Arrange the tuna like spokes of a wheel in a large shallow dish. Pour in the broth, cover, and microwave on HIGH for 4 minutes.

While tuna is cooking, blend together the remaining ingredients. Serve a tablespoon of the mustard sauce with each portion of tuna.

Nutritional Information
(as a percentage of daily intake)

9% (174) calories
11% (7 g) fat
1% (2 g) carbohydrates
40% (30 g) protein

9% (204 mg) sodium
4% (35 mg) calcium
20% (3 mg) iron

This fish stew, made with orzo (the rice-shaped pasta), is one of my favorite dishes for informal entertaining. Serve in large bowls, with toasted sourdough bread, for a hearty one-bowl meal. Even guests who claim they don't like fish love this stew.

Serves 8

1 quart Fish Stock (page 46) or Chicken Broth (page 42)

1 large onion, peeled and finely chopped

3 garlic cloves, peeled and finely chopped

2 tablespoons canned chopped mild green chilies

½ cup crushed tomatoes in puree or Chunky Tomato Sauce (page 107)

12 small littleneck clams, scrubbed

6 medium-size shrimp, shelled and deveined

¼ pound bay scallops

1 ½-pound grouper or haddock fillet, cut into 1-inch cubes

1 cup orzo, cooked conventionally in boiling water until just barely tender (about 6 minutes)

½ cup tightly packed fresh parsley leaves, finely chopped

In a very large bowl, combine stock, onion, and garlic; microwave on HIGH, uncovered, for 12 minutes. Stir in the chilies, tomatoes, and clams; microwave on HIGH until clams begin to open, about 6 minutes. Add the remaining ingredients, stir, and microwave on HIGH, uncovered, for 5 minutes. Stir and ladle into a large bowl. Serve at once.

*Nutritional Information
(as a percentage of daily intake)*

14% (279) calories
3% (2 g) fat
12% (32 g) carbohydrates
45% (34 g) protein

23% (543 mg) sodium
13% (102 mg) calcium
4% (27 mg) iron

MICROWAVING NOTE

Tiny pastas, like orzo, become soft and gummy when cooked in the microwave, so conventional cooking is recommended.

Poultry

Chicken, turkey, and game birds, if cut into pieces, stay tender and moist when microwaved. A breast takes only about 2 minutes to cook. A whole chicken, cut up and smothered in a sauce, will cook in less than half an hour.

But most startling to me is how incredibly well a microwave-convection oven can roast whole chickens, turkey breasts or whole turkeys, even geese. With the combination of dry heat (convection) and microwaves, roasted poultry is wonderfully moist with crisp, golden brown skin. However, because most homes do not yet have a microwave-convection oven, only two of the more than 25 recipes and variations in this chapter require a microwave-convection oven—one for a roast turkey breast and the other for a roast goose.

There are elegant recipes here such as Chicken with Red and Yellow Peppers and Fresh Herbs and Chicken with Spinach and Leeks that are easy to make. The flavors and colors are bright, the tastes distinct and complementary. There are recipes for quick family meals, such as the chicken cooked with barbecue sauce. And there are several recipes for chicken smothered in thick sauces, such as the chicken with curried onions, the chicken in a rich and mildly spicy tomato sauce enriched with a fresh tomato salsa, and the chicken with mushrooms. There's a ground chicken ragoût made with mushrooms and broccoli and flavored with Thai fish sauce for the adventurous, and there is a microwave version of an old favorite, Deviled Thighs.

Turkey microwaves quickly and easily, and for family eating there are turkey drumsticks marinated in an Asian-style sauce. There is a breast of turkey with an Italian-style tomato gravy and an herbed meat loaf made with turkey. For the holidays there is a grand whole turkey breast roasted to perfection in a microwave-convection oven.

Game recipes include Duck with Cherry Sauce—tender, slightly pink breast of duck in a microwave cherry sauce, Pheasant with Mustard Juices—pheasant breast with lightly flavored mustard juices, and a whole goose for the holidays roasted in a microwave-convection oven.

For a quick chicken breast, or whenever you need some cooked chicken, microwave poaching produces the fullest flavor and plumpest, juiciest chicken.

Serves 2; makes 2 cups diced chicken

¾-pound boneless and skinless chicken breast, all visible fat removed, cut in half lengthwise

1 cup hottest possible tap water

In a large bowl, combine the chicken and water. Separate the chicken pieces as much as possible to ensure even cooking. Cover and microwave on HIGH for 4½ minutes, then allow to cool in the liquid for 5 minutes. Drain and serve or refrigerate until needed.

Nutritional Information
(as a percentage of daily intake)

10% (193) calories
3% (2 g) fat
0% (0 g) carbohydrates
45% (34 g) protein

5% (114 mg) sodium
3% (20 mg) calcium
7% (1 mg) iron

If you buy the chicken already cut into serving pieces, then all you have to do for this recipe is to remove the skin and visible fat, add some milk or broth, and 14 minutes later you have a perfectly poached chicken for a simple family meal. Because there is no skin, the chicken will look plain, so I suggest you serve it with one of the following sauces: Winter Green Salsa (page 112), Emerald Sauce (page 98), Harissa (page 132), or Golden Onion Relish (page 155).

Serves 6

3½-pound chicken, cut into serving pieces, skin and all visible fat removed

2 cups Chicken Broth (page 42) or water

Arrange the chicken in a very large shallow rectangular dish, the thick meaty pieces placed toward the corners and edges of the dish, the wings and bone ends of the drumsticks near the center of the dish. Add the broth and cover. Microwave on HIGH for 13 minutes. Serve.

Nutritional Information
(as a percentage of daily intake)

7% (130) calories
3% (2 g) fat
0% (0 g) carbohydrates
36% (27 g) protein

3% (77 mg) sodium
2% (13 mg) calcium
7% (1 mg) iron

Here's an instant family favorite that takes about 6 minutes to prepare and cook. The chicken is moist and tender and robustly flavored with the barbecue sauce.

Serves 4

½ cup store-bought barbecue sauce or from the recipe on page 229

2 skinless and boneless chicken breasts (about 1¼ pounds), cut in half lengthwise, narrow fillets on the underside of each half breast removed and saved for another use, all visible fat removed

Pour the barbecue sauce into a large shallow dish. Coat the chicken all over with the barbecue sauce and then arrange like spokes of a wheel, the narrower ends pointed toward the center. Cover and microwave on HIGH for 5 minutes. Serve with some of the barbecue sauce spooned over each portion.

Nutritional Information
(as a percentage of daily intake)

9% (182) calories
5% (3 g) fat
1% (3 g) carbohydrates
45% (34 g) protein

15% (351 mg) sodium
0% (23 mg) calcium
7% (1 mg) iron

Chicken Salad with Tomatoes, Avocado, and Herbs

Here bright summer-fresh flavors, such as lemon, parsley, cilantro, crisp celery, and tomatoes, combine with chicken in an avocado and garlic dressing to make a festive chicken salad.

Serves 6

¾-pound boneless and skinless chicken breast, all visible fat removed, cut in half lengthwise

1 cup hottest possible tap water

1 medium-size avocado, peeled and pitted

2 garlic cloves, peeled

juice of 1 lemon

2 scallions, cut into 2-inch lengths

1 small bunch of cilantro, thick stems removed (about 1 cup tightly packed)

1 cup tightly packed fresh parsley leaves

1 large vine-ripened tomato, cored and cut into ¼-inch dice

3 celery ribs, finely diced

a little salt and freshly ground black pepper to taste

Place the chicken, spaced as far apart as possible, in a large shallow rectangular dish or large bowl and add the water. Cover and microwave on HIGH for 4½ minutes. Allow to cool, covered, in the water for at least 10 minutes.

In a food processor, puree the avocado and garlic with the lemon juice. Add the scallions, cilantro, and parsley and pulse until very finely chopped with a texture as thick as sour cream.

When chicken has cooled, remove from the water, pat dry, and dice. Combine with the avocado mixture, tomato, and celery. Mix well and season with salt and pepper. Serve immediately or cover and refrigerate until needed.

Variation

Piquant Herbed Chicken Salad: Substitute lime juice for the lemon juice and puree ½ to 1 jalapeño pepper with the avocado. Season generously with freshly ground black pepper.

Nutritional Information
(as a percentage of daily intake)

7% (130) calories   3% (66 mg) sodium
9% (6 g) fat   5% (38 mg) calcium
2% (5 g) carbohydrates   13% (2 mg) iron
20% (15 g) protein

The mild curry flavor of this salad shadows the ingredients, rather than overwhelming them. This is a cool, pale green curried chicken salad perfect for warm-weather lunches or dinners.

Serves 4

¾-pound boneless and skinless chicken breast, all visible fat removed, cut in half lengthwise

1 cup hottest possible tap water

1 large sweet yellow bell pepper, cored and cut into 2-inch chunks

3 celery ribs, with leaves if possible, cut into 2-inch lengths

3 scallions, trimmed and cut into 2-inch lengths

½ cup tightly packed fresh parsley leaves

2 garlic cloves, peeled

1-inch piece of fresh ginger, peeled and quartered

juice of 1 lime

⅓ cup golden raisins, coarsely chopped

½ cup plain nonfat yogurt

2 teaspoons curry powder

a little salt and freshly ground black pepper to taste

Place the chicken, spaced as far apart as possible, in a large shallow dish and add the water. Cover and microwave on HIGH for 4½ minutes. Allow to cool, covered, in the water, for 5 to 10 minutes.

Meanwhile, in a food processor, coarsely chop the yellow pepper, celery, and scallions. Transfer to a large bowl. Without rinsing the food processor, finely chop the parsley, garlic, and ginger. Add to the other vegetables.

Drain and dice the chicken and add to the vegetables with the lime juice, raisins, yogurt, and curry powder. Mix well and season to taste with salt and pepper. Refrigerate until serving time.

Nutritional Information
(as a percentage of daily intake)

10% (191) calories

3% (2 g) fat

8% (21 g) carbohydrates

32% (24 g) protein

5% (114 mg) sodium

15% (119 mg) calcium

20% (3 mg) iron

Chicken with Red and Yellow Peppers and Fresh Herbs

The sweet flavors of the red and yellow peppers, accented by the herbs, mellow to make a fragrant, textured sauce for the chicken. Serve with a simple green vegetable, like broccoli or asparagus (see recipes on pages 106 and 99), which will add color and on which the extra sauce can be spooned. No salt or pepper is necessary in this recipe.

Serves 4

1 large sweet red bell pepper, cored and cut into 2-inch pieces

1 large sweet yellow bell pepper, cored and cut into 2-inch pieces

1 small onion, peeled and halved

1 large garlic clove, peeled

¼ cup tightly packed fresh parsley leaves

¼ cup tightly packed fresh basil

juice of ½ lemon

2 boneless and skinless chicken breasts (about 1¼ pounds), all visible fat removed, each cut in half lengthwise

In a food processor, in batches, chop the peppers, onion, garlic, parsley, and basil with the lemon juice. Transfer to a large shallow dish, cover, and microwave on HIGH for 5 minutes. Arrange the chicken on the pepper mixture like spokes of a wheel, cover, and microwave on HIGH for 6 minutes. Serve with the peppers spooned over the chicken as a thick sauce.

Nutritional Information
(as a percentage of daily intake)

8% (154) calories

3% (2 g) fat

5% (13 g) carbohydrates

31% (23 g) protein

3% (65 mg) sodium

5% (36 mg) calcium

20% (3 mg) iron

Even in a simple glass baking dish this recipe is attractive enough to go straight to the table. The leeks are cooked in the dish, then the spinach is cooked on top of them, and finally the chicken and tomatoes are arranged over the bed of spinach. This layering allows the vegetables to keep their individual identities, with the flavors melding together playfully in the mouth.

Serves 4

3 medium-size leeks (about 1 pound), white parts only, split in half lengthwise, washed thoroughly and thinly sliced

2 large garlic cloves, peeled and finely chopped

juice of ½ lemon

½ pound fresh spinach, thick stems removed, washed and coarsely chopped

2 boneless and skinless chicken breasts (1¼ to 1½ pounds), all visible fat removed, cut in half lengthwise, narrow fillets on the underside of each half breast removed

1 large ripe tomato, cored and cut into ½-inch dice

Mix leeks, garlic, and lemon juice in a large shallow dish. Cover and microwave on HIGH for 4 minutes. Pack the spinach on top, cover, and microwave on HIGH for 3 minutes.

Arrange the chicken on top of the spinach like spokes of a wheel, tips pointed toward the center. Place a quarter of the diced tomato between each 2 chicken pieces. Cover and microwave on HIGH for 7 minutes.

Nutritional Information
(as a percentage of daily intake)

9% (172) calories

3% (2 g) fat

3% (8 g) carbohydrates

41% (31 g) protein

6% (132 mg) sodium

11% (89 mg) calcium

13% (3 mg) iron

Here a whole chicken, cut into pieces, is smothered in a thick tomato sauce that has been made mildly spicy with onions, garlic, and salsa. The chicken is exceptionally moist and tender, and the sauce is thick and mildly spicy.

Serve with rice (see recipes on pages 50–60).

Serves 6

1 medium-size onion, finely chopped

3 large garlic cloves, finely chopped

3½-pound chicken, cut into serving pieces, all skin and visible fat removed, back discarded (remove skin from the large joint of the wing only)

½ teaspoon crushed dried oregano

½ cup chopped fresh parsley

1½ cups Fresh Tomato Salsa (page 102) or Winter Green Salsa (page 112) *or* 12 ounces fine-quality jarred salsa

3 cups Chunky Tomato Sauce (page 107)

a little salt and freshly ground black pepper to taste

In a food processor, finely chop the onion and garlic. Transfer to a large bowl, cover, and microwave on HIGH for 2 minutes.

While onions are cooking, arrange the chicken in a very large shallow rectangular dish, the thick meaty pieces placed toward the corners and edges of the dish, the wings and bone ends of the drumsticks near the center of the dish.

Stir the oregano, parsley, salsa, and tomato sauce into the cooked onions. Spread over the chicken. Cover and place in the oven on a large pie plate or on an inverted shallow dish to elevate the chicken 1 to 2 inches off the floor of the oven to ensure even cooking. Microwave on HIGH for 19 minutes. Arrange the chicken on plates, smothered in the sauce, with rice on the side.

Nutritional Information
(as a percentage of daily intake)

13% (261) calories

5% (3 g) fat

6% (16 g) carbohydrates

59% (44 g) protein

5% (129 mg) sodium

8% (64 mg) calcium

20% (3 mg) iron

This microwave chicken fricassee is heady with onions, green peppers, and fresh mushrooms.

Serves 6

1 large onion, peeled and cut into eighths

1 large sweet green bell pepper, cored and cut into eighths

2 large garlic cloves, peeled

½ cup tightly packed fresh parsley leaves

3½-pound chicken, cut into serving pieces, skin and all visible fat removed

¾ pound fresh mushrooms (cultivated, firm wild such as cremini or shiitake, or a combination), washed and thickly sliced

2 cups Chunky Tomato Sauce (page 107)

In a food processor, coarsely chop the onion, green pepper, garlic, and parsley. Transfer to a medium bowl and cover. Microwave on HIGH for 5 minutes.

While onion mixture is cooking, arrange the chicken in a very large shallow rectangular dish, the thick meaty pieces placed toward the corners and edges of the dish, the wings and bone ends of the drumsticks near the center of the dish.

Stir the mushrooms and tomato sauce into the cooked onion mixture and spread evenly over the chicken. Cover and microwave on HIGH for 16 minutes.

To serve, arrange the chicken on plates. Stir the sauce together and spoon over the chicken.

Nutritional Information
(as a percentage of daily intake)

5% (104) calories

2% (1 g) fat

3% (8 g) carbohydrates

21% (16 g) protein

2% (58 mg) sodium

4% (30 mg) calcium

13% (2 mg) iron

Chicken Smothered in Curried Onions

Tender, moist pieces of chicken are smothered in slightly crunchy curried onions that have a gentle sweet-and-sour flavor and a light aroma of curry, ginger, and garlic. This is a spicy, but not a hot spicy, recipe. The golden color of the onions compensates for the lack of coloring in the chicken.

Serves 6

2 pounds onions, peeled
4 large garlic cloves, peeled
½ jalapeño pepper
3-inch piece of fresh ginger, peeled and quartered
2 tablespoons curry powder
3½-pound chicken, cut into serving pieces, skin and all visible fat removed

juice of 1 lemon
juice of 1 lime
2 tablespoons honey
¼ cup golden raisins

In a food processor, in several batches, chop the onions, garlic, pepper, ginger, and curry powder. Place in a large bowl, cover, and microwave on HIGH for 10 minutes.

While the onions are cooking, arrange the chicken in a very large shallow rectangular dish, the thick meaty pieces placed toward the corners and edges of the dish, the wings and bone ends of the drumsticks near the center of the dish.

Stir the lemon juice, lime juice, honey, and raisins into the cooked curried onions and spread evenly over the chicken. Cover and microwave on HIGH for 15 minutes. Serve smothered in the onions.

Nutritional Information
(as a percentage of daily intake)

14% (279) calories
3% (3 g) fat
9% (26 g) carbohydrates
52% (39 g) protein

8% (189 mg) sodium
10% (76 mg) calcium
20% (3 mg) iron

James Beard, the late dean of American cookery, considered deviled thighs one of his all-time favorite recipes, perhaps because of the slightly risqué implications of the title. In this recipe, which is based on a Beard recipe, the chicken is coated in an herb, caper, and mild mustard sauce and dusted in bread crumbs, which add an implication of crispness (really crisp food is not possible in the microwave) to these thighs.

Serve these hot from the oven or chill and use for quick hot-weather meals or for picnics.

Serves 6

2 tablespoons hot Dijon mustard
2 tablespoons coarse mustard
1 large garlic clove, peeled
1 tablespoon drained capers, rinsed
1 teaspoon dried tarragon
½ teaspoon dried oregano

a little freshly ground black pepper to taste
juice of ½ lime
6 chicken thighs (1¾ pounds), skin and all visible fat removed
1½ cups plain dried bread crumbs

In a food processor, combine all ingredients except chicken and bread crumbs and process until garlic and capers are chopped and everything is well mixed. Transfer to bowl.

Coat the chicken with the mustard mixture, then roll in the bread crumbs. Arrange like spokes on a very large plate or in a shallow round dish and microwave on HIGH, uncovered, for 10 minutes. Serve or cool, cover, and refrigerate until needed.

Nutritional Information
(as a percentage of daily intake)

8% (157) calories
6% (4 g) fat
5% (13 g) carbohydrates
21% (16 g) protein

15% (357 mg) sodium
5% (37 mg) calcium
13% (2 mg) iron

SPECIAL NOTE

In the recipe for deviled thighs, all legs (drumsticks), or a combination of legs and thighs, or an equal weight of breasts (all skin and visible fat removed), can be used.

Tender, moist pieces of chicken are buried under a thick layer of celery flavored with onions, leeks, garlic, fresh basil, and lime juice to make an emerald-colored, garden-fresh-tasting topping.

A little crunch will be left in some of the celery, which will add textural interest to the chicken. For a hot sparkle to the dish, add the optional jalapeño pepper.

Serves 6

1 large onion, peeled and cut into eighths

2 leeks, white part only, split lengthwise, washed thoroughly, and cut in half

3 large garlic cloves, peeled

1 small jalapeño pepper (optional)

2 teaspoons crushed dried rosemary

3½-pound chicken, cut into serving pieces, skin and all visible fat removed

1 small (1-pound) celery stalk, with leaves if possible, sliced ½ inch thick

1 cup coarsely chopped fresh basil

juice of 1½ limes

In a food processor, finely chop the onion, leeks, garlic, jalapeño, and rosemary. Transfer to a large bowl, cover, and microwave on HIGH for 4 minutes.

While onions are cooking, arrange the chicken in a very large shallow rectangular dish, the thick meaty pieces placed toward the corners and edges of the dish, the wings and bone ends of the drumsticks near the center of the dish.

Mix the cooked onions with the celery and spread evenly over the chicken. Cover and microwave on HIGH for 14 minutes. Transfer the chicken to serving plates and mix the basil and lime juice with the celery mixture and cooking juices. Spread over the chicken and serve.

Nutritional Information
(as a percentage of daily intake)

14% (278) calories

8% (5 g) fat

2% (6 g) carbohydrates

67% (50 g) protein

8% (180 mg) sodium

7% (58 mg) calcium

20% (3 mg) iron

Spicy Ground Chicken with Mushrooms and Broccoli

The Thai fish sauce, nuoc mam, a salty, clear, poignantly fish-flavored condiment, is combined with garlic, ginger, and anise seeds to make a sweetly spicy, slightly salty sauce in which the chicken is cooked. When combined with the broccoli and mushrooms, this ragoût bursts with unexpected flavors and textures, is brightly colored, and deserves a bed of rice (see recipes on pages 50–60) or perhaps some traditionally cooked bean thread noodles (about ¼ pound) to accompany it.

Because supermarket chicken is so undependable in quality, cooking a chicken breast in one piece is always a little iffy—sometimes it is juicy and perfect; other times, through no fault of the cook, it is dry and flavorless. This recipe seems not to care. The chicken always comes out moist and tender and full of sweet flavor.

Serves 8

1 medium-size onion, peeled and quartered

2 large garlic cloves, peeled

2-inch piece of fresh ginger, peeled

¼ cup nuoc mam (available in Asian groceries and some supermarkets)

⅔ cup Chicken Broth (page 42)

1 tablespoon cornstarch

¼ teaspoon anise seeds

4 or 5 grinds of black pepper

1¼ pounds boneless and skinless chicken breasts, all visible fat removed, coarsely ground in a food processor or meat grinder

1 small (1-pound) bunch of broccoli, cut into ½-inch flowerets, stems reserved for another recipe

½ pound fresh cultivated mushrooms, bottoms trimmed, cut into ½-inch wedges

2 scallions, chopped

½ cup tightly packed finely chopped cilantro leaves

freshly ground black pepper to taste

In a food processor, finely chop the onion, garlic, and ginger. In a blender, combine the nuoc mam, chicken broth, cornstarch, anise seeds, and pepper and blend well. Pour over the onions, stir, cover, and microwave on HIGH for 4 minutes. Whisk sauce thoroughly (it will become cloudy and thicken), then stir in the chicken. Cover and microwave on HIGH for 7 minutes, stirring once midway to ensure even cooking.

While chicken is cooking, place the broccoli and mushrooms in a large bowl and cover. After chicken is removed from the oven, microwave broccoli and mushrooms on HIGH for 5 minutes.

Combine chicken mixture with broccoli and mushrooms and the chopped scallions and cilantro. Mix well, season with pepper, cover, and reheat if necessary. Serve over rice or noodles.

Variation

Spicy Ground Turkey with Broccoli and Mushrooms: Substitute turkey for the chicken.

Nutritional Information
(as a percentage of daily intake)

5% (105) calories

5% (127 mg) sodium

2% (1 g) fat

6% (51 mg) calcium

3% (8 g) carbohydrates

13% (2 mg) iron

23% (17 g) protein

Here the turkey is microwaved with tomato sauce and forms what my Italian friends call a tomato gravy, a rich tomato sauce with a turkey flavor.

This is a quick and easy recipe, especially if you have tomato or barbecue sauce (see variation) on hand.

Serves 4

1¼-pound boneless turkey breast roast (plastic timer removed), rinsed under cold running tap water and patted dry

½ cups Chunky Tomato Sauce (page 107)

Place the turkey in a large bowl and pour the tomato sauce over it. Cover and microwave on HIGH for 18 minutes, stirring once midway through the microwaving to prevent a burned tomato crust from forming on the edge of the bowl. Let the turkey rest at room temperature for 5 to 10 minutes, then cover, remove the skin, slice, and serve with some of the tomato gravy spooned over each portion.

Variation

Sliced Turkey with Barbecue Sauce: Substitute barbecue sauce, page 229, for the tomato sauce.

Nutritional Information
(as a percentage of daily intake)

12% (244) calories
11% (7 g) fat
0% (0 g) carbohydrates
56% (42 g) protein

5% (108 mg) sodium
5% (37 mg) calcium
20% (3 mg) iron

The marinade of Chinese oyster sauce, soy sauce, garlic, and ginger lightly flavors the turkey. This is definitely family fare, best eaten with your fingers. It is especially popular with children and teenagers who don't mind getting their fingers into their food.

Serves 4

4 turkey drumsticks (about 3 pounds), skin and all visible fat removed
⅓ cup Chinese oyster sauce
3 tablespoons soy sauce or tamari
3 large garlic cloves, peeled

1½-inch piece of fresh ginger, peeled
grated zest of ½ orange
a little freshly ground black pepper to taste

With a small, sharp knife, loosen all the skin and tendons around the bottom of each drumstick by cutting through to the bone. This will prevent the meat from tightening up and unattractively pulling away from the bone.

Combine the remaining ingredients in a blender or food processor and puree until smooth. Pour over the drumsticks and marinate in the refrigerator overnight, turning once or twice.

Arrange the drumsticks like spokes of a wheel in a large shallow dish, with the bottoms of the drumsticks meeting at the center. Pour marinade into dish, cover, and microwave on HIGH for 14 minutes.

Variation

For 3 drumsticks (about 2¼ pounds): Prepare as directed, but microwave on HIGH for only 11 minutes.

Nutritional Information
(as a percentage of daily intake)

14% (278) calories
15% (10 g) fat
1% (3 g) carbohydrates
56% (42 g) protein

17% (415 mg) sodium
7% (56 mg) calcium
27% (4 mg) iron

Whole Turkey Breast Roasted with Lemon

A Microwave-Convection Recipe

A microwave-convection oven roasts a breast of turkey better than an ordinary oven—the skin is crisp and mahogany-colored, and the meat is juicier and more tender than with ordinary roasting. For the holidays this recipe produces a spectacular roasted breast that can be presented on a platter at the table. And because you are dealing with only the breast, the carving is very simple—just cut thin vertical slices down each side of the breast.

In this recipe the cavity of the turkey is filled with lemon and garlic, which will lightly flavor the meat as it cooks, and the skin is rubbed with a little oil, lemon, and herbs to scent and flavor the skin, should you wish to eat it. Salt and pepper should be added after cooking, if you wish, because the salt will inhibit even browning and the flavor of pepper greatly intensifies during microwaving, so it is best controlled by adding it after the bird is cooked.

Most ovens overcook if allowed to cook for the computer-set time, so here you are instructed to test the turkey for doneness after 30 minutes.

Serves 8

1 whole 5- to 5½-pound turkey breast, bone in
1 large lemon, cut into 1-inch pieces
3 garlic cloves, very finely chopped
1 tablespoon olive oil
juice of ½ lemon
½ teaspoon crushed dried thyme
½ teaspoon crushed dried oregano
½ teaspoon crushed dried rosemary

Rinse the turkey under cold running tap water, remove the plastic thermometer if there is one, pat dry, and trim away any visible fat. Mix the lemon pieces and chopped garlic and place inside the cavity on the underside of the breast, covering with the flaps of skin that hang over the edges of the breast. Place on a microwave-safe roasting rack, meat side up. Mix together the oil, lemon juice, thyme, oregano, and rosemary. Rub all over the outside of the turkey.

Place in a microwave-convection oven and set to cook automatically, following the manufacturer's directions, on the poultry setting. After 30 minutes, test for doneness by inserting an instantly registering thermometer into the thickest part of the meat without touching bone. The turkey is done when the thermometer registers 140 degrees. If not done, return to the oven and continue to cook on the microwave-convection poultry setting until done.

Remove from the oven and allow to stand at room temperature for 10 minutes to allow the juices to settle back into the meat.

Nutritional Information
(as a percentage of daily intake)
per 4-ounce serving without the skin

11% (219) calories
8% (5 g) fat
0% (0 g) carbohydrates
56% (42 g) protein

4% (89 mg) sodium
3% (27 mg) calcium
13% (2 mg) iron

This light, herb-scented turkey meat loaf is a quick family pleaser. Serve it hot from the oven or refrigerate it and use it for sandwiches.

The meat loaf will shrink considerably during cooking; juices that surround the meat loaf in the pan after it is cooked can be spooned over the sliced meat loaf when it is served. The top of the meat loaf may be a little crusty or have some blemishes from the cooking, so if you want to present the whole meat loaf at the table unsliced, flip it over onto a serving plate and present the bottom as the top.

Serve with Chunky Tomato Sauce (page 107) and mashed potatoes (page 139) for a simple family meal.

Serves 6

1 pound ground turkey
1 egg white
⅓ cup skim milk
2 to 3 slices soft commercial whole wheat bread
1 small onion, peeled and cut in half
1 celery rib, cut into 2-inch pieces
1 cup tightly packed fresh parsley leaves

½ teaspoon dried thyme
½ teaspoon dried oregano
1 teaspoon dried basil
¼ teaspoon hot red pepper sauce
1 tablespoon Dijon mustard
a little salt and freshly ground black pepper to taste

Combine the turkey, egg white, and skim milk in a mixing bowl. In a food processor, process the bread to form soft bread crumbs. Add 1 cup of the bread crumbs to the bowl with the turkey. Again in the food processor, without rinsing the bowl, finely chop the onion, celery, parsley, thyme, oregano, and basil. Add to the mixing bowl with the hot red pepper sauce and mustard and blend well with your hands. Season to taste with salt and pepper. Spread evenly in a glass meat loaf pan (9 by 5 by 3 inches), cover, and microwave on MEDIUM (50%) for 24 minutes.

Nutritional Information
(as a percentage of daily intake)

13% (260) calories
20% (13 g) fat
3% (8 g) carbohydrates
37% (28 g) protein

10% (229 mg) sodium
9% (75 mg) calcium
20% (3 mg) iron

With the microwave, in just 4 minutes, two breasts are cooked and ready to serve. The duck is moist, tender, almost buttery, consistently better than with ordinary cooking. The trade-off, however, is that the outside of the duck turns gray rather than an attractive brown. To overcome this, the duck should be sliced before serving.

Here a quick cherry juice is made in the microwave and is then used to poach the duck breasts. After the breasts are cooked, the juices are thickened into a sauce to serve with the duck.

Serves 4

1-pound package frozen dark sweet cherries
juice of ½ lemon

2 boneless duck breasts (about 1¼ pounds), skin and all visible fat removed, split in half lengthwise
1 teaspoon cornstarch

Combine the cherries and lemon juice in a medium bowl, cover, and microwave on HIGH for 10 minutes. Strain juice and discard cherries.

While cherries are cooking, arrange the duck in a large shallow dish like spokes of a wheel with the narrower ends pointed toward the center. Pour the strained cherry juice over the duck, cover, and microwave on HIGH for 4 minutes. Uncover and remove ½ cup of the juices. Blend 1 tablespoon of those juices with the cornstarch to dissolve, then mix into the ½ cup of juices. Microwave on HIGH, uncovered, for 2 minutes.

Slice the duck on the bias into ¼-inch slices, arrange on plates, and spoon a quarter of the sauce over each serving.

Variation

Duck with Blackberry Sauce: Use frozen blackberries instead of cherries.

Nutritional Information
(as a percentage of daily intake)

7% (137) calories
5% (3 g) fat
5% (15 g) carbohydrates
17% (13 g) protein

2% (36 mg) sodium
1% (10 mg) calcium
20% (3 mg) iron

Duck Salad with Oranges and Red Onion

Oranges and red onion bounce around in this salad of diced duck breast flavored with capers and herbs and dressed only with lime juice. The different flavors all seem to blend together to form a new taste—with an emphatic flavor here and there jumping out at you. This is an amazingly light, fresh-tasting salad. The texture is best when all the ingredients are cut into small pieces.

This makes a fine appetizer before a fish entrée or a quick but grand light lunch—the whole salad, including cooking the duck, takes less than 20 minutes to prepare. I sometimes add ½ cup of cooked white beans to this salad and surround it with bright microwave-cooked broccoli flowerets.

Serves 4 as an entrée, 6 as an appetizer

2 boneless duck breasts (about 1¼ pounds), skin and all visible fat removed, split in half lengthwise

1 cup Chicken Broth (page 42)

2 juice oranges, thickly peeled so no white pith remains and cut with a sharp serrated knife between the white membranes to release just the orange segments

1 large ripe tomato, cored, seeded, and cut into ¼-inch dice

½ small red onion, finely chopped

juice of 1 large lime

1 tablespoon drained capers, rinsed and coarsely chopped

1 tablespoon finely chopped fresh chives

1 tablespoon finely chopped fresh parsley

a little salt and freshly ground black pepper to taste

Place the duck breasts, arranged like spokes of a wheel, in a large shallow dish and add the broth. Cover and microwave on HIGH for 5 minutes. Uncover and allow to cool to room temperature, then cut into ¼-inch dice. Toss with the oranges, tomato, red onion, lime juice, capers, chives, and parsley. Season with a little salt and pepper. Serve at room temperature or refrigerate and serve cold.

Nutritional Information
(as a percentage of daily intake)
per entrée serving

6% (119) calories	8% (185 mg) sodium
5% (3 g) fat	3% (29 mg) calcium
3% (9 g) carbohydrates	20% (3 mg) iron
21% (14 g) protein	

Pheasant has a light color and mild flavor similar to a leg of turkey. Here the breast is spread with two different mustards and cooked very quickly. The pan juices act as a light sauce.

This is a quick (preparation and cooking take only 5 minutes) entrée to serve with Celery Root and Potato Puree (page 124) and a simple green vegetable during autumn for game-loving guests.

Purchasing Note: Pheasant breasts are available from specialty butchers.

Serves 2

1 teaspoon Dijon mustard
1 teaspoon coarse mustard

1 pheasant breast (¾ pound), skin and all visible fat removed, split in half lengthwise

Mix the 2 mustards and spread evenly over the bone side (not the flat skin side) of the breast pieces. Place, skinned side down, in a large shallow dish, cover, and microwave on HIGH for 3 minutes. Uncover and serve half a breast with some of the mustard juices that have accumulated under the pheasant during cooking spooned over each portion.

Nutritional Information
(as a percentage of daily intake)

12% (239) calories
9% (6 g) fat
0% (1 g) carbohydrates
56% (43 g) protein

12% (256 mg) sodium
3% (19 mg) calcium
13% (2 mg) iron

A Microwave-Convection Recipe

With its crisp skin and deep mahogany color, a roast goose is the most festive of all holiday entrées. The taste is rich, sweet, and mildly gamy, a little stronger than the flavor of duck. All of the meat on a goose is dark, even the breast.

Although goose fell into disfavor because of its fattiness and the resultant difficulty in cooking it, now, with America's farm-raised, reduced-fat geese, a goose is easier to roast than a large turkey and most of the greasiness is gone.

The finest roast goose is cooked in a microwave-convection oven. The combination of microwaves and dry heat produces a crisp skin with a dark mahogany color and tender, moist meat. The goose is less greasy and more flavorful when microwave-convection-cooked than with ordinary roasting.

Serves 6

12-pound goose
1 large lemon, cut into ¾-inch
  chunks
3 garlic cloves, chopped
2 tablespoons olive oil

½ teaspoon crushed dried thyme
½ teaspoon crushed dried rosemary
½ teaspoon crushed dried oregano
a little salt and freshly ground black
  pepper to taste

Remove the string or rubber bands that hold the legs and wings in place. Remove all the excess fat from the cavity of the goose, as well as the giblets and neck. Rinse under cold running water, inside and out, and pat dry. Mix the lemon chunks and garlic and stuff into the body cavity of the goose. With the point of a small sharp knife, prick the goose all over. Prick at 1-inch intervals on the breast and ½-inch intervals on the rest of the bird.

Place on a microwave-safe rack in a microwave-convection oven and set to cook on microwave-convection at 375 to 380 degrees. Cook for 1 hour and 15 minutes, then test for doneness by inserting an instantly registering thermometer into the thickest part of the meat between the leg and thigh. The goose is done when the temperature registers 165 degrees. If goose needs additional cooking, estimate that time by the rule of thumb that the temperature will rise about 1 degree a minute.

When done, drain the cavity of fat and allow the goose to rest at room temperature for 15 minutes before carving and serving.

Nutritional Information
(as a percentage of daily intake)
per 4-ounce serving without the skin

7% (143) calories
12% (8 g) fat
0% (0 g) carbohydrates
23% (17 g) protein

2% (48 mg) sodium
1% (8 mg) calcium
13% (2 mg) iron

Goose has a rich, gamy flavor, but the geese of today are not nearly as fatty as they once were. And goose breasts, which are lower in cholesterol than chicken breasts, are now available from gourmet butchers, so it is no longer necessary to cook a whole goose every time you want to serve this all-American bird.

Serve with Golden Onion Relish (page 155) or Holiday Three-Berry and Beet Compote (page 306) and Sweet and Sour Red Cabbage with Hidden Shiitakes (page 117).

Butcher's Note: A breast of goose can be ordered from specialty butchers, albeit at quite a hefty price. Ask that the skin be removed, leaving the breast in two pieces.

Serves 4

2 large garlic cloves, very finely chopped
½ teaspoon crushed dried marjoram
¼ teaspoon crushed dried rosemary
4 or 5 grinds of black pepper

1 tablespoon balsamic vinegar
1 goose breast (1¾- to 2-pound), skin and all visible fat removed
½ cup Chicken Broth (page 42) or water

Combine the garlic, marjoram, rosemary, pepper, and vinegar and rub all over the goose. Arrange in a large rectangular shallow dish, cover, and allow to marinate in the refrigerator for 2 hours.

Add the broth to the goose, cover, and microwave on HIGH for 7½ minutes. Slice thinly, spooning some of the juices that accumulated under the goose over each portion.

Nutritional Information
(as a percentage of daily intake)
per 4-ounce serving without the skin

7% (143) calories
12% (8 g) fat
0% (0 g) carbohydrates
23% (17 g) protein

2% (48 mg) sodium
1% (8 mg) calcium
13% (2 mg) iron

Meat

A microwave oven is not well suited to cooking lean red meats, but there are a few cuts of beef that do well, particularly those that are flat, such as flank steaks and London broil. Some recipes for ground beef also cook well in the microwave. Pork tenderloins cook exceedingly well. I have included in this chapter recipes for a great Wild Mushroom Chili, an exceptionally flavorful meat loaf that is a snap to make, two flank steak recipes, one plain and the other marinated, and several recipes for pork tenderloins. There is a recipe for a cold beef salad, flavored with herbs and sun-dried tomatoes, that uses cooked (top round) London broil and is one of my favorite cold summer salads.

A microwave-convection oven, however, roasts red meat, such as prime rib and leg of lamb, beautifully and much faster than a conventional oven. Just season those roasts as you normally would, then set the oven to cook them automatically. For my taste, most of the preprogrammed cooking times are too long, and roasts overcook. Always set the roast to cook rare, then test with an instantly registering or microwave-safe thermometer and adjust the cooking time as needed. The microwave-convection ovens I have experimented with cook the roast to medium-rare or medium on the rare setting.

I have experimented with microwave browning skillets and do not believe that they perform as well as cooking in a skillet. I also believe that it is a bad idea to try to duplicate sautéing in the microwave.

This is a sweet, tender-in-your-mouth chili, with a deep tomato flavor and the scent and flavor of a dozen herbs and spices, including a few unexpected spices that sweeten the spice combination: cinnamon, coriander, ginger, and cloves. As you taste the chili, note that the mushrooms retain their integrity.

Both beef and pork are used to soften the taste of the red meats, but all beef could be used if you'd prefer.

With wild mushrooms, this chili loses its casual character and becomes a dish for informal company entertaining. Try serving it from a large silver bowl rather than portioning it onto plates in the kitchen.

Don't be intimidated by the length of the ingredients list in this recipe; most of it is just a list of seasonings.

Serves 8

1 pound lean ground beef
½ pound lean ground pork loin
1 large onion, peeled and quartered
5 garlic cloves, peeled
2 large leeks, white part only, split lengthwise, washed thoroughly, and cut in half
2 shallots, peeled
1 pound fresh shiitake or cremini mushrooms, cut into 1-inch chunks
1 28-ounce can crushed tomatoes in puree
1 6-ounce can tomato paste

3 cups cooked kidney, pink, or white beans (page 69–71)
3 tablespoons chili powder
1 teaspoon ground cumin
1 teaspoon crushed dried marjoram
1 teaspoon crushed dried oregano
½ teaspoon ground cinnamon
½ teaspoon ground coriander
½ teaspoon ground ginger
¼ teaspoon ground cloves
½ teaspoon cayenne pepper (optional)
a little salt and freshly ground black pepper to taste

Crumble the beef and pork into a large shallow dish. Cover and microwave on HIGH for 7 minutes. Set aside.

While meats are cooking, in a food processor finely chop the onion, garlic, leeks, and shallots. Transfer to a very large bowl, cover, and microwave on HIGH for 6 minutes.

Drain the cooked meats, crumble into small pieces, and add to the bowl of cooked vegetables with the mushrooms, crushed tomatoes, tomato paste, beans, and seasonings. Mix well, cover, and microwave on HIGH for 25 minutes, stirring once midway through the cooking. Stir and season with salt and pepper.

Nutritional Information
(as a percentage of daily intake)

20% (397) calories
23% (15 g) fat
12% (34 g) carbohydrates
44% (33 g) protein

11% (267 mg) sodium
11% (87 mg) calcium
40% (6 mg) iron

This large, spectacular salad is great for picnics, buffets, summer meals, and outdoor entertaining, even for office parties. All of the opulent flavors of the sun-dried tomatoes, herbs, capers, and mustard blend with the contrasting tastes and textures of the meat and potatoes.

Serves 8

2 pounds (4 large) red potatoes, washed

1¼-pound top round London broil, all visible fat removed

½ pound (about 3 medium-size) carrots, trimmed and scrubbed

2 scallions, trimmed and cut into 2-inch lengths

1 cup tightly packed fresh parsley leaves

½ cup tightly packed fresh dill

½ cup coarsely chopped sun-dried tomatoes

2 tablespoons drained capers, rinsed

1½ tablespoons coarse mustard

2 tablespoons raspberry vinegar *or* the juice of 1 small lime

freshly ground black pepper to taste

Place the potatoes, evenly spaced, on the floor of the microwave and microwave on HIGH for 10 minutes. Remove and set aside to cool, then cut into ¾-inch dice.

Place the London broil in a shallow dish, cover, and microwave on MEDIUM for 10 minutes, turning the meat over midway through the cooking to ensure even doneness. Cool and cut into ½-inch dice.

Place the carrots in a medium bowl or shallow dish, cover, and microwave on HIGH for 5 minutes. Cool under cold running water, then drain.

In a food processor, finely chop the scallions, parsley, and dill.

In a very large bowl, combine the potatoes, beef, carrots, scallions, parsley, dill, sun-dried tomatoes, capers, mustard, and vinegar or lime juice. Mix well and season with pepper. Refrigerate until needed.

Nutritional Information
(as a percentage of daily intake)

11% (221) calories

8% (5 g) fat

11% (31 g) carbohydrates

23% (17 g) protein

4% (98 mg) sodium

7% (52 mg) calcium

27% (4 mg) iron

Meat Loaf

The microwave is a great way to prepare this family favorite quickly and without having to turn on a conventional oven and heat up the kitchen.

The meat loaf here is seasoned with chili powder and Worcestershire sauce and is topped with tomato sauce. Should you want a milder-flavored meat loaf, try the variation below.

Serves 6

1 small onion, peeled and quartered
2 garlic cloves, peeled
1 pound lean ground beef such as ground round
1 cup freshly made soft whole wheat or white bread crumbs (made from 3 slices soft commercial bread)
½ cup skim milk

1 egg white
1 tablespoon Worcestershire sauce
2 tablespoons ketchup
2 teaspoons chili powder
1 teaspoon crushed dried oregano
a little salt and freshly ground black pepper to taste
¾ cup Chunky Tomato Sauce (page 107)

In a food processor, finely chop the onion and garlic. In a large mixing bowl, combine the chopped onion and garlic with the beef, bread crumbs, milk, egg white, Worcestershire sauce, ketchup, chili powder, and oregano and blend well with your hands. Season to taste with salt and pepper. Press lightly and evenly into a glass meat loaf pan (9 by 5 by 3 inches). Spread the tomato sauce across the top of the meat loaf. Cover and microwave on MEDIUM for 23 minutes.

Variation

A Mild-Mannered Meat Loaf: Use only 1½ teaspoons Worcestershire sauce, 1 tablespoon ketchup, and ½ teaspoon oregano; substitute ½ teaspoon crushed dried thyme for the chili powder and add ½ cup very finely chopped fresh parsley to the mixture.

12% (240) calories   6% (148 mg) sodium
20% (13 g) fat   7% (58 mg) calcium
4% (10 g) carbohdyrates   13% (2 mg) iron
27% (20 g) protein

ADAPTING MEAT LOAF RECIPES TO THE MICROWAVE

To adapt your favorite meat loaf recipe to the microwave, use 1 pound ground beef, 1 cup bread crumbs, ½ cup skim milk, and 1 egg white and flavor with onions, carrots, celery, and seasoning, or whatever you like, using your own recipe as a guide by adjusting the proportions to 1 pound of meat.

Here is the basic recipe for a quick London broil for four. It cooks in just 10 or 12 minutes. The meat can be marinated before cooking, following your favorite recipe, if you wish. Here it is seasoned lightly with garlic and lemon juice.

Serves 4

1 garlic clove, very finely chopped
1 tablespoon fruity olive oil
4 to 5 generous grinds of black
 pepper

1 1¼-pound top round London broil,
 all surface fat removed

Mix together the garlic, oil, and pepper and rub all over the meat. Place in a shallow dish, cover, and microwave on MEDIUM for 10 minutes, turning once midway through the cooking to ensure even doneness, for rare, 12 minutes for medium rare. Allow to rest for 5 to 10 minutes before serving. Slice across the grain and serve, spooning some of the cooking juices over the meat if you wish.

Nutritional Information
(as a percentage of daily intake)

14% (272) calories
24% (16 g) fat
 0% (0 g) carbohydrates
53% (40 g) protein

3% (66 mg) sodium
1% (7 mg) calcium
27% (4 mg) iron

Because the microwave doesn't brown meats, cuts like flank steak, which are served sliced, and thus have no need for a browned appearance (though the additional flavor of the browning might be nice), make good candidates for microwaving. This recipe cooks a flank steak in only 10 minutes.

You can marinate the flank steak before cooking, using your own marinade, if you wish.

Serves 4 to 6

1-pound flank steak, trimmed of all visible fat
juice of ½ lemon

a little freshly ground black pepper to taste

Rub the steak all over with the lemon juice, then season with pepper. Place in a shallow dish or on a round plate large enough to hold it flat, cover, and microwave on MEDIUM for 8 minutes for rare, 10 minutes for medium-rare.

Nutritional Information
(as a percentage of daily intake)

8% (162) calories
14% (9 g) fat
0% (0 g) carbohydrates
36% (27 g) protein

2% (44 mg) sodium
0% (3 mg) calcium
20% (3 mg) iron

COOKING TIMES FOR FLANK STEAKS (1 POUND REFRIGERATOR-COLD STEAKS)

Rare: 8 minutes on HIGH

Medium-rare: 10 minutes on HIGH

Medium: 12 minutes on HIGH

Flank Steak Teriyaki

This dish makes cooking a flank steak easier than ever—just slip the dish used to marinate the steak into the microwave, and 10 minutes later—with no splattering and no greasy aluminum foil to clean up, the flank steak is perfectly cooked.

Marinating a simple flank steak in a teriyaki marinade gives the steak a play of flavors: a little garlic, a touch of ginger, and a gentle burst of the slightly licorice flavor of the anise seed. Spoon some of the marinade and cooking juices over the sliced steak, if you wish, for extra flavor.

Serves 6

⅓ cup soy sauce
3 tablespoons brown sugar
3 large garlic cloves, peeled
2 teaspoons ground ginger
1 teaspoon anise seeds

¼ teaspoon freshly ground black
  pepper
1-pound flank steak, trimmed of all
  visible fat

Combine everything but the flank steak in a blender and blend well. Pour half the teriyaki sauce into a large shallow rectangular dish, place the flank steak in the dish, and pour the remaining marinade over the steak. Seal airtight with plastic wrap and marinate overnight or up to 24 hours in the refrigerator.

Microwave on MEDIUM without uncovering, for 10 minutes for medium-rare, 12 minutes for medium.

Carefully uncover, slice on the bias, and serve, with some of the marinade spooned over the steak if you wish.

Nutritional Information
(as a percentage of daily intake)

10% (204) calories
14% (9 g) fat
 4% (10 g) carbohydrates
36% (27 g) protein

24% (575 mg) sodium
 2% (18 mg) calcium
20% (3 mg) iron

Marinated Pork Tenderloins with Mustard Juices

Tender and moist, these marinated pork tenderloins are one of the most successful red meat dishes I have prepared in the microwave.

The pork is marinated for a day or 2 in a combination of mustard and apple juice flavored with ginger and garlic. The sweetness of the apple juice, rather than wine or oil, acts as the base for the marinade. And the pork is cooked directly in the marinade to increase its moistness.

Serves 6

½ cup Dijon mustard
1½ cups apple juice
2-inch piece of fresh ginger, peeled and quartered
4 garlic cloves, peeled

2 pork tenderloins (1½ pounds), all visible fat and silver membranes removed, slashed on the bias ¼-inch deep so the pork will absorb flavor from the marinade and cook without shrinking

In a blender, combine the mustard, apple juice, ginger, and garlic and blend well. Arrange the pork in a large shallow dish and cover with the mustard marinade. Cover and refrigerate for 1 to 2 days. Push the pork tenderloins to opposite sides of the dish, as far apart as possible to ensure even cooking, cover, and microwave on MEDIUM for 22 minutes.

Slice and serve immediately, with some of the cooking juices spooned over each serving.

Nutritional Information
(as a percentage of daily intake)

9% (188) calories
8% (5 g) fat
0% (0 g) carbohydrates
44% (33 g) protein

14% (341 mg) sodium
3% (24 mg) calcium
7% (1 mg) iron

Here pork tenderloins are studded with garlic (like a leg of lamb) and rubbed with ground herbs and seeds for a fragrant, fresh taste. The pork needs to marinate for at least 2 hours, though overnight will allow the marinade to penetrate more deeply. Serve with mustard on the side.

Serves 6

1½ pounds pork tenderloins, all visible fat and any thin silvery membranes trimmed away

2 large garlic cloves, peeled and slivered

1 teaspoon dried rosemary

½ teaspoon dried thyme

1 teaspoon fennel seeds

1 teaspoon celery seeds

4 black peppercorns

juice of 1 lime

1 cup Chicken Broth (page 42)

With the point of a small sharp knife, pierce deeply into the pork about every 1½ inches. Slide a sliver of garlic into each hole. Place in a large shallow dish.

In a spice mill, grind the rosemary, thyme, fennel seeds, celery seeds, and peppercorns to a powder. Mix with the lime juice and rub over the pork. Cover and refrigerate for 2 hours or overnight.

Add the broth to the pork, cover, and microwave on MEDIUM for 16 minutes. Slice and serve.

Nutritional Information
(as a percentage of daily intake)

10% (196) calories

9% (6 g) fat

0% (1 g) carbohydrates

44% (33 g) protein

14% (85 mg) sodium

3% (2 mg) calcium

7% (1 mg) iron

In this simple family recipe, a thick uncooked barbecue sauce is mixed together and poured over the roast. After cooking, the sauce is spooned over the pork.

Serves 4

⅔ cup ketchup

1 tablespoon plus 1 teaspoon Worcestershire sauce

½ teaspoon hot red pepper sauce

2 teaspoons chili powder

½ teaspoon crushed dried oregano

½ teaspoon onion powder

½ teaspoon garlic powder

several generous grinds of black
  pepper

1 1¼-pound boneless pork loin roast,
  trimmed of all visible fat

To Make the Quick Barbecue Sauce: Blend together everything but the pork. Place the pork in a rectangular loaf pan and pour the barbecue sauce evenly over the roast. Cover and microwave on MEDIUM for 23 minutes. Slice the meat, stir the sauce, ignoring any crusted sauce around the edges of the dish, and spoon over the sliced pork.

Nutritional Information
(as a percentage of daily intake)

10% (204) calories

9% (6 g) fat

1% (4 g) carbohydrates

44% (33 g) protein

16% (387 mg) sodium

1% (10 mg) calcium

7% (1 mg) iron

SIMPLE LOIN OF PORK ROAST

Season the outside of the roast with herbs, such as thyme, rosemary, and oregano, or spices, such as paprika and cumin. For a 1½-pound roast, microwave on MEDIUM for 25 minutes. For pork roasts larger than 1½ pounds, roast conventionally or in a microwave-convection oven.

Breakfast

The microwave cooks a bowl of hot cereal in just seconds. It poaches fruits magnificently. It also cooks breakfast grains easily and makes some of the best-ever jams and jellies (see "Jams, Jellies, Preserves, and Other Condiments"). All in all, the microwave can make a major contribution to breakfast, the most underrated and underattended meal of the day.

There are recipes here for dried and fresh fruits cooked in the microwave. The Figs Cooked in Spiced Apple Cider sparkle with the fragrance of cinnamon, ginger, and coriander. Cold from the refrigerator, they can be part of a quick breakfast with a thick slice of toasted bread. The Tender Pineapple Chunks, cooked in a light syrup, have a simple, uncomplicated taste with a slight tartness that gives them a peppy breakfast appeal. The Poached Plums make a less lively cooked fruit for breakfast but will seem friendly early in the morning. And the Prunes Cooked with Lemon Slices are my favorite—tender, sweet prunes surrounded by slices of lemon in a light syrup, the sweetness of the prunes contrasting playfully with the tart lemon slices.

There is a recipe for a wild rice breakfast cereal that I make occasionally for myself or for guests. The nutty, toasted flavor of the wild rice, sweetened with a little maple syrup and garnished with fresh raspberries, is the most unusual cereal I have ever eaten and one of the best.

There are two oatmeal recipes, one using steel-cut oatmeal, the second for an apricot- and orange-flavored oatmeal that uses rolled oats.

The microwave can also be used to make breakfast drinks. You'll find a fragrant, spiced coffee recipe, an apple cider recipe, and a hot chocolate recipe. Each develops a unique flavor and texture from being cooked in the microwave.

The microwave isn't the perfect answer to a modern breakfast, but it can be used to add some interesting variety to the first meal of the day.

I love the slightly granular, sensual texture and sweet, fruity flavor of dried figs. Here they are cooked in a spiced apple juice that adds a bold aroma to these intensely flavored dried fruits. Serve the figs cold, with a little of the spiced cooking liquid spooned over them, for warm-weather breakfasts, or serve them warm for cold-weather breakfasts.

Buying Note: When you're buying dried figs, whether they are the straw- to honey-colored varieties or the purple-blue-black Mission figs, which I prefer for this recipe, always choose figs that are plump and moist, figs that feel somewhat tender when gently squeezed.

Serves 8

1½ pounds dried figs (see note above)
2 cups apple cider or apple juice
1½ teaspoons dried grated lemon peel
 ***or* the grated zest of 1 large lemon**
2 teaspoons dried grated orange peel
 ***or* the grated zest of 1 large orange**

½ teaspoon ground cinnamon
¼ teaspoon ground ginger
¼ teaspoon ground coriander

Combine all the ingredients in a large bowl. Mix well and seal airtight with plastic wrap. Microwave on HIGH until figs are tender when pierced with the tip of a knife, about 15 to 20 minutes.

Carefully uncover, strain cider into a large bowl, and microwave on HIGH, uncovered, until slightly thickened and reduced by about half, approximately 10 minutes. Strain and pour over the figs. Serve warm or refrigerate to serve cold.

Nutritional Information
(as a percentage of daily intake)

13% (266) calories
2% (1 g) fat
25% (68 g) carbohydrates
4% (3 g) protein

1% (14 mg) sodium
17% (138 mg) calcium
13% (2 mg) iron

Tender chunks of sweet, juicy pineapple make a perfect winter breakfast, either before a small bowl of mixed grain cereal or with a bran muffin. Thanks to the microwave, the pineapple here remains fresh-tasting, cooked until tender without losing its natural tartness or texture.

Serve with a little of the cooking liquid spooned over the pineapple or, for more formal breakfasts, with a tablespoon or two of Apple Juice Glaze (page 280) or Cranberry Sauce (page 276).

Serves 6

1 medium-size pineapple, peeled   **⅔ cup water**
½ cup sugar

Quarter the pineapple lengthwise, remove the fibrous core, and cut into ½-inch chunks. Mix the pineapple, sugar, and water in a medium bowl or shallow dish. Cover and microwave on HIGH for 11 minutes. Serve warm or refrigerate and serve cold.

Nutritional Information
(as a percentage of daily intake)

5% (92) calories   0% (2 mg) sodium
2% (1 g) fat   1% (11 mg) calcium
8% (23 g) carbohydrates   7% (1 mg) iron
1% (1 g) protein

As a child, I was occasionally lucky enough to spend a day or 2 at my aunt's country house, where there was always a jar of poached prunes in the refrigerator. I was as intrigued by the slices of lemon used to flavor the poaching syrup as by the tender pitted prunes.

Although the country house in the Poconos is now a large housing development and my aunt lives in Florida, a jar of poached prunes, with a dozen or so slices from a large lemon, is a frequent visitor to my refrigerator and an occasional guest at my breakfast table on days when I am not in the mood for cereal.

Cooked in the microwave, the prunes become puffy without becoming mushy.

Childhood memories aside, these prunes are addictive. It is not a question of whether or not you can eat just one; it's a question of whether or not you can eat just one bowl.

Serves 8

1½ pounds pitted prunes   **3 cups water**
1 large lemon, very thinly sliced   **1 cup sugar**

In a large bowl or shallow dish, mix all the ingredients. Cover and microwave on HIGH for 11 minutes. Serve cold with a lemon slice added to each portion.

Nutritional Information
(as a percentage of daily intake)

6% (119) calories   0% (2 mg) sodium
0% (0 g) fat   3% (20 mg) calcium
11% (33 g) carbohydrates   7% (1 mg) iron
1% (1 g) protein

Icy cold, tender poached plums, with their soft centers and slight sweetness, make a simple breakfast with a piece of sourdough bread or a small bowl of cereal. I prefer Damson or small red plums to black Friars for this recipe.

Serves 4

3 cups hottest possible tap water
1 cup sugar
1 tablespoon vanilla extract

1 pound (6 to 8, depending on the variety) plums

In a very large bowl, stir together the water, sugar, and vanilla. Microwave on HIGH, uncovered, for 8 minutes. Carefully remove from the oven, add the plums, and microwave on HIGH, uncovered, for 5 minutes. With a slotted spoon, transfer the plums to a bowl or dish where they can rest in a single layer. Pour the cooking liquid over the plums, cover, and refrigerate until very cold.

Variation

Poached Apricots: Substitute 1 pound apricots (8 to 10) for the plums and poach for 4 minutes.

Nutritional Information
(as a percentage of daily intake)

6% (120) calories
2% (1 g) fat
11% (30 g) carbohydrates
1% (1 g) protein

0% (0 mg) sodium
1% (6 mg) calcium
0% (0 mg) iron

Like ham with red-eye gravy, grits are a part of many southern family breakfasts. On their own, grits are quite bland, so they have become little more than a vehicle for eating salt and butter. But if you use just a little salt and butter, the quiet flavor of the corn can be tasted.

Grits are not popular throughout the South. One southern Virginian friend admitted that she had never cooked grits. "Virginians don't eat grits," she declared. "They're popular in North and South Carolina and Georgia, I think, but not Virginia."

When thinking about grits, Louis Mahoney, one of the South's most dedicated southern newspaper food editors, says we must always remember, "There is no such thing as instant grits.*"

For many southerners, the best way to serve grits is to refrigerate them in a loaf pan until firm, then slice, sauté in butter until brown (like polenta), and serve for breakfast with maple syrup.

Grits are ground hominy; hominy is dried corn with its hull and germ removed.

Serves 6

3½ cups skim milk **1 tablespoon unsalted butter**
1 cup grits (not instant)
a little salt and freshly ground black
  pepper to taste

Combine the milk and grits in a medium bowl, cover, and microwave on HIGH for 5 minutes. Stir until smooth, then microwave on HIGH, uncovered, for 2½ minutes. Season with salt and pepper, spoon onto plates, top each serving with ½ teaspoon butter, and serve.

Nutritional Information
(as a percentage of daily intake)

8% (163) calories   4% (89 mg) sodium
3% (2 g) fat   22% (178 mg) calcium
10% (28 g) carbohydrates 7% (1 mg) iron
9% (7 g) protein

*Instant grits are very finely ground hominy that has been cooked and dehydrated, a process that completely destroys the flavor and texture of the grits.

Wild Rice Cereal

I was startled the first time I was served wild rice for breakfast. But with a handful of raspberries and a drizzle of maple syrup, it makes a great, boldly flavored, slightly chewy breakfast cereal. The berries add a soft, sweet, moist contrast to the texture of the wild rice and add a little tang to the flavor of the cereal that balances with the sweetness of maple syrup.

All 3 ingredients are indigenous to Minnesota, and this was a traditional cereal of that state's north-country Indians. Cream was added to the cereal in the original recipe, but the lighter flavor of milk is better, for it doesn't mask the subtleties of the wild rice with butterfat.

Serves 4

¾ cup cold cooked wild rice, cooked in water (see box below)
1½ cups hottest possible tap water

1 cup fresh raspberries
¼ to ½ cup maple syrup
1 cup low-fat milk

Combine the wild rice and water in a large bowl. Seal airtight with plastic wrap and microwave on HIGH until rice is tender and the water is absorbed, about 25 minutes. Drain and cool under cold running water.

Combine the wild rice and raspberries in cereal bowls and drizzle with maple syrup to taste. Add ¼ cup milk to each bowl and serve.

Nutritional Information
(as a percentage of daily intake)

6% (129) calories
3% (2 g) fat
9% (26 g) carbohydrates
5% (4 g) protein

1% (35 mg) sodium
14% (116 mg) calcium
7% (1 mg) iron

BASIC PREPARATION OF WILD RICE

Makes 2½ cups

1 cup wild rice   **2 cups water**

Combine wild rice and water in a medium bowl and seal airtight with plastic wrap. Microwave on HIGH until tender, about 27 minutes. Carefully uncover and drain.

Either reheat or refrigerate to use later.

After you have sampled this lightly sweetened, corn- and pecan-flavored mixed grain cereal with golden raisins, you'll want to quadruple the ingredients to make enough of this dry cereal mix to last the whole winter (store in an airtight container for up to 6 months).

You can vary the dried fruit as you wish. Try dried apricots or peaches instead of the raisins; or use dried cherries or cranberries, and almonds instead of the pecans.

Makes 5 cups, serving 10

1 cup quick (not instant) oat flakes
1 cup whole wheat flakes
½ cup corn bran
½ cup oat bran

1 cup powdered (dry) nonfat milk
⅔ cup chopped pecans
½ cup golden raisins or currants
2 tablespoons light brown sugar

Blend everything together. Store until needed in an airtight container.

For 1 Serving: Mix ½ cup cereal with ½ cup skim milk in a cereal bowl. Microwave on HIGH, uncovered, for 1½ minutes. Stir and serve.

For 2 Servings: Mix 1 cup cereal with 1 cup skim milk and microwave on HIGH, uncovered, for 2 minutes and 20 seconds.

Nutritional Information
(as a percentage of daily intake)

7% (149) calories
9% (6 g) fat
8% (22 g) carbohydrates
7% (5 g) protein

2% (52 mg) sodium
15% (117 mg) calcium
13% (2 mg) iron

OATS AND OATMEAL

I love oatmeal. I loved it before it was chic and before I knew of its important fibrous nature. It was the creamy texture and nutty flavor I always liked.

There are three kinds of oats. Steel-cut oats—oat kernels cut into pieces with a steel blade—have the finest texture and flavor and make the best oatmeal. Next best are rolled oats, sometimes called oat flakes, which are flattened oat kernels—less chewy, but still textured and flavorful. And finally there are instant oats, which are rolled oats that have been cooked and dehydrated so that they turn into cereal almost instantly when heated with water or milk. Instant oats make a bland mush when cooked; avoid them except for camping.

It's the steel-cut oats that make this the greatest bowl of oatmeal ever. It has a full, toasty, nutty oat flavor and a variety of chewy and creamy textures.

Although I am fondest of this oatmeal plain or with just a little maple syrup, and occasionally with a few golden raisins, you can add the flavoring ingredients from the Apricot-Orange Oatmeal recipe on page 243 or the Lemon and Golden Raisin Porridge variation.

Note on Cooking Time: The highest-quality steel-cut oats, which have very few broken pieces, take longer to cook than less expensive brands.

Serves 2

1 cup steel-cut oatmeal   **3 cups skim milk**

Combine the oatmeal and milk in a very large bowl. Microwave on HIGH, uncovered, until tender yet crunchy, about 25 to 35 minutes. Stir well and serve.

Nutritional Information
(as a percentage of daily intake)

14% (284) calories   8% (190 mg) sodium
5% (3 g) fat   59% (474 mg) calcium
16% (45 g) carbohydrates   13% (2 mg) iron
25% (19 g) protein

Apricot-Orange Oatmeal

Made with rolled oats, scented with orange, and flavored with dried apricots, this is a quick oatmeal recipe with a creamy texture and a mild oat flavor.

Serves 2

1½ cups skim milk
1 cup rolled oats (oat flakes)
¼ teaspoon dried grated orange peel
  or 1 teaspoon freshly grated orange zest

2 tablespoons chopped dried apricots
  (about 8 half apricot pieces)
1 teaspoon sugar (optional)

Combine everything in a very large bowl and microwave on HIGH, uncovered, for 5 minutes. Stir well and serve.

Variations

Lemon and Golden Raisin Porridge: Substitute lemon peel and golden raisins for the orange peel and apricots.

Plain Oatmeal: Prepare as directed, without the orange peel or apricots. Brown sugar or maple syrup can be substituted for the white sugar.

Nutritional Information
(as a percentage of daily intake)

12% (249) calories
 5% (3 g) fat
16% (44 g) carbohydrates
17% (13 g) protein

4% (96 mg) sodium
32% (256 mg) calcium
13% (2 mg) iron

Scented Coffee

The elegantly scented, lightly sweetened coffee of a Saudi Arabian friend inspired me to blend coriander, cinnamon, and ginger to make this fragrant, gently sweetened brew. It is fine black and equally good with a little low-fat milk. It makes the best-ever iced coffee.

Use dark, French-roasted coffee beans so that the coffee will be strong enough in flavor to stand up to the heady spices.

Making coffee in the microwave gives the coffee a thickness, an added body, a viscosity not found in coffee made by any other brewing method. Some people prefer it as an evening dessert coffee, though I like it best at breakfast.

Makes 6 6-ounce cups

1½ quarts hottest possible tap water
¾ cup finely ground coffee
1 teaspoon ground cinnamon

1 teaspoon ground coriander
1 teaspoon ground ginger
3 tablespoons brown sugar

In a large bowl, gently stir everything together until coffee grinds are moistened. Cover and microwave on HIGH for 8 minutes. Strain through a lined coffee filter or a sieve lined with 2 layers of paper toweling or a thin, clean kitchen towel. Reheat and serve very hot or refrigerate until cold.

Nutritional Information
(as a percentage of daily intake)

2% (33) calories
0% (0 g) fat
3% (9 g) carbohydrates
0% (0 g) protein

0% (9 mg) sodium
5% (38 mg) calcium
13% (2 mg) iron

When the skim milk in this cocoa recipe is whirled in a blender, it whips like cream, forming a froth that rises like a soufflé in the microwave oven, then settles down a bit when poured into a mug. With a little foamy head atop each serving, this hot cocoa is reminiscent of cappuccino.

Use the finest-quality Dutch or Swiss cocoa powder for the best-flavored hot chocolate. The cinnamon is almost imperceptible in the drink, though it strengthens the chocolate flavor in a quiet, subtle way. If you are a cinnamon lover, feel free to double the amount recommended in the recipe.

Serves 3

½ cup cocoa powder
½ cup powdered (dry) nonfat milk
2¾ cups skim milk

3 tablespoons brown sugar
½ teaspoon ground cinnamon
1 teaspoon vanilla extract

Combine all the ingredients in the jar of a blender, and holding the lid very securely in place, blend on high speed for 30 seconds to aerate the drink mixture.

Pour the drink into a very large bowl, seal airtight with a double layer of plastic wrap, and microwave on HIGH for 6 minutes. Carefully uncover, stir to deflate about half the foam, then ladle into mugs and serve.

Nutritional Information
(as a percentage of daily intake)

10% (205) calories
5% (3 g) fat
13% (37 g) carbohydrates
19% (14 g) protein

8% (183 mg) sodium
55% (440 mg) calcium
13% (2 mg) iron

Gently spiced with lemon and orange overtones, this hot apple cider is an eye-opener on cold winter days or can be served cold for breakfast in summer instead of orange juice.

Serves 8, makes 2 quarts

2 quarts apple cider
1 tablespoon dried grated orange peel
 or the grated zest of 1 large orange
1 teaspoon ground cinnamon

½ teaspoon ground ginger
¼ teaspoon ground coriander
pinch of ground cloves
½ lemon, thinly sliced

Stir everything together in a very large bowl, cover, and microwave on HIGH until steaming hot, about 12 to 15 minutes. Strain.

Serve hot in mugs or refrigerate until cold and serve in tall glasses. Use the cooked lemon slices as garnish for some of the servings.

Nutritional Information
(as a percentage of daily intake)

6% (119) calories
0% (0 g) fat
11% (30 g) carbohydrates
0% (0 g) protein

0% (7 mg) sodium
3% (25 mg) calcium
7% (1 mg) iron

Desserts

The microwave cooks fruit desserts magnificently, intensifying both the fruit color and flavor. It makes incomparably flavored dessert sauces. It makes wonderful puddings in half the time and with none of the mess of ordinary cooking. And the microwave can be used to prepare cold desserts, such as sorbets and ice creams and mousses.

The microwave-convection oven cooks fine pies and cobblers—with brown, crisp crusts and fruit fillings that are fresher than ever before.

There are modern microwave versions of four old-fashioned puddings in this chapter. Puddings left our culinary vocabulary in the 1980s in favor of restaurant recipes for rich mousses, terrines, flourless cakes, and frozen soufflés. But with the aid of the microwave, easy-to-prepare old friends can now be welcomed back to the table. There's a simple Chocolate Pudding that is comforting family fare. There's a Tapioca Pudding with Blackberry Sauce that is elegant enough to serve at a company dinner. There's a Rice Pudding with Dark Sweet Cherry Sauce; the pudding is light and creamy like an old-fashioned rice pudding baked for hours in the oven, and the sauce adds a glistening sheen and an intense fruit flavor to the recipe. And there is a pineapple bread pudding with a nutty flavor and fresh pineapple taste.

The microwave is a fine asset for making sorbets, light ice creams, and mousses. The Soft Kiwifruit Sorbet is a soothing pale green color and has an elegant and formal air. The Rhubarb and Blackberry Ice Cream with Strawberry Sauce is my favorite recipe in this chapter. The Light Raspberry Ice Cream and Vanilla Bean Ice Cream are so emphatically flavored and so creamy that no one will suspect they are reduced-fat ice creams. The Cranberry Mousse with Strawberry Sauce melts in your mouth, and the Lemon Snow with Blueberry Sauce is the lightest and most refreshing recipe in the chapter.

Because the microwave makes intensely flavored fruit sauces so easily, there are three desserts here using fresh fruit topped with microwave sauces. Pineapple and Raspberries with Strawberry Sauce is a classic combination, and here it becomes company fare with the addition of the sauce. The unusual combination of fresh strawberries and lichees becomes a showstopper with the cranberry sauce. And you'll be surprised at how dramatic and delicious an ordinary-sounding dish like Strawberries with Pineapple Sauce is thanks to the microwave.

The microwave cooks and poaches fresh fruit with remarkable finesse. Fruits become tender without losing their texture. The complex, varied, and subtle flavors and aromas of fruit are intensified, not diminished, with microwave cooking. And the colors often become emphatic rather than dull. Here you'll find tender poached peaches with a light cheese mousse, a Fresh

Pear Compote with an exceptionally natural texture and an apple juice glaze. There's a microwave version of cooked whole pears with raspberry sauce, and there are the palest of golden-orange-colored poached apricots. There are recipes for poached cherries and for tenderly cooked orange slices.

In general, I believe that cakes, cupcakes, muffins, and cookies are best prepared in a conventional oven. These items cook very quickly in a microwave, I admit, but at a great sacrifice. Microwaving turns cakes, cupcakes, and muffins rubbery, destroying the fragile crumbs that would have made them delicious. And cookies, because they do not brown and because only four to six can be cooked at a time, are a time-consuming nuisance to cook in the microwave. However, the Individual Cheesecakes with Pineapple Sauce recipe, which cooks in the blink of an eye, actually 3 minutes, is an exception to the rule.

There are four cobblers here that can be prepared in a microwave-convection oven with fine results. There's a Golden Peach Cobbler with Blackberries, an Apple Cobbler with Cranberries, a Pear Cobbler with Ginger, and a stunning Rhubarb and Hidden Strawberry Cobbler. There are special notes on making cobblers in a microwave-convection oven on page 251.

With the microwave, light fresh fruit desserts with intense natural flavors and textures are now possible with just a few minutes of cooking.

PUDDINGS

Chocolate Pudding

Two decades of grand, dense, bold chocolate mousses, soufflés, terrines, and tortes have caused Americans to lose sight of the fact that chocolate was once a comforting food for children, not a mania for adults.

Here is a plea for a return to chocolate as comfort food, a return to simple homemade chocolate pudding, missing from most contemporary cookbooks. Don't get any ideas about adding anything to this recipe. No nuts, no chunks of white chocolate. Nothing. It's perfect just the way it is.

Serves 4

3 tablespoons cornstarch
½ cup sugar
2 cups skim milk
1 ounce unsweetened chocolate, broken into several pieces

1 egg white
1 egg
1 teaspoon vanilla extract

In a very large bowl, combine everything but the vanilla and whisk until well blended. Microwave on HIGH, uncovered, for 9 minutes, whisking until well blended midway through the cooking to minimize lumping.

Add the vanilla and whisk until smooth. The edges of the pudding will be thicker than the center. The pudding should have thickened to the consistency of a loose sour cream. If not, microwave on HIGH for 1 more minute, then whisk until smooth.

Pour into 4 custard cups. Cover with plastic wrap and refrigerate until cold.

Nutritional Information
(as a percentage of daily intake)

11% (220) calories
6% (4 g) fat
15% (40 g) carbohydrates
9% (7 g) protein

4% (95 mg) sodium
20% (162 mg) calcium
7% (1 mg) iron

Tapioca Pudding with Blackberry Sauce

For most people, tapioca pudding is old-fashioned comfort food. But I once attended an elegant outdoor party in Aspen, given in honor of one of Japan's most important corporate leaders, and the hostess served tapioca pudding with a homemade wild blackberry sauce for dessert. The tapioca pudding was the hit of the meal; everyone talked about it for weeks.

So whether it's for a family dinner or an elegant company meal, try reviving this classic. You'll be surprised at how warmly it will be received.

Serves 6

¼ cup quick-cooking tapioca
¼ cup sugar
1 large egg

3 cups skim milk
1 teaspoon vanilla extract
Blackberry Sauce (recipe follows)

Combine the tapioca, sugar, egg, and milk in a large bowl and whisk until well blended. Microwave on HIGH, uncovered, for 10 minutes. Whisk until smooth, then return to the oven and microwave on HIGH, uncovered, until boiling, about another 3 to 4 minutes. Stir in the vanilla. Pour into 6 individual serving cups, cover with plastic wrap, and refrigerate.

Serve with 2 tablespoons Blackberry Sauce spooned over each portion or pass the sauce separately.

Variations

Tapioca Pudding with Raspberry Sauce: Serve with Raspberry Sauce (page 282) instead of Blackberry Sauce.

Tapioca Pudding with Cherry Sauce: Serve with Dark Sweet Cherry Sauce (page 256) instead of Blackberry Sauce.

Tapioca Pudding with Ginger: Add 1 tablespoon very finely chopped preserved or crystallized ginger with the vanilla.

*Nutritional Information
(as a percentage of daily intake)
per serving without the sauce*

6% (110) calories   3% (75 mg) sodium
2% (1 g) fat   26% (157 mg) calcium
7% (70 g) carbohydrates   0% (0 mg) iron
7% (45 g) protein

MICROWAVE NOTE

Whole pearl tapioca turns into a rubbery sheet when cooked in the microwave, so be sure to use only quick-cooking tapioca.

Blackberry Sauce

This quick and easy sauce is intensely flavored, not too sweet, and can be used with dozens of different kinds of desserts.

Serves 8

1 pound unsweetened individually quick-frozen blackberries
⅓ cup sugar

1 tablespoon dried grated orange peel *or* **the grated zest of 1 large orange**

Combine the blackberries, sugar, and orange peel in a large bowl. Cover and microwave on HIGH for 10 minutes. Carefully ladle into a strainer, allowing the clear sauce to drain into a clean bowl. With the back of the ladle, very gently press on the blackberry pulp to extract all the liquid. Do not push hard enough to force the tender pulp through the strainer. Discard the pulp.

Cover sauce and refrigerate until cold.

Nutritional Information
(as a percentage of daily intake)
per 3-tablespoon serving

3% (63) calories
0% (0 g) fat
6% (16 g) carbohydrates
1% (1 g) protein

0% (1 mg) sodium
2% (15 mg) calcium
0% (0 mg) iron

Rice Pudding with Dark Sweet Cherry Sauce

The old-fashioned rice pudding made with only rice, milk, and a little sugar cannot be improved on. None of the rich modern-day versions, saturated with cream and egg yolks, does anything to enhance this great classic. In this light version, which uses skim milk instead of whole milk, the milk is so reduced during the 90 minutes of cooking that the pudding tastes just as creamy as it would with whole milk.

I like the pudding with just a little vanilla. However, rice pudding aficionados sometimes add raisins (use golden raisins), and some are willing to flavor the pudding with a dash of nutmeg or a spritz of orange flower or rose water. For them, there are variations below listing proper quantities.

While this recipe cannot be called "quick-cooking" (it takes 1¾ hours), that's half the time it would have taken in a conventional oven.

Make this recipe with a medium-grain white rice, such as Italian *Arborio rice*, not long-grain rice, which produces the wrong texture.

Serves 4

1 quart skim milk
¼ cup medium-grain rice
⅓ cup sugar

¼ teaspoon vanilla extract
Dark Cherry Sauce (recipe follows)

Mix the milk, rice, and sugar together in a large bowl. Microwave on DEFROST, uncovered, for 90 minutes. Stir the pudding, mixing in the skin that has formed on the surface. Return to the oven, still uncovered, and continue microwaving on DEFROST until thick and creamy, another 5 to 15 minutes. Watch closely and do not overcook: 3 or 4 minutes too long and the creamy rice pudding will turn into a burned, coagulated mess. Stop the microwaving when the pudding appears to be thick, has deepened in color, and has lost any semblance of soupiness.

Stir in the vanilla and serve immediately. Pass the cherry sauce separately.

Variations

Nutmeg-Flavored Rice Pudding: Stir ¼ teaspoon freshly grated nutmeg into the pudding when it comes from the oven.

Rose or Orange Flower Water: For an exotic fragrance, mix ⅛ to ¼ teaspoon orange or rose flower water into the pudding instead of the vanilla. This unusual flavoring, of which I am occasionally fond, comes from a suggestion by my friend and colleague Marion Cunningham.

Rice Pudding with Golden Raisins: Combine ½ cup golden raisins with enough apple juice to cover in a small bowl or 1-cup glass measure. Microwave on HIGH for 4 minutes, then cool to room temperature. Drain and mix with the milk, rice, and sugar.

Rice Pudding for 2: Combine 2½ cups skim milk with 3 tablespoons medium-grain rice and 3 tablespoons sugar in a large bowl. Microwave on HIGH, uncovered, for 70 to 75 minutes, until a very thick, very creamy texture forms. Stir, flavor gently with vanilla, nutmeg, or orange or rose flower water, if you wish, and serve.

Rice Pudding with Winter Blackberry Sauce: Serve with Blackberry Sauce (page 253) instead of the cherry sauce

Rice Pudding with Raspberry Sauce: Serve with Raspberry Sauce (page 282) instead of the cherry sauce.

Nutritional Information
(as a percentage of daily intake)
per serving without the sauce

10% (192) calories
0% (0 g) fat
14% (38 g) carbohydrates
12% (9 g) protein

5% (127 mg) sodium
38% (305 mg) calcium
0% (0 mg) iron

Dark Sweet Cherry Sauce

This shiny, deep-burgundy-colored sauce is intensely flavored with dark cherries, and has hints of lemon and orange.

Serves 8

1 pound unsweetened individually quick-frozen dark sweet pitted cherries

⅓ cup sugar

1 teaspoon dried grated orange peel *or* the grated zest of ½ large orange

1 teaspoon dried grated lemon peel *or* the grated zest of ½ lemon

Combine everything in a large bowl. Cover and microwave on HIGH for 10 minutes. Carefully ladle the cherries into a strainer, allowing the clear sauce to drain, pressing gently on the cherry pulp to extract all the liquid. Do not push hard enough to force the tender pulp through the strainer. Discard the pulp and refrigerate the sauce until cold.

Nutritional Information
(as a percentage of daily intake)
per 3-tablespoon serving

5% (104) calories

0% (0 g) fat

9% (26 g) carbohydrates

1% (1 g) protein

0% (1 mg) sodium

1% (11 mg) calcium

0% (0 mg) iron

The first time I was served this pudding, it was made with white bread, cream, egg yolks, and about ½ pound of butter. And it was justifiably called "Pineapple Mess." I have lightened it, given it a little more body and texture and a slight nuttiness in flavor by changing to whole wheat bread, as Cousin Karen suggested I do. Now it's a quick, easy family favorite.

As the pudding cools, juices from the pineapple will accumulate in the bottom of the dish. Just spoon some of the juices over each serving.

This pudding also works as an accompaniment for glazed ham or turkey at the holidays.

Serves 6

2 tablespoons unsalted butter, cut into 4 pieces

8 slices soft commercial whole wheat bread, crusts removed

2 cups Pineapple Sauce (page 258)

1 cup skim milk

¼ cup sugar

1 egg white

1 teaspoon vanilla extract

Place the butter in a glass meat loaf pan and microwave on HIGH, uncovered, for 1 minute to soften and melt (butter does not have to melt completely). Brush butter onto one side of each slice of bread and stack the bread. Spread any butter that remains evenly over the inside of the pan. Cut bread into 1-inch cubes and combine with the pineapple sauce in the buttered pan.

Combine the milk, sugar, egg, and vanilla and whisk until thoroughly blended. Pour it over the pineapple and bread mixture and microwave on HIGH, uncovered, for 9 minutes.

Although you can serve this hot from the oven, it is best allowed to cool and stiffen for 15 to 20 minutes. It can also be covered and refrigerated, then reheated to warm just before serving.

Variations

Ginger Pineapple Bread Pudding: Add ½ teaspoon ground ginger to the milk sugar mixture.

Pineapple Bread Pudding with Fruit Sauce: Serve with Raspberry Sauce (page 282), Blackberry Sauce (page 253), or Dark Sweet Cherry Sauce (page 256).

Pear Pudding: Follow the recipe for Fresh Pear Compote on page 279, cutting the pears into ¼-inch dice. Drain and substitute 2 cups pears for the pineapple.

Nutritional Information
(as a percentage of daily intake)

13% (265) calories	11% (272 mg) sodium
9% (6 g) fat	12% (92 mg) calcium
18% (50 g) carbohydrates	13% (2 mg) iron
9% (7 g) protein	

Pineapple Sauce

More highly textured than applesauce, this pineapple sauce is a sweetly tangy side dish for chicken, game, or pork. It is also a welcome midwinter breakfast fruit.

Serves 6

2 large ripe pineapples, peeled, cored, and cut into 2-inch chunks

In a food processor, in several batches, puree the pineapple. (There should be about 6 cups.) Transfer puree to a large bowl and microwave on HIGH, uncovered, for 45 minutes, stirring once midway through the cooking. Cover and refrigerate until needed.

Variation

Maple-Flavored Pineapple Sauce: Mix ¼ cup maple syrup into the cooked pineapple sauce before refrigerating.

Nutritional Information
(as a percentage of daily intake)

6% (127) calories

2% (1 g) fat

12% (32 g) carbohydrates

1% (1 g) protein

0% (3 mg) sodium

2% (18 mg) calcium

7% (1 mg) iron

ICE CREAMS, SORBETS, AND MOUSSES

Soft Kiwi Sorbet

No, you cannot make a sorbet in the microwave, however much some people want you to think you can do anything in a microwave. But you can use your oven to make the hot syrup for the meringue.

With its fuzzy, funny brown skin, its emerald flesh, its sweet flavor with a slight tartness in its finish, and its jet-black-speckled interior, the kiwi is one of the most beautiful of the exotic fruits.

This soft, creamy-textured, palest-of-greens green kiwifruit sorbet is flecked with the fruit's tiny tender black seeds.

Serves 10

2 egg whites
1 cup sugar
½ cup hottest possible tap
   water

3 pounds (about 18) kiwis, peeled and
   pureed in a food processor (4
   cups puree)
juice of ½ lime

Place the egg whites in the bowl of an electric mixer and set in place on the mixer.

In a bowl that will hold at least 8 cups, stir together the sugar and water. (An 8-cup glass measuring cup with a handle is extremely useful.) Microwave on HIGH, uncovered, for 3 minutes. Stir until all the sugar is dissolved, then cover and microwave on HIGH for 5 minutes.

After 4½ minutes of cooking, begin to beat the egg whites at medium speed. The egg whites need to be at a thin, fully frothed texture, almost soft peaks, when the hot syrup is added.

Using a pot holder, remove syrup from the oven. Be careful; the bowl will be very hot.

With the electric mixer beating, gradually pour the syrup into the egg whites in a very thin stream. Egg whites will become a glossy meringue.

Beat at medium-high speed until cooled to room temperature, 5 minutes or more. Add the kiwi puree and lime juice and beat on slowest speed until just blended, or fold gently together with a large rubber spatula.

Freeze in an ice cream maker according to the manufacturer's directions.

Variations

Pear Sorbet: Cook 5 large pears as directed for Fresh Pear Compote (page 279), extending the cooking time to 10 minutes. Puree pears to make 4 cups puree. Substitute for the kiwi puree.

Raspberry Sorbet: Substitute about 4 cups pureed fresh raspberries (from about 2½ pints) for the pureed kiwis and substitute the juice of 1 lemon for the lime juice.

Nutritional Information
(as a percentage of daily intake)

8% (162) calories

0% (0 g) fat

15% (40 g) carbohydrates

3% (2 g) protein

1% (13 mg) sodium

5% (36 mg) calcium

0% (0 mg) iron

During midsummer, small, lusciously sweet red and purple plums can be found in farmer's markets. Their juicy texture and delicate flavor make them an ideal candidate for flavoring a sorbet.

In this recipe the microwaved plums color the puree to make a pale purple-blue or cranberry red sorbet with an elegant, delicate plum flavor.

Because ripe sweet peaches and raspberries are at their prime at the same time as sweet plums, I often mix three peaches, cut into ½-inch dice and tossed with a squirt or two of lemon to prevent discoloring, with a cup or so of fresh raspberries and spoon those onto plates next to this plum sorbet. That extends the recipe to serve eight or nine.

Serves 6

2 pounds small, sweet plums, pitted **½ cup sugar**
1 egg white **¼ cup hottest possible tap water**

In a food processor, puree the plums until smooth. Transfer to a medium bowl, cover, and microwave on HIGH for 6 minutes. Stir and refrigerate until cold.

Place the egg white in the bowl of an electric mixer and set in place on the mixer.

In a bowl that will hold at least 8 cups, stir together the sugar and water. (An 8-cup glass measuring cup with a handle is extremely useful.) Microwave on HIGH, uncovered, for 3 minutes. Stir until all the sugar is dissolved, then cover and microwave on HIGH for 4 minutes.

About 1 minute before the sugar is finished microwaving, begin to beat the egg white at medium speed. The egg white needs to be at a thin, fully frothed texture, almost soft peaks, when the hot syrup is added.

Using a pot holder, remove syrup from the oven. Be careful, the bowl will be very hot.

With the electric mixer beating, gradually pour the syrup into the egg white in a very thin stream. The egg white will become a glossy meringue.

Beat at medium speed until cooled to room temperature, 5 minutes or more. Add the puree and beat on slowest speed until just blended, or fold gently together with a large rubber spatula.

Freeze in an ice cream maker according to the manufacturer's directions.

7% (147) calories

2% (1 g) fat

13% (36 g) carbohydrates

3% (2 g) protein

0% (8 mg) sodium

1% (6 mg) calcium

0% (0 mg) iron

A ripe midsummer cantaloupe, sweet and luscious but thin in texture, is combined here with a mango, which gives the overall flavor roundness, adds smoothness to the texture, and enhances the color. The ginger adds a subtle balance to the sweetness of this sorbet. Serve garnished with some sweet fresh blueberries.

Remove this sorbet from the freezer about 10 minutes before serving so the texture can soften and the fragrance of the melon can return.

Serves 8

3-pound ripe cantaloupe, peeled and seeded

1 large ripe mango, peeled and flesh cut off the seed

juice of 1 small lemon

1½-inch piece of fresh ginger, peeled

1 egg white

½ cup sugar

¼ cup hottest possible tap water

For Garnish
1 cup fresh blueberries

In a blender, puree the cantaloupe and mango with the lemon juice and ginger until smooth. Transfer to a medium bowl, cover, and refrigerate.

Place the egg white in the bowl of an electric mixer and set in place on the mixer.

In a bowl that will hold at least 8 cups, stir together the sugar and water. (An 8-cup glass measuring cup with a handle is extremely useful.) Microwave on HIGH, uncovered, for 3 minutes. Stir until all the sugar is dissolved, then cover and microwave on HIGH for 4 minutes.

About 1 minute before the sugar is finished microwaving, begin to beat the egg white at medium speed. The egg white needs to be at a thin, fully frothed texture, almost soft peaks, when the hot syrup is added.

Using a pot holder, remove syrup from the oven. Be careful, the bowl will be very hot.

With the electric mixer beating, gradually pour the syrup into the egg white in a very thin stream. The egg white will become a glossy meringue.

Beat at medium-high speed until cooled to room temperature, 5 minutes or more. Add the pureed cantaloupe mixture and beat on slowest speed until just blended, or fold together gently with a large rubber spatula.

Freeze in an ice cream maker according to the manufacturer's directions.

Nutritional Information
(as a percentage of daily intake)

2% (91) calories

0% (0 g) fat

9% (22 g) carbohydrates

0% (1 g) protein

0% (10 mg) sodium

2% (17 mg) calcium

0% (0 mg) iron

Rhubarb and Blackberry Ice Cream with Strawberry Sauce

This low-fat ice cream has all the rich creaminess of regular ice cream and two perfectly mated fruit flavors in just the right proportions. A friend says that this recipe alone is worth the price of the book, and I tend to agree with him.

If you are not familiar with fresh rhubarb, you may not have had a grandmother to warn you that the leaves are poisonous.

Serves 8

1 pound unsweetened individually quick-frozen blackberries

1 cup sugar

2 tablespoons dried grated orange peel *or* the grated zest of 1 orange

1 pound fresh rhubarb, ends trimmed, all leaves discarded, cut into ½-inch pieces

2 cups light sour cream

1 egg white

1 tablespoon sugar

Strawberry Sauce (recipe follows)

Mix berries, 1 cup sugar, and orange peel in a medium bowl. Cover and microwave on HIGH for 10 minutes. Strain into a large bowl, pressing gently on the blackberries to extract all the juice (but do not push the pulp through the strainer). Discard pulp. Place the rhubarb in the bowl with the blackberry syrup. Cover and microwave on HIGH for 6 minutes. Puree in a blender or food processor and refrigerate until cold.

When rhubarb is cold, mix well with the sour cream.

Beat the egg white in an electric mixer until frothy, add the tablespoon of sugar, and continue beating until a stiff, shiny meringue forms. Gently fold into the rhubarb puree and freeze in an electric ice cream maker according to the manufacturer's directions.

Serve the ice cream with the Strawberry Sauce on the side.

Nutritional Information
(as a percentage of daily intake)
per serving without the sauce

10% (195) calories   3% (70 mg) sodium
3% (2 g) fat   8% (60 mg) calcium
15% (40 g) carbohydrates   0% (0 mg) iron
4% (3 g) protein

Strawberry Sauce

This rich, deep red, glossy strawberry sauce has an intense strawberry flavor.

Serves 8

2 1-pound packages frozen sliced   **juice of ½ lemon**
sweetened strawberries

Place the strawberries in a medium bowl, cover, and microwave on HIGH for 10 minutes. Pour into a strainer and allow to drain. Press gently on the berries to extract the liquid, but not so hard that the pulp is pushed through the strainer.

Mix the lemon juice into the strawberry sauce. Refrigerate until cold.

Nutritional Information
(as a percentage of daily intake)
per 3-tablespoon serving

1% (26) calories   0% (2 mg) sodium
0% (0 g) fat   2% (12 mg) calcium
3% (7 g) carbohydrates   0% (0 mg) iron
0% (0 g) protein

Light Raspberry Ice Cream

With its lush raspberry flavor and thick, creamy texture, no one will ever know this is a low-fat ice cream. The raspberries are microwaved with the sugar to produce an intensely flavored raspberry essence, which is then mixed with light sour cream and milk to make the ice cream.

Serves 10

2 1-pound packages unsweetened individually quick-frozen raspberries
1½ cups sugar

1 quart light sour cream
½ cup skim milk
juice of 1 lemon

In a large bowl, combine the berries and sugar, cover, and microwave on HIGH for 12 minutes. Stir to dissolve the sugar. Strain, pressing lightly on the berries to extract all the juice, but not so hard that the berries push through the strainer. Cover the raspberry juice and refrigerate until cold.

Whisk together the chilled raspberry juice, sour cream, skim milk, and lemon juice until no specks of white remain. Transfer to an ice cream maker and freeze according to the manufacturer's directions.

Variations

Blackberry Ice Cream: Substitute blackberries for the raspberries.

Raspberry-Blackberry Ice Cream: Use ¾ pound raspberries and ¼ pound of blackberries (either or both fresh or frozen).

Nutritional Information
(as a percentage of daily intake)

13% (263) calories
5% (3 g) fat
19% (53 g) carbohydrates
5% (4 g) protein

4% (104 mg) sodium
4% (30 mg) calcium
7% (1 mg) iron

The simplicity of the ingredients and the need for a pure flavor in this recipe requires that only a fragrant, moist vanilla bean be used and that the brand of sour cream be the best and the vanilla extract the finest.

Serves 6

¾ cup sugar

1 5- to 6-inch-long plump, moist vanilla bean, split lengthwise and cut into ½-inch pieces

½ cup skim milk

2 cups light sour cream

1 teaspoon finest-quality vanilla extract

In a food processor, combine the sugar and vanilla bean and process until bean is almost pulverized and the sugar becomes a dirty brown color with only tiny particles of the bean remaining. Transfer to a large bowl, stir in the milk, cover, and microwave on HIGH for 5 minutes. Strain and refrigerate until cold.

Mix the cold vanilla milk with the sour cream and vanilla. Transfer to an ice cream maker and freeze according to the manufacturer's directions.

Nutritional Information
(as a percentage of daily intake)

9% (170) calories

5% (3 g) fat

11% (31 g) carbohydrates

4% (3 g) protein

4% (91 mg) sodium

3% (25 mg) calcium

0% (0 mg) iron

This elegant, smooth, pale-burgundy-colored mousse has a very creamy texture. It is one of my favorite late autumn desserts. Served with Strawberry Sauce, this is a spectacular dessert.

Serves 6

4 extra-large egg whites
¼ cup sugar
2 cups Cranberry Sauce (see variation; page 276) refrigerator-cold

1 recipe Strawberry Sauce (page 267)

With an electric mixer, beat the egg whites until they are very frothy and have about doubled in volume. Continue beating, gradually adding the sugar. Beat until a shiny meringue forms that holds a soft, droopy peak when the beater is lifted out of the meringue or just until the egg whites will no longer slip when the bowl is tilted.

Pour the cranberry sauce into the meringue and beat at the slowest speed of the mixer until just blended to an even color with no streaks of cranberry sauce visible. Do not overbeat.

Pour into an ice cream maker and freeze according to the manufacturer's directions. Serve with Strawberry Sauce passed separately.

Variations

Frozen Blackberry Mousse (serves 4): Use 3 extra-large egg whites, 3 tablespoons sugar, and 1 recipe Blackberry Sauce (page 253) to make the mousse. Serve without an accompanying sauce.

Frozen Raspberry Mousse with Strawberry Sauce (serves 4): Use 3 extra-large egg whites, 3 tablespoons sugar, and 1 recipe Raspberry Sauce (page 282) to make the mousse. Serve with Strawberry Sauce as directed.

Frozen Strawberry Mousse with Strawberry or Raspberry Sauce (serves 4): Use 3 extra-large egg whites, 3 tablespoons sugar, and 1 recipe Raspberry Sauce (page 282) to make the mousse. Serve with Strawberry Sauce as directed or with Raspberry Sauce (page 282).

Nutritional Information
(as a percentage of daily intake)
without the sauce

11% (226) calories
 0% (0 g) fat
20% (56 g) carbohydrates
 3% (2 g) protein

1% (35 mg) sodium
1% (8 mg) calcium
0% (0 mg) iron

These billowy mounds of lemon-flavored meringue are so light, they're almost like not having dessert at all. After a rich meal, this is the perfect dessert. When there just isn't room for another bite, a peak of lemon snow can be served.

This recipe needs to be prepared a day ahead.

Serves 6

1 envelope (2½ teaspoons) unflavored gelatin
¼ cup cold water
¾ cup sugar
1 cup hot tap water

juice of 3 large lemons
3 large egg whites
Blackberry Sauce (see variation; page
  253)

In a small bowl, sprinkle gelatin over cold water and set aside to soften.

In a medium bowl, mix the sugar and hot water and microwave on HIGH, uncovered, until just boiling, about 4 to 5 minutes. Stir to dissolve all the sugar.

Stir lemon juice into softened gelatin, then mix gelatin into sugar and water. Refrigerate, uncovered, until cold but not set, about 1½ hours.

In the bowl of an electric mixer, combine the cold lemon gelatin and the egg whites and beat until a stiff, shiny meringue forms. This could take as long as 20 to 25 minutes.

Scoop billowy heaps of the soft lemon snow into large deep serving bowls. Cover with plastic wrap and refrigerate overnight.

Serve with Blackberry Sauce, either spooned over the lemon snow, spooned around the lemon snow, or passed separately.

Variation

Lemon Snow with Cranberry Sauce: Substitute Cranberry Sauce (page 276) for the Blackberry Sauce.

Nutritional Information
(as a percentage of daily intake)
per serving without the sauce

6% (112) calories

0% (0 g) fat

9% (26 g) carbohydrates

4% (3 g) protein

1% (27 mg) sodium

0% (3 mg) calcium

0% (0 mg) iron

POACHED AND FRESH FRUITS

Pineapple and Raspberries with Strawberry Sauce

This classic—and instant—combination of sweet yet slightly acidic fruits is one of the best matches in the fruit kingdom. With the addition of Strawberry Sauce, this dessert becomes at once a family favorite and a fine clean finish after a long or rich company dinner.

Serves 6

1 ripe pineapple, peeled, cored, and cut into 1-inch chunks

½ pint fresh raspberries
1 recipe Strawberry Sauce (page 267)

Combine the pineapple and raspberries and pass the sauce separately.

Nutritional Information
(as a percentage of daily intake)
per serving without the sauce

4% (86) calories
2% (1 g) fat
8% (22 g) carbohydrates
1% (1 g) protein

0% (2 mg) sodium
2% (16 mg) calcium
7% (1 mg) iron

Strawberries and Lichees with Cranberry Sauce

If you have never eaten a lichee, you are in for a surprise. The milky color and moist interior of this sweet, mildly flavored fruit is a sensual delight. It is the single perfect complement to the strawberry, and this is one of my favorite summer desserts, particularly in midsummer, when rich, red, luscious strawberries are available at the same time as fresh lichees (which can be found in some gourmet markets or Asian groceries).

Serves 6

2 pints fresh strawberries, hulled, refrigerator-cold

1 pound fresh lichees, carefully shelled, halved, and seeded, *or* approximately 1 pound canned lichees, drained, refrigerator-cold

1 recipe Cranberry Sauce (recipe follows)

Arrange the strawberries and lichees on plates. Serve with Cranberry Sauce passed separately.

Nutritional Information
(as a percentage of daily intake)
per serving without the sauce

4% (72) calories
2% (1 g) fat
6% (17 g) carbohydrates
1% (1 g) protein

0% (1 mg) sodium
2% (14 mg) calcium
0% (0 mg) iron

This thin, shiny sauce is lightly sweetened and has a deep cranberry flavor.

Makes 1 cup

¾ pound fresh or frozen cranberries, picked over and any bruised berries discarded

½ cup water
¾ cup sugar
juice of ½ small lemon

In a large bowl, mix together the berries, water, and sugar. Cover and microwave on HIGH for 12 minutes. Strain, pressing hard on the berries to extract all the juice; discard the pulp. Mix the lemon juice into the cranberry juice. Refrigerate until cold.

Variation

For 2 Cups Cranberry Sauce: Double the ingredients; cover and microwave on HIGH for 18 minutes in a very large bowl. Strain and mix with the juice of 1 small lemon.

Nutritional Information
(as a percentage of daily intake)
per 3-tablespoon serving

7% (130) calories
0% (0 g) fat
12% (34 g) carbohydrates
0% (0 g) protein

0% (1 mg) sodium
0% (2 mg) calcium
0% (0 mg) iron

Here whole ripe strawberries are arranged on plates with an incredibly fresh-tasting, bright yellow chunky Pineapple Sauce. This is a simple, elegant combination of flavors and textures.

Serves 6

2 pints ripe fresh strawberries, hulled and cored   **1½ cups Pineapple Sauce (page 258)**

Decoratively arrange the berries and pineapple sauce on plates and serve.

Nutritional Information
(as a percentage of daily intake)

5% (106) calories

2% (1 g) fat

9% (26 g) carbohydrates

1% (1 g) protein

0% (3 mg) sodium

3% (25 mg) calcium

7% (1 mg) iron

The microwave is extraordinary at poaching fresh fruits.

This quick mousse tastes like a cross between a cheesecake and the French Valentine classic, *coeur à la crème*, only it is considerably lighter.

Serves 6

3 cups hottest possible tap water
1½ cups sugar
juice of 1 lemon
6 medium-size (2 pounds) freestone peaches, cut in half and pits removed

½ cup light ricotta cheese
¼ cup light cream cheese
3 tablespoons powdered sugar
grated zest of ½ lemon
½ teaspoon vanilla extract

In a very large bowl, stir together the water, sugar, and lemon juice. Microwave on HIGH, uncovered, for 10 minutes. Stir and add the peaches. Microwave on HIGH, uncovered, for 4 minutes. Cover and refrigerate until cool.

Combine the remaining ingredients in a food processor or electric mixer and blend thoroughly. Refrigerate until peaches are cooled.

With a slotted spoon, transfer 2 peach halves to each serving plate. Drop a tablespoon of the cheese mousse onto each half.

Variations

Poached Peaches with Almond Cheese Mousse: Substitute almond extract for the vanilla and eliminate the lemon zest.

Poached Peaches with Ginger: Poach the peaches as directed and serve cold, sprinkled with about ½ teaspoon per person very finely shredded crystallized ginger.

Nutritional Information
(as a percentage of daily intake)

6% (114) calories
6% (4 g) fat
7% (18 g) carbohydrates
4% (3 g) protein

2% (43 mg) sodium
8% (65 mg) calcium
0% (0 mg) iron

Fresh Pear Compote with Apple Juice Glaze

Here 4 pears become a tender, cooked compote in only 10 minutes. The flowery fragrance and naturally flecked texture of the pears are amplified by microwave cooking; they taste more intense than ever before.

This easy recipe makes a light, clean finish to a family meal. It can be dressed up a bit, if you have time, by serving it with the Apple Juice Glaze.

To tell when a pear is ripe, press two fingers gently at the stem end. When ripe, the pear will yield, or seem to withdraw, from the pads of your fingers. The same test can be used for a peach, pressing anywhere on that fruit.

This compote is also good for breakfast.

Serves 4

juice of 1½ limes
⅓ cup sugar
4 large (½ pound) ripe Comice or Anjou pears

1 recipe Apple Juice Glaze (recipe follows) (optional)

Combine the lime juice and sugar in a large bowl. Peel, core, and cut pears into ½- to ¾-inch dice, then toss with the lime juice and sugar. Cover and microwave on HIGH for 10 minutes. Drain, cover, and refrigerate until needed. To serve, drizzle a tablespoon or so of the Apple Juice Glaze over each portion.

Nutritional Information
(as a percentage of daily intake)
per serving without the glaze

7% (144) calories
2% (1 g) fat
13% (36 g) carbohydrates
1% (1 g) protein

0% (0 mg) sodium
3% (22 mg) calcium
0% (0 mg) iron

This thick glaze is a barely caramelized sauce made by reducing fresh apple cider in an open bowl until it becomes thick and deeply colored.

During the fall and early winter, when new, unfiltered, unpasteurized fresh apple cider is available, use it for this sauce to produce a dark caramel-apple-flavored glaze. At other times of the year, choose a dark brown, opaque apple juice, or, if that's not available, a translucent golden-colored apple juice.

Serves 4

1½ cups apple cider or apple juice (see note above)

Pour cider into a large glass bowl or measuring cup and microwave on HIGH, uncovered, until reduced to about ½ cup and a thick saucelike glaze is formed, about 20 minutes. Watch carefully during the last 5 minutes as sauce quickly caramelizes and burns if cooked too long.

This glaze should be served at room temperature, but it can be stored for a week or so, covered tightly, in the refrigerator.

Nutritional Information
(as a percentage of daily intake)
per 2-tablespoon serving

2% (42) calories	0% (6 mg) sodium
0% (0 g) fat	1% (5 mg) calcium
4% (10 g) carbohydrates	0% (0 mg) iron
0% (0 g) protein	

The large Comice pears of autumn are my favorites for this recipe, because they are big and easy to handle, but Anjous, which are slightly smaller, can be substituted. Anjous will cook in 7 minutes, not 8. Boscs have a buttery texture, and a richer fragrance and texture than Comice and Anjous. Boscs need only 6 minutes to cook.

Serves 4

4 large, firm pears (about 8 ounces each), with stems

½ lemon
Raspberry Sauce (page 282)

Cut a thin slice off the bottom of each pear so it will sit straight up when placed on a plate. Peel with a vegetable peeler, leaving the stem in place. Repeat with the remaining pears, rubbing each with the cut side of the lemon to prevent discoloration.

Arrange the pears in the corners of a large shallow square dish. Drape with plastic wrap, sealing under the dish but leaving the package loose and baggy on top. Microwave on HIGH for 8 minutes. Immediately uncover and refrigerate to cool.

Because the pears are tender, they will crush if the plastic film is allowed to shrink around the fruits.

Serve cold on plates surrounded by Raspberry Sauce or pass the sauce separately.

Variations

Pears with Blackberry Sauce: Serve with Blackberry Sauce (page 253) instead of Raspberry Sauce.

Pears with Dark Sweet Cherry Sauce: Serve with Dark Sweet Cherry Sauce (page 256) instead of Raspberry Sauce.

Nutritional Information
(as a percentage of daily intake)
per serving without the sauce

6% (120) calories
2% (1 g) fat
11% (30 g) carbohydrates
1% (1 g) protein

0% (0 mg) sodium
3% (22 mg) calcium
0% (0 mg) iron

This is a real sauce, not an uncooked raspberry puree, made thick with the pulpy flesh of crushed raspberries. The sauce shines, adding a formal finish and an intense raspberry flavor to desserts. I generally prefer frozen raspberries for this sauce, but a pint of very ripe fresh raspberries can be used.

Serves 8

1 pound unsweetened individually quick-frozen raspberries
⅓ cup sugar

2 teaspoons dried grated lemon peel or the grated peel of ½ orange

Combine the raspberries, sugar, and lemon peel in a large bowl. Seal airtight with plastic wrap and microwave on HIGH for 10 minutes. Carefully ladle into a strainer, allowing the clear sauce to drain. With the back of the ladle, very gently press on the raspberry pulp to extract all the liquid. Do not push hard enough to force the tender pulp to puree and fall through the strainer into the sauce. Discard the pulp and refrigerate until chilled.

Nutritional Information
(as a percentage of daily intake)
per 3-tablespoon serving

3% (51) calories
0% (0 g) fat
5% (13 g) carbohydrates
0% (0 g) protein

0% (0 mg) sodium
1% (8 mg) calcium
0% (0 mg) iron

Poached Apricots with Dark Sweet Cherry Sauce

Small pale orange fresh apricots poach beautifully in the microwave. Serve plain for a family dessert (or even for breakfast) or with the cherry sauce for a company meal.

Serves 4

3 cups hottest possible tap water
1 cup sugar
1 tablespoon vanilla extract
1 pound (8 to 10) small firm fresh apricots

1 recipe Dark Sweet Cherry Sauce (page 256)

In a very large bowl, stir together the water, sugar, and vanilla. Microwave on HIGH, uncovered, for 8 minutes. Carefully remove from the oven, add the apricots, and microwave on HIGH, uncovered, for 2 minutes. Transfer the apricots to a shallow dish just large enough to hold them in a single layer and add enough of the poaching liquid to cover and prevent discoloration. Cover and refrigerate until serving time.

Nutritional Information
(as a percentage of daily intake)
per serving without the sauce

4% (79) calories
0% (0 g) fat
7% (19 g) carbohydrates
3% (2 g) protein

0% (1 mg) sodium
2% (17 mg) calcium
7% (1 mg) iron

Strawberries and Poached Cherries with Blackberry Sauce

Poached cherries are firmer and more flavorful than raw cherries and offer a contrast in appearance and texture that brings out the sweetness and tenderness of the strawberries.

Serve with the sauce for a company meal or without the sauce for a quick family dessert. Or place the strawberries and cherries in a large plastic bag to transport to picnics or potluck dinners.

Serves 6

2 pints ripe fresh strawberries, cored (and cut in half if large)
1 recipe Poached Cherries (page 286)

1 recipe Blackberry Sauce (page 253)

Mix the berries and cherries and spoon a little of the Blackberry Sauce over each portion or pass sauce separately.

Nutritional Information
(as a percentage of daily intake)
per serving without the sauce

4% (76) calories
2% (1 g) fat
7% (18 g) carbohydrates
1% (1 g) protein

0% (1 mg) sodium
3% (20 mg) calcium
0% (0 mg) iron

Tender Orange Slices
in Orange Sauce

This simple dish of tender poached orange slices in orange sauce is full of crisp, clean flavors. Served cold from the refrigerator, it is one of the most refreshing of summer desserts.

Use large, sweet navel oranges, not juice oranges, for the best result.

Serves 6

1½ cups freshly squeezed orange juice
¼ cup sugar

6 large fresh navel oranges, peeled, sliced, and seeded

In a large bowl, stir together the orange juice and sugar. Add the orange slices and cover. Microwave on HIGH for 6 minutes. With a slotted spoon, transfer the orange slices to another bowl and set aside. Return the cooking juices to the oven and microwave on HIGH, uncovered, for 10 minutes to concentrate the flavors. Pour sauce over the orange slices, cover, and refrigerate until cold.

Nutritional Information
(as a percentage of daily intake)

7% (145) calories
0% (0 g) fat
13% (36 g) carbohydrates
3% (2 g) protein

0% (1 mg) sodium
10% (79 mg) calcium
0% (0 mg) iron

Poached Cherries

These tender poached sweet cherries are like traditional brandied cherries, but the rich complementary flavor of cranberry-raspberry juice is used to make the syrup rather than brandy.

Late spring to early summer is the best time to make this recipe, when dark sweet cherries are plentiful and very dark in color. The darker the color, the sweeter the cherry and the more easily it will pit.

Unfortunately, there are about 20 tedious minutes of work involved here pitting the cherries. A simple inexpensive cherry pitter can be purchased at many kitchen shops to facilitate the job. I suggest that you buy two pitters and invite a friend or have the kids do the job for you. You can also open a paper clip and bend it into an S-shape to pit the cherries.

Poached cherries can be covered tightly and stored in the refrigerator for up to 3 weeks.

Serves 8

1 quart cranberry-raspberry juice
½ cup sugar
juice of 1 lemon
1 tablespoon vanilla extract

2 pounds dark sweet cherries, stems removed, any bruised or damaged cherries discarded, washed thoroughly under cold running water, and pitted

Place the juice in a large glass measuring cup and microwave on HIGH, uncovered, until reduced to 2 cups, about 40 minutes. Stir in the sugar and microwave on HIGH for 2 minutes. Stir in the lemon juice and vanilla. Place the cherries in a large bowl, pour the flavored syrup over the cherries, cover, and microwave on HIGH for 5 minutes. Refrigerate until cold.

Nutritional Information
(as a percentage of daily intake)

5% (105) calories
2% (1 g) fat
9% (25 g) carbohydrates
1% (1 g) protein

0% (2 mg) sodium
2% (18 mg) calcium
0% (0 mg) iron

CAKES AND COBBLERS

Individual Cheesecakes with Pineapple Sauce

These light, individual cheesecakes, because they are cooked in a micro-wave, will not form a puffed top crust, but rather collapse slightly when cooled. Still, they are delicious and quick—only about 5 minutes of preparation and about 3 minutes of cooking—so I am willing to forgive the irregularities in their appearance. And the pineapple sauce, spooned on top of the cheesecakes, hides the blemishes.

If you don't have time to make the sauce, top each cheesecake with a few ripe fresh berries.

Serves 6

vegetable oil cooking spray
⅓ cup graham cracker crumbs,
    approximately, for dusting the
    muffin pan
1¼ cups light ricotta cheese

3 tablespoons sugar
3 tablespoons flour
⅛ teaspoon baking powder
¼ teaspoon vanilla extract
¾ cup Pineapple Sauce (page 258)

Lightly spray a microwave muffin pan (with 6 sections, each holding ⅓ cup) with cooking spray and place about a tablespoon of crumbs in each indenta-tion. Shake around so muffin pan is evenly coated with crumbs, then invert over the sink and rap to remove excess crumbs.

In a large bowl, combine the cheese, sugar, flour, baking powder, and vanilla. Mix very well. Scoop ¼ cup of the cheese mixture into each indentation. Wet your fingers and pat the top of each cheesecake flat.

Microwave on HIGH for 3 minutes and 10 seconds. Remove from the oven, cool for 10 minutes in the pan, then invert, rap, and the cheesecakes will fall out. Cool completely on a rack. Arrange on plates and spoon a heaping tablespoon of Pineapple Sauce onto each.

Nutritional Information
(as a percentage of daily intake)

8% (166) calories   4% (102 mg) sodium
8% (5 g) fat   19% (148 mg) calcium
9% (25 g) carbohydrates   7% (1 mg) iron
9% (7 g) protein

A Microwave-Convection Recipe

This is one of my favorite summer desserts. The combination of blackberries and peaches is one of the season's best. Use peaches that are firm but ripe, bright yellow in color, and full of fragrance. And don't peel them. The color added by the skins, as well as the fiber and nutrients, is an important part of this cobbler.

Serves 8

¾ cup flour
¼ cup sugar
¼ cup unsalted butter, cut into 4 pieces
1 large egg white
grated zest of ½ lemon

3 pounds ripe but firm yellow peaches
1 cup fresh or unsweetened individually quick-frozen blackberries
juice of 1 lemon
⅓ cup flour
⅔ cup sugar

Prepare the crust by combining the ¾ cup flour, the ¼ cup sugar, the butter, egg white, and lemon zest in a food processor and process just until a ball of dough forms on top of the blades. Do not overprocess. Dough will be soft. Remove and flatten into a circle (about ¼ inch thick) between 2 sheets of plastic wrap. Refrigerate while the filling is prepared.

To prepare the filling, wash the peaches and cut into ¾-inch dice, discarding the pits. In a large bowl, combine diced peaches with the blackberries, lemon juice, the ⅓ cup flour, and the ⅔ cup sugar. Toss well.

Transfer to a medium bowl that is just large enough to hold all the filling (2 quarts). Do not use a larger bowl.

Between 2 sheets of plastic wrap, roll out the dough so it is just slightly larger than the top of the bowl. Carefully lift the top sheet of plastic wrap off the dough; then, holding the other piece of plastic wrap, invert the dough over the bowl and press gently around the edge to secure in place. Small cracks in the dough are normal. Make a hole in the center of the crust plus 4 decorative cuts to allow the steam to vent.

Place in a microwave-convection oven and set to cook at 450 degrees for 30 minutes on the microwave-convection setting. Crust will be lightly browned and cobbler ready to eat, but it is best if allowed to cool to room temperature before serving.

Variation

White Peach Cobbler: Substitute juicy ripe white peaches for the yellow peaches and increase the flour that is mixed with the peaches to ½ cup.

Nutritional Information
(as a percentage of daily intake)

12% (247) calories

9% (6 g) fat

18% (49 g) carbohydrates

4% (3 g) protein

0% (7 mg) sodium

2% (18 mg) calcium

7% (1 mg) iron

MAKING COBBLERS IN THE MICROWAVE-CONVECTION OVEN

The difference between a pie and a cobbler is not so much in the recipe, but in the serving. Pies are served in wedges; cobblers are served in bowls. And indeed, these fruit cobblers should be served in bowls.

Because I adore the flavor of a butter crust, I am unwilling to make any of those alternative-fat toppings or crusts. Instead I make a real butter crust, but very little of it in proportion to the amount of filling. Then each serving of one of these cobblers gets a cup of cooked fruit filling and just over a teaspoon of butter (in the crust). Changing the proportion and the balance of what we eat, not necessarily the ingredients, allows us to eat foods like butter in a balanced diet with no remorse.

Cooking the Cobblers:

Note that these are microwave-convection recipes. They require a microwave-convection oven, not a regular microwave. Convection heat is necessary to brown and cook a crust properly. And with the addition of microwave heat, the cobbler cooks in less than half an hour—less than half the time it would take ordinarily. The fruit flavors are more intense, the fruit textures firm and tender, not mushy as with ordinary oven cooking.

If you do not have a microwave-convection oven, you could bake these cobblers in a traditional oven at 375 degrees until done, about 1 hour.

About the Crust:

This is not a traditional flaky American pastry, but rather a simple butter cookie dough. The cookie dough is easier to make, easier to roll out, and tastes rich and buttery. If you prefer a flaky crust, just use the ingredients in the list and prepare as you would your favorite flaky pastry. Also, when cooked the crust will brown most around the edge of the dish and will conform to the shape of the fruit, developing a homey appearance.

A Microwave-Convection Recipe

Firm, tart apples are accented by tender, tiny whole cranberries in this cobbler, and the crust is flavored with almond extract. The three flavors together make an unexpected apple cobbler with a bold, assertive personality. No cinnamon or traditional apple pie spices to complicate the flavors—just pure, lightly sweetened apples and cranberries.

In autumn and early winter, fresh cranberries and the best apples are available for this cobbler, but the rest of the year, use frozen cranberries (it is almost impossible to taste the difference) or, in summer, substitute either blackberries or raspberries (again, either fresh or frozen).

Serves 8

¾ cup flour	3 pounds firm, tart cooking apples
¼ cup sugar	1 cup fresh or unsweetened individ-
¼ cup unsalted butter, cut into 4	ually quick-frozen cranberries
pieces	juice of 1 lemon
1 large egg white	⅓ cup flour
⅛ teaspoon vanilla extract	¾ cup sugar
¼ teaspoon almond extract	

Prepare the crust by combining the ¾ cup flour, the ¼ cup sugar, the butter, egg white, and vanilla and almond extracts in a food processor and process just until a ball of dough forms on top of the blades. Do not overprocess. Dough will be soft. Remove and flatten into a circle (about ¼ inch thick) between 2 sheets of plastic wrap. Refrigerate while the filling is prepared.

To prepare the filling, peel, core, and cut the apples into ½-inch dice. In a large bowl, combine diced apples with the cranberries, lemon juice, the ⅓ cup flour, and the ¾ cup sugar. Toss well.

Transfer to a medium bowl that is just large enough to hold all the filling (2 quarts).

Between 2 sheets of plastic wrap, roll out the dough so it is just slightly larger than the top of the bowl. Carefully lift the top sheet of plastic wrap off the dough; then, holding the other piece of plastic wrap, invert the dough over the bowl and press around the edge to secure in place. Make a hole in the center of the crust plus 4 decorative cuts to allow the steam to vent.

Place in a microwave-convection oven and set to cook at 450 degrees for 30 minutes on the microwave-convection setting. Remove from the oven and cool before serving.

Nutritional Information
(as a percentage of daily intake)

15% (304) calories
9% (6 g) fat
23% (62 g) carbohydrates
3% (2 g) protein

0% (9 mg) sodium
2% (18 mg) calcium
7% (1 mg) iron

A Microwave-Convection Recipe

Luscious, fragrant Comice pears make this ginger-flavored cobbler a fine and unexpected change from cold-weather apple pies and cobblers. Comice pears give this chunky cobbler the richest fragrance and best texture. The crust has been left unflavored, except for its butteriness, which adds to the sense of richness in the pears.

Serves 8

¾ cup flour
¼ cup sugar
¼ cup unsalted butter, cut into 4 pieces
1 large egg white
3 pounds ripe but firm Comice pears

2 tablespoons chopped tender pieces of crystallized ginger or preserved ginger
juice of 1 lemon
⅓ cup flour
¾ cup sugar

Prepare the crust by combining the ¾ cup flour, the ¼ cup sugar, the butter, and egg white in a food processor and process just until a ball of dough forms on top of the blades. Do not overprocess. Dough will be soft. Remove and flatten into a circle (about ¼ inch thick) between 2 sheets of plastic wrap. Refrigerate while the filling is prepared.

To prepare the filling, peel, core, and cut the pears into ¾-inch dice. In a large bowl, combine diced pears, ginger, lemon juice, the ⅓ cup flour, and the ¾ cup sugar. Toss well.

Transfer to a medium bowl that is just large enough to hold all the filling (2 quarts).

Between 2 sheets of plastic wrap, roll out the dough so it is just slightly larger than the top of the bowl. Carefully lift the top sheet of plastic wrap off the dough; then, holding the other piece of plastic wrap, invert the dough over the bowl and press around the edge to secure in place. Make 4 decorative cuts in the crust to vent the steam.

Place in a microwave-convection oven and set to cook at 450 degrees for 30 minutes on the microwave-convection setting. Remove from the oven and cool before serving.

Nutritional Information
(as a percentage of daily intake)

19% (379) calories
9% (6 g) fat
29% (81 g) carbohydrates
4% (3 g) protein

0% (7 mg) sodium
3% (25 mg) calcium
7% (1 mg) iron

Rhubarb and Hidden
Strawberry Cobbler

Here tender chunks of rhubarb are cooked in an intensely flavored strawberry sauce, leaving the cobbler with a rhubarb texture and the flavor and scent of strawberries, but without the mushy texture of baked strawberries.

Serves 8

¾ cup flour
¼ cup sugar
¼ cup unsalted butter, cut into 4 pieces
1 large egg white
1 pound unsweetened individually quick-frozen whole strawberries

1½ cups sugar
½ cup flour
3 pounds rhubarb, ends trimmed, all leaves discarded (the leaves are toxic), cut into ½-inch slices

Prepare the crust by combining the ¾ cup flour, the ¼ cup sugar, the butter, and egg white in a food processor and process just until a ball of dough forms on top of the blades. Do not overprocess. Dough will be soft. Remove and flatten into a circle (about ¼ inch thick) between 2 sheets of plastic wrap. Refrigerate while the filling is prepared.

Combine the strawberries and 1½ cups sugar in a medium bowl, cover, and microwave on HIGH for 10 minutes. Stir to dissolve all the sugar, then strain juices into a blender jar, discarding the pulp. Add the ½ cup flour and blend until smooth. Pour back into the medium bowl and microwave on HIGH, uncovered, until bubbly, about 5 minutes. Add the rhubarb and mix well with a large spoon.

Between 2 sheets of plastic wrap, roll out the dough so it is just slightly larger than the top of the bowl. Carefully lift the top sheet of plastic wrap off the dough; then, holding the other piece of plastic wrap, invert the dough over the bowl and press around the edge to secure in place. Make a hole in the center of the crust to vent the steam.

Place in a microwave-convection oven and set to cook at 500 degrees for 26 minutes on the microwave-convection setting. Remove from the oven and cool before serving. Scoop deeply into the dish when serving as some of the sweet strawberry juices settle to the bottom.

Nutritional Information
(as a percentage of daily intake)

17% (335) calories
9% (6 g) fat
25% (68 g) carbohydrates
5% (4 g) protein

1% (17 mg) sodium
21% (169 mg) calcium
7% (1 mg) iron

Jams, Jellies, and Other Condiments

The luxury of long days spent in the kitchen canning and preserving are gone forever. But thanks to the microwave, even without those long days in the kitchen you can still have great preserves.

There is no better way, no easier way, to make jellies, jams, preserves, fruit butters, relishes, and chutneys than with the microwave. The microwave makes canning simple, easy, and foolproof. Within an hour, and with just one bowl to clean up, you can have a batch of the best preserves you've ever made. If you are a first-time preserver, there are no complicated techniques to learn, and no special equipment is needed.

Best of all, the flavor of microwaved preserves is fuller, fresher, and more intense than with ordinary preserving.

It's so simple, in fact, that you will find yourself preserving year-round, not just in the summer. In autumn I make applesauce, in spring I make strawberry preserves, in winter I make dried fruit jams such as Winter Apricot Jam, and for the holidays I make relishes and compotes, such as the Holiday Three-Berry and Beet Compote. And in summer I make all kinds and combinations of fresh berry jams, jellies, and preserves.

The microwave makes applesauce with a pure flavor and natural apple texture, even after the long cooking.

This recipe calls for sweet apples such as Gala or Delicious, and so no sugar is added. Use yellow or red apples. Yellow apples will produce a golden-colored sauce, red a pink applesauce. If you have tart apples, such as pippins or greenings, sweeten after pureeing with ¼ cup to ¾ cup of sugar and microwave on HIGH for 5 minutes, uncovered; then stir and store.

I prefer plain applesauce—just the pure apple flavor, no spices, and especially no horseradish. For those who prefer a spiced, scented applesauce, the variation below is provided. Horseradish can be added at your own risk.

Serves 14

12 large sweet apples, quartered   **juice of 1 lemon**

Place the apples in a very large bowl, cover, and microwave on HIGH for 35 minutes.

Push through a strainer or food mill, discarding the skins, cores, seeds, and stems. There may be a few pieces of not quite tender apple; puree them too. If sauce seems thin, microwave on HIGH, uncovered, for 5 to 10 minutes to thicken.

Stir in the lemon juice. Cover and refrigerate for up to 3 weeks or freeze for up to 3 months.

Variations

Spiced Applesauce: Mix 2 teaspoons ground cinnamon, 1 teaspoon ground ginger, ¼ teaspoon ground nutmeg, and ⅛ teaspoon ground cloves into the recipe just after the apples are pureed. Microwave on HIGH, uncovered, for 1 minute to blend the flavors, unless a final cooking is indicated.

Pear Sauce: Substitute large sweet Comice pears for the apples.

Nutritional Information
(as a percentage of daily intake)
per ½-cup serving

6% (119) calories	0% (0 g) protein	2% (15 mg) calcium
2% (1 g) fat	0% (0 mg) sodium	0% (0 mg) iron
11% (31 g) carbohydrates		

My friend and colleague Arlene Wanderman suggested the idea for this almost instant, seemingly effortless, very-fresh-tasting applesauce. The apples are cored, pureed, and then cooked—with their skins. Since it takes less than 5 minutes to prepare and only 10 minutes to cook, you can have fresh applesauce any time you need it.

Thin-skinned yellow apples, such as Washington State Golden Delicious or the tender, sweet, highly perfumed varieties of New York State, are best for this recipe. When hot, the texture of this applesauce is identical to regular applesauce, but when cold, the bits of skin can be felt on the tongue, so I prefer not to use red apples, whose thicker skins are sometimes a little bitter.

Serves 6

juice of ½ lemon

3 sweet yellow apples (see note above), cored and cut into roughly 1-inch chunks

Squeeze the lemon juice into the bowl of a food processor. Turn on the food processor and drop the apples, a few pieces at a time, through the feed tube. Puree very finely, almost to a sauce, letting the machine process for 2 or 3 minutes.

Transfer to a large bowl, cover, and microwave on HIGH for 10 minutes. Stir and serve or stir, cover, and refrigerate until needed.

Variation

10-Minute Pear Sauce: Substitute medium-large pears (Anjou pears, with their thin skins, are best) for the apples.

Nutritional Information
(as a percentage of daily intake)
per ½-cup serving

2% (43) calories	0% (0 mg) sodium
0% (0 g) fat	1% (5 mg) calcium
4% (11 g) carbohydrates	0% (0 mg) iron
0% (0 g) protein	

Traditional apple butter darkens as it thickens during cooking. That is not the case with microwave apple butter, which would be blond, not caramel, in color, were it not for the addition of the spices.

Most country or homemade apple butters are too heavily spiced, hiding the flavor of the apple under a cinnamon and spice mask. This apple butter is only lightly spiced, so the full flavor of the apples is emphasized, not diminished.

Makes about 3 cups

1 recipe Applesauce (page 301)
2 teaspoons ground cinnamon
1 teaspoon ground ginger
½ teaspoon ground coriander

½ teaspoon ground cardamom
¼ teaspoon freshly grated nutmeg
¼ teaspoon ground allspice

Mix applesauce with spices. Place in a shallow rectangular dish and microwave on HIGH, uncovered, so it reduces, for 40 minutes. Stir every 10 minutes to prevent a crust from forming on the edges of the dish and to ensure even cooking.

Variation

Pear Butter: Substitute Pear Sauce from the variation with the Applesauce recipe.

Nutritional Information
(as a percentage of daily intake)
per 2-tablespoon serving

3% (59) calories
0% (0 g) fat
6% (16 g) carbohydrates
0% (0 g) protein

0% (0 mg) sodium
1% (7 mg) calcium
0% (0 mg) iron

This is a ripe-apricot-flavored jam strengthened by the taste of the orange juice and sweetened by the raisins. It is thick but spreads easily. The variations for Winter Peach Jam and Prune Butter, which are made in the same way as the apricot jam, are not to be missed.

Makes about 3 cups

¾ **pound dried apricots**
½ **cup golden raisins**
2 **cups orange juice**

¾ **cup sugar**
½ **teaspoon ground cinnamon**
¼ **teaspoon ground ginger**

Combine apricots, raisins, and orange juice in a medium bowl. Seal airtight with plastic wrap and microwave on HIGH for 12 minutes. Carefully uncover and puree in a food processor. Add the sugar, cinnamon, and ginger and process until well blended. Refrigerate or freeze until needed.

Variations

Winter Peach Jam: Substitute dried peaches for the apricots and apple juice for the orange juice.

Prune Butter: Substitute pitted prunes for the apricots, apple juice for the orange juice, and eliminate the raisins and spices.

Nutritional Information
(as a percentage of daily intake)
per 2-tablespoon serving

3% (64) calories
0% (0 g) fat
6% (16 g) carbohydrates
0% (0 g) protein

0% (0 mg) sodium
1% (8 mg) calcium
0% (0 mg) iron

This is a classic cranberry relish in texture and appearance, but with the added flavor of raspberries. It is perfect for holiday meals or just to have on hand at other times to spread on morning toast or to moisten and flavor sandwiches.

You can use both fresh cranberries and fresh raspberries, or both berries can be frozen, or one can be fresh and the other frozen. It makes no difference to the taste and texture of the relish.

Makes 2 cups

¾ **pound fresh or unsweetened individually quick-frozen cranberries, picked over**

10 to 12 ounces unsweetened individually quick-frozen raspberries *or* 1 pint fresh raspberries, picked over

1 cup sugar

juice of ½ lemon

Combine the cranberries, raspberries, and sugar in a large bowl and cover. Microwave on HIGH for 10 minutes. Stir and return to the oven uncovered. Microwave on HIGH until a thick relish forms, about 15 minutes. Stir in the lemon juice and refrigerate until needed.

Nutritional Information
(as a percentage of daily intake)
per 2-tablespoon serving

4% (76) calories
0% (0 g) fat
7% (20 g) carbohydrates
0% (0 g) protein

0% (0 mg) sodium
1% (5 mg) calcium
0% (0 mg) iron

Holiday Three-Berry and Beet Compote

This sweet, fresh-tasting compote, with its deep purple color and subtle vegetable flavors, uses frozen berries rather than fresh, so it can be made all winter. The beets add a deep purple color and a smoothness to the texture.

Serve with turkey or ham for Thanksgiving or Christmas. Serve with chicken, game (everything from quail to boar and venison), or pork to make nonholiday dinners a special event.

Makes 2 cups

1 medium-size red onion, peeled and quartered

1 medium-size beet, peeled and quartered

2-inch piece of fresh ginger, peeled and halved

2 large garlic cloves, peeled

juice of 1 large orange

⅓ cup sugar

2 cups (about ¾ pound) unsweetened individually quick-frozen raspberries

1 cup (about 6 ounces) unsweetened individually quick-frozen blackberries

1 cup (about 6 ounces) unsweetened individually quick-frozen blueberries

grated zest of 1 large lemon

freshly ground black pepper to taste

In a food processor, finely chop the onion, beet, ginger, and garlic. Transfer to a large bowl and stir in the orange juice, sugar, and berries. Cover and microwave on HIGH for 10 minutes. Uncover and microwave on HIGH until virtually all the liquid has evaporated and a thick compote has formed, about 30 minutes, stirring after 20 minutes of cooking and again after 25 minutes to prevent scorching.

Stir in the lemon zest and season very lightly with pepper. Cover and store in the refrigerator.

Variations

A *Slightly Fruitier Holiday Compote:* Substitute unsweetened individually quick-frozen dark sweet cherries for the raspberries for a fruitier flavor. Do not season with pepper.

Nutritional Information
(as a percentage of daily intake)
per 2-tablespoon serving

3% (67) calories   0% (2 mg) sodium
0% (0 g) fat   2% (13 mg) calcium
6% (17 g) carbohydrates 0% (0 mg) iron
0% (0 g) protein

FRESH BERRY PRESERVES

In about an hour you can have 3 or 4 cups of fresh berry preserves with almost no effort beyond cleaning the berries. And the taste will be fresher and more intense than with traditional preserving methods.

You may want to make fresh berry preserves several times during the summer months, when berries are at their prime. For the best preserves, of course, use the best, freshest berries. Vine-ripened berries, with lush sweet flavors and aromas, are available in farmer's markets throughout the country.

Instead, I recommend that you refrigerate some of the preserves for current use and freeze the rest until needed. Refrigerate for up to 1 month or freeze for up to 4 months. If you're a traditionalist and prefer the time-consuming method of canning preserves using sterile jars and a water bath, you can do so with any of the preserves, jam, or jelly recipes that follow.

In the recipes here the amount of sugar has been reduced dramatically from traditional proportions (half sugar and half berries). But the preserves will still taste sweet if you use vine-ripened rather than commercial berries. Each of the recipes adds lemon juice at the end of the cooking to give a fresh edge to the preserves.

Testing Berry Preserves for Doneness:

The recommended cooking time for the berries will produce a thick but not hard preserve. Test the preserves toward the end of the cooking time by placing a little on a teaspoon and setting the spoon in the freezer, uncovered, for 5 minutes to chill. Look at the texture and taste the cold preserves. If you want a thicker preserve, return the bowl to the microwave, uncovered, and cook for another 5 minutes; then retest.

Strawberry Preserves

In about an hour you can have these thick, intensely flavored preserves, with little more effort than it takes to clean the berries and divide the preserves into jars! The flavor will be fresher than you have ever tasted in a strawberry preserve.

Makes 3 cups

**2 quarts ripe, juicy dark sweet straw-
  berries, hulled**

**1 cup sugar
juice of 1 lemon**

In a very large bowl, mix the strawberries and sugar. Cover and microwave on HIGH for 20 minutes. Uncover and microwave on HIGH for 25 minutes.

Preserves will be very thick and bubbly. Test for doneness (see note on page 307).

When preserves are ready, stir in the lemon juice and carefully ladle the preserves into containers that can be sealed airtight. Refrigerate some for current use and freeze the rest.

Variations

Strawberry Jelly (makes about 1½ cups): Proceed as directed, but strain the preserves before bottling, pressing on the berries to extract all the jelly.

Strawberry Jam (makes about 2 cups): Proceed as directed in the recipe above. After adding the lemon juice, force the preserves through a strainer to remove the seeds.

For 4 Cups Strawberry Preserves: Use 3 quarts strawberries, 3 cups sugar, and the juice of 1½ lemons. Extend the final, uncovered cooking time to 40 minutes.

*Nutritional Information
(as a percentage of daily intake)
per 2-tablespoon serving*

2% (47) calories

0% (1 mg) sodium

0% (0 g) fat

1% (7 mg) calcium

4% (12 g) carbohydrates

0% (0 mg) iron

0% (0 g) protein

This dark purple-blue preserve of tiny cooked blueberries is alive with bright blueberry flavor.

Makes 3 cups

2 quarts fresh blueberries, picked over   **juice of 1½ lemons**
1 cup sugar

In a very large bowl, mix the blueberries and sugar. Cover and microwave on HIGH for 15 minutes. Uncover and microwave on HIGH for 35 minutes.

Preserves will be very thick and bubbly. Test for doneness (see note on page 307).

When preserves are ready, stir in the lemon juice and carefully ladle the preserves into containers that can be sealed. Refrigerate some for current use and freeze the rest.

Nutritional Information
(as a percentage of daily intake)
per 2-tablespoon serving

3% (59) calories

0% (0 g) fat

5% (15 g) carbohydrates

0% (0 g) protein

0% (3 mg) sodium

0% (3 mg) calcium

0% (0 mg) iron

Raspberry Preserves

My favorite berry is used to make these thick, luscious preserves, with no chance of burning or scorching as with traditional preserve making.

Makes 3 cups

2 quarts fresh raspberries, picked over   **juice of 1 lemon**
1½ cups sugar

In a very large bowl, mix the raspberries and sugar. Cover and microwave on HIGH for 20 minutes. Uncover and microwave on HIGH for 20 minutes.

Preserves will be very thick and bubbly. Test for doneness (see note on page 307).

When preserves are ready, stir in the lemon juice and carefully ladle the preserves into containers that can be sealed airtight. Refrigerate some for current use and freeze the rest.

Variations

Raspberry Jelly (makes about 1½ cups): Proceed as directed, but strain the preserves before bottling, pressing on the berries to extract all the jelly.

Raspberry Jam (makes about 2 cups): Proceed as directed. After adding the lemon juice, force the preserves through a strainer to remove the seeds.

Nutritional Information
(as a percentage of daily intake)
per 2-tablespoon serving

3% (52) calories   0% (0 mg) sodium
0% (0 g) fat   1% (9 mg) calcium
5% (13 g) carbohydrates   0% (0 mg) iron
0% (0 g) protein

A thick preserve with a depth of flavor unrivaled in the world of preserves. Blackberries have more character as a preserve than strawberries, raspberries, or blueberries.

Makes 3 cups

2 quarts fresh blackberries, picked over

1½ cups sugar
juice of 1 lemon

In a very large bowl, mix the blackberries and sugar. Cover and microwave on HIGH for 20 minutes. Carefully uncover and return to the oven. Microwave on HIGH for 25 minutes.

Preserves will be very thick and bubbly. Test for doneness (see note on page 307).

When preserves are ready, stir in the lemon juice and carefully ladle the preserves into containers that can be sealed airtight. Refrigerate some for current use and freeze the rest.

Variation

Blackberry Jelly (makes about 1½ cups): Proceed as directed, but strain the preserves before bottling, pressing on the berries to extract all the jelly.

Nutritional Information
(as a percentage of daily intake)
per 2-tablespoon serving

4% (73) calories
0% (0 g) fat
7% (19 g) carbohydrates
0% (0 g) protein

0% (0 mg) sodium
2% (15 mg) calcium
0% (0 mg) iron

Small black raspberries, with cherry and burgundy wine aromas and a deep, sweet raspberry flavor, make my favorite summer preserve. Because black raspberries have less water than red raspberries, the preserves are denser.

Makes about 4 cups

**2 quarts fresh black raspberries,   ½ cup sugar
  picked over**

In a very large bowl, mix the black raspberries and sugar. Cover and microwave on HIGH for 15 minutes. Carefully uncover, stir, and return to the oven. Microwave on HIGH for 20 minutes.

Preserves will be very thick and bubbly. Test for doneness (see note on page 307).

When preserves are ready, carefully ladle into containers that can be sealed airtight. Refrigerate some for current use and freeze the rest.

*Nutritional Information
(as a percentage of daily intake)
per 2-tablespoon serving*

3% (68) calories   0% (0 mg) sodium
0% (0 g) fat   1% (9 mg) calcium
6% (16 g) carbohydrates   0% (0 mg) iron
0% (0 g) protein

Tiny tart cherries are preserved whole in this recipe, with a very light coating of cherry jelly around them. This is not an easily spreadable jam, but rather a homey, chunky breakfast preserve.

The cherries will take about 45 minutes to pit, if you are working alone, about an hour if you ask a preschooler to help you.

Makes about 3 cups

2 quarts fresh sour cherries, pitted   **1½ cups sugar**

In a very large bowl, combine the cherries and sugar. Cover and microwave on HIGH for 10 minutes. Stir and microwave on HIGH, uncovered, for 45 minutes.

Cherries will have shrunk and become preserved, and there will be some clear cherry liquid bubbling in the bowl. Test for doneness (see note on page 307).

When preserves are ready, carefully ladle into containers that can be sealed airtight. Refrigerate some for current use and freeze the rest.

Nutritional Information
(as a percentage of daily intake)
per 2-tablespoon serving

4% (72) calories   0% (0 mg) sodium
0% (0 g) fat   1% (7 mg) calcium
7% (18 g) carbohydrates   0% (0 mg) iron
0% (0 g) protein

Notes on Microwave Cooking and Cookware

It Doesn't Matter How a Microwave Works

Most people have never considered how a traditional electric oven works. A traditional electric oven converts electricity into heat through the use of a resistance coil, and the dry heat cooks the food by direct and indirect molecular conduction. But you don't need to know how an electric oven works in order to cook in it.

A microwave oven converts electricity into radio waves (microwaves) through the use of a magnetron tube, and the microwaves heat the food by increasing the molecular energy in the food. And you don't need to know how a microwave oven works in order to cook in it.

There are, however, two simple techniques you will need for microwave cooking, and a word needs to be said about the debate over how to properly cover a dish or bowl.

Basic Techniques

The two basic microwave skills used in this book that are essential to good cooking in the microwave are sealing dishes airtight, when necessary, and arranging food to maximize microwave heating. Both are simple to learn and will become second nature to you in a short time. Sealing is explained in the introduction to the soup chapter, where it is used extensively, and arranging food, with the meatiest parts around the outside of the dish or with the food arranged in a circle or as spokes of a wheel, is explained in the directions to recipes where it is used.

Covering a Dish or Bowl: Debates have raged over which is the best of the three ways to cover a bowl or dish for microwave cooking. Is it best to seal the dish airtight with plastic wrap; or to cover it with plastic wrap, a corner of which is left open to produce a vent for the steam; or to cover the dish tightly with a lid, cover, or plate? In some cases, such as making soups, it is essential to seal airtight with plastic wrap; otherwise, the answer, quite simply, is that it doesn't matter. Use whichever technique you find easiest. All three techniques produce the same quality of cooking in the same time. All three produce steam, so be careful when uncovering the dish or bowl; be especially careful with an airtight seal.

Adjusting Quantities and Cooking Times

Until you are an experienced microwave cook, it is best not to try adjusting the quantities in a microwave recipe, for the rules by which we adjust recipes by quantity and cooking time are complex.

Look at the general rules of thumb for adjusting the quantities and cooking times in conventional cooking. When vegetables, fruits, fish, and meats are poached, steamed, boiled, or stewed, the cooking times remain basically the same even when recipes are halved or doubled. In sautéing, broiling, and grilling, the timing remains the same as long as the food is not increased in thickness. With soups, doubling or halving the recipes generally does not change the cooking time.

General rules of thumb for microwave cooking are that you add 50 percent more time when you double the quantity and that you reduce the cooking time by a third when you halve a recipe when cooking vegetables, fruits, fish, meats, and many cereals and grains. With the soup recipes in this book, however, doubling the quantities is more than the microwave can handle, and halving the recipes will reduce the cooking times only slightly. With dry beans, lentils, and split peas, doubling or halving the recipes does not change the cooking times or changes them only slightly.

Just as the experienced cook understands how to adjust recipes in conventional cooking, experience with the microwave will teach you how to adjust quantities and cooking times, and bowl sizes when necessary, when cooking in this dynamic appliance.

Power Ratings

You don't have to worry about power ratings anymore. Virtually all full-size microwave ovens now have ratings between 600 and 750 watts, and the recipes in this book will cook properly in any of them. The recipes in this book were not meant to be cooked in small ovens.

If you have an older microwave, or if the timing seems in error when you try a recipe from this book, do check to see that your oven is power-rated in the 600- to 750-watt range. If not, you may have to extend the cooking times. An oven with a 500-watt rating will need about a third to half more cooking time than indicated in the recipes.

Power Settings

None of the recipes in this book are dependent on any of the barrage of special features, like probes and sensors, that have been added to microwave ovens in recent years. The recipes do, however, use three power settings: HIGH; MEDIUM; and DEFROST. Consult the manufacturer's directions to set your oven to those powers.

You and Your Timer

Because digital timers are used on microwave ovens, the recipes give exact cooking times. Sometimes, however, you may want to remove a dish from the oven early to check for doneness, as you would in a conventional oven, or just because you have stood in front of the oven watching the digital readout countdown for 20 seconds and by the time it reaches 10 or 8 you are so frustrated you open the door and pull out the food. So be it. A few seconds lost won't matter for the recipes in this book.

Preparing More Than One Recipe from This Book

To prepare two recipes from this book for a single meal, cook the recipes sequentially just before serving, then reheat the first on HIGH for about 1 to 3 minutes when the second, which will stay hot if left covered, comes out of the oven. If you're preparing three or more recipes, perhaps for a holiday meal, replace any plastic wrap used to cover the dishes with aluminum foil and reheat in a conventional oven.

Microwave Cookware

Most of the cookware needed for microwave cooking already exists in a well-equipped kitchen, and the few pieces of cookware that are missing are reasonably priced and readily available in supermarkets, hardware stores, restaurant supply houses, and gourmet cookware shops.

Throughout this book I have used the simple descriptive words *small, medium, large,* and *very large* to describe bowls and dishes. I have chosen to do this to take some of the pseudo-scientific jargon and unnecessary persnickitiness out of the recipes. I have also chosen not to use the word *microwave-safe* in the recipes. I believe it is reasonable to assume that the cook knows not to use an unsafe piece of cookware, a plastic dish in a conventional oven or a metal dish in a microwave oven.

All of the cookware used to test this book falls into three categories: measuring cups, shallow-sided dishes, and bowls.

Measuring Cups: These are traditional heat-resistant glass liquid-measuring cups. A 1-cup, 2-cup, 4-cup, and 8-cup measure are all that would ever be needed. That is a traditional set that most kitchens already have. But only the 2-cup and 8-cup are essential, because anything prepared in a 1-cup measure could be prepared in a 2-cup measure, and anything prepared in a 4-cup measure could also be prepared in an 8-cup measure.

In microwave cooking it is generally safe to use a bowl or dish one size larger than that called for. The opposite, however, is not true. Using smaller bowls will sometimes cause dramatically uneven heating.

Shallow-Sided Dishes and Plates: These are heat-resistant glass baking dishes. Most homes have at least one of these, a (meat) loaf pan (about 8 to 9 inches by 4 to 5 inches by 3 inches), which because of its shape is sometimes very useful for microwave cooking. In addition, three shallow-sided glass baking dishes (all about 2 inches deep) should be considered a part of a complete microwave cookware set. These are an 8- to 9-inch square dish (large), a rectangular dish approximately 11 inches by 7 inches (large), and a deep round dish that measures about 11 inches across the top (large). A microwave-safe serving plate, approximately 12 inches in diameter (very large), can be substituted for the round dish in recipes that do not require the dish to hold large amounts of liquid.

Note that the large shallow-sided dish must be able to fit into your microwave oven. Measure the inside dimensions of your oven before purchasing a large dish. For many ovens, 11 inches by 7 inches is the largest size that will fit.

Bowls: These are simply heat-resistant glass bowls. A complete microwave cookware set would include a small bowl (approximately 2 cups), a medium bowl (approximately 2 quarts), a large bowl (approximately 3 quarts), and a very large bowl (approximately 6 quarts). Essential, however, are only the large and very large bowl. Whenever a small bowl is required, the 2-cup glass measure can be used, and whenever a medium bowl is needed, the 8-cup glass measure can be used. In all recipes plain soufflé dishes or large ramekins can be used for bowls.

Note that the very large bowl is not a standard-size glass bowl. I use a large white porcelain bowl that has always been in my kitchen, used previously for mixing large salads and for holding bread dough that needed to rise. This very large bowl takes the place of a spaghetti pot and a soup kettle for microwave cooking, in addition to being essential for many other recipes that produce enough to serve six people—2 pounds of spinach, for example, will not fit into a smaller bowl.

Index